EDUCATING STUDENTS IN A
MEDIA-SATURATED CULTURE

John Davies

EDUCATING STUDENTS in a MEDIA-SATURATED CULTURE

TECHNOMIC
PUBLISHING CO., INC
LANCASTER · BASEL

Educating Students in a Media-Saturated Culture

a **TECHNOMIC**®publication

Published in the Western Hemisphere by
Technomic Publishing Company, Inc.
851 New Holland Avenue, Box 3535
Lancaster, Pennsylvania 17604 U.S.A.

Distributed in the Rest of the World by
Technomic Publishing AG
Missionsstrasse 44
CH-4055 Basel, Switzerland

Printed in the United States of America
10 9 8 7 6 5 4 3 2

Main entry under title:
  Educating Students in a Media-Saturated Culture

A Technomic Publishing Company book
Bibliography: p. 261
Includes index p. 295

Library of Congress Catalog Card No. 95-61804
ISBN No. 1-56676-365-7

In Memory of
Kathryn Meath and Edna Cleere

For
Rox, Christian, and Harrison

CONTENTS

Chapter 5: Lessons on Life:
The Media and Social Development   **83**

Chapter 6: Growing Up on the Media:
Does It Affect Physical Development?   **117**

Chapter 7: Playing to Emotions:
The Media and Affective Development   **133**

Chapter 8: Myths Created by the Media   **149**

Writing a book is rarely a solitary endeavor. It is impossible to thank everyone who has in some way contributed to this effort. I am indebted to my colleagues at Miami Country Day School, particularly those who edited various chapters: Fredlyn Rosenfeld, Mary Ellen Cassini, Virgil Rogers, and Beth Paul. Dr. Sarah Pell and Sheryl Piper contributed to this effort as well. A number of individuals active in promoting media literacy provided insights, support, and encouragement, especially Marieli Rowe of the National Telemedia Council, Kathleen Tyner of Strategies for Media Literacy, Dr. Cynthia Mee, Cynthia Grey, Nick Doob, and Linda Atkinson. Alex Knapp provided me with invaluable computer assistance. I am also profoundly grateful to Dr. Joseph Eckenrode for his comments, suggestions, and support for *Educating Students in a Media-Saturated Culture* as a worthwhile project and to Dr. David Elkind, whose book *The Hurried Child* first stimulated my interest in this subject many years ago. Last, but not least, I wish to thank my wife Roxane for her continual encouragement and enduring patience as I ventured off to the library to do research or sat at the computer into the late hours of the night.

Preliminary versions of some of this material appeared in *Transescence,* published by Educational Leadership Institute, Inc. and the *Journal of Health Education,* published by the American Alliance for Health, Physical Education, Recreation & Dance.

Every new medium of communication has in its time aroused anxiety—
the cinema, radio, and at one time (a chastening thought) even reading.
Now it is the turn of television.

H. Himmelweit, S. N. Oppenheim, and P. Price,
authors of *Television and the Child,* 1958

In a national poll, over 1000 adults were asked what were the most
positive and most negative influences on children today. Of the five
negative influences identified by respondents, four were mass media.
Named were MTV, politicians, movies, television, and popular music
(Edwards, 1990/91). The conventional wisdom that the media are "bad"
represents a sort of precarious situation for today's students. It is a situation layered with irony. On the one hand, there has been considerable
discussion about the negative influences of the media on young people.
At the same time, developments in communication technology have
greatly increased students' accessibility to the media. It is not unusual
for a young person to spend as much as eight hours a day with various
types of media. And so, while concern mounts regarding the impact of
the media on society, as evidenced by the latest round in the media and
violence debate, the student who sits in our classroom today is consuming more media than ever. The amount of time spent with the media by
students represents another level of irony. The printed word excepted,
much of the media use of children and adolescents requires no literacy
per se. Television, video, film, and popular music require no particular
skills to be used. Listening/viewing can be done by anybody at any
time! The price paid for this arrangement is that, without the skills to

decode the meanings behind the media, we leave students, as well as ourselves, in the untenuous position of allowing the media to construct our reality for us. This has profound implications for society politically, socially, economically, and from an educational perspective as well.

It would not be an exaggeration to say that today's culture is a media-saturated culture. It is virtually impossible to live in today's society without encountering the media throughout the day. Concerned parents with small children will attest to this fact. The persistent image of the media as a negative influence can only serve to exacerbate this concern. Educators routinely identify the media, particularly television, as the culprit for everything from a diminished attention span to loss of reading time. What is a teacher to do?

The ubiquity of the media makes censorship virtually impossible; moreover, this approach raises constitutional issues as well. By now, we are all accustomed to hearing the "free speech" and "free press" arguments emanating from the media industry. In lieu of censorship, two other avenues for addressing concerns about the impact of media on children and adolescents are available, however. The first is a critical examination of what the research really says regarding the power of the media. While the media are tremendously powerful, they do not constitute the omnipotent monolithic system we are often led to believe. Here, the news may not be as bad as we think. The second is a recognition that students can be taught to "read" the media and become critical media consumers in their own right.

The media have been variously described as "the other curriculum," "the hidden curriculum," and a "parallel school system." It has been suggested that as much as 80% of our learning is visual, most of that media-related. Indeed, there is a "reschooling" taking place every day. Given the prevalence of media in our lives, how could anything else be the case? Again, it is ironic that, despite the recognition that young people are learning a great deal from the media, our educational system has been largely unresponsive in trying to teach students how to decode and understand the media messages that they receive countless times in a day. Therefore, this book is written specifically for those who work in schools. It seeks to provide educators with an overview of the media research as it relates to students, as well as to examine those issues that are particularly relevant to teachers and administrators. I would like to state my position as directly as possible: if we are not teaching the students sitting in our classrooms today to be media literate, then we are doing them a grave disservice. Not only are we doing them a disservice, but we are also missing a wonderful opportunity. If this position seems strong, it is meant to be. The United States lags far behind countries like Great Britain, Canada, and Australia, which have already realized this point. This is not to say that media literacy has not gained ground in this country. The number of converts in education is growing. Since 1953 the National Telemedia Council has promoted media literacy. Several states now have some media literacy initiative in progress. New Mexico, for example, is developing a K–12 curriculum at present and has already begun training teachers. In some cases, local school districts have begun the process on their own, as in Billerica, Massachusetts. For media literacy to become a mainstream part of education, it will fall to teachers and administrators to push for its adoption in the curriculum. The compelling reason for this book is to convince educators that this is a worthwhile endeavor.

After the dust has settled over the debate of media effects and their impact on students, it is unlikely that media literacy will have become part of curriculum if efforts to make this a reality have depended solely on countering the negative impact of the media. A reading of the history of the mass media over the last 100 years reveals that concerns over negative media effects are not new. The Payne studies, conducted during the Depression, stirred considerable concern about the susceptibility of young people to the pernicious effects of movies. Similar concerns have been raised about radio, comic books, television, and, most recently, MTV. However, as Anderson and Ploghoft (1993) note, an inoculation approach to media education has not proven sufficient over the last two decades to sustain teacher interest and curriculum development. Clearly then, it is time to move beyond the "media are bad" approach. As educators, we need to reposition ourselves regarding the media. This is not to say that we should pretend that the media are neutral. In fact, this book offers considerable evidence that the media do have effects, some of them negative. But there is more. Because of the pervasiveness of the media, there is virtually no aspect of our culture and society that goes untouched. The media then become a continual point of reference, often, the starting point for helping students learn about their world; moreover, the media represent a relevant point of departure for capturing students' interest. These constitute positive reasons for incorporating media literacy into the curriculum. Some of the earliest media literacy efforts, what were termed *critical receiver-ship skills* for television, emphasized the positive reasons for teaching media literacy. The most compelling reason for education to pursue media literacy in the curriculum may be the idea that the ultimate goal of education and media literacy are virtually one and the same. The cornerstone for both is the creation of independent thinkers. Mainstream education seeks to teach students to be critical thinkers in order to be problem solvers, decision makers, and responsible citizens. Media literacy asks nothing less. At the heart of all of the various elements of media literacy is critical analysis. The media then provide a vast laboratory for helping students to become thinkers in the deepest sense and all that means in terms of character, responsible citizenship, and the other aims of education. Only by recognizing that media literacy represents both a responsibility, as well as an opportunity for educators, will these much needed skills find their way into the curriculum.

To date, there are several thousand studies on the use, effects, and content of the mass media. Unless noted, the research cited was conducted in this country. While there is common ground among the media experiences across the globe, there are differences as well. Television, for example, is different abroad. Generally, it contains less violence, and the pace is not so rapid. The majority of these studies relate to young people, students who come to school every day. Much of the research resides in scholarly journals, with little effort being made to make it available to teachers. This is a point worth considering. There exists a large body of research that relates to young people, yet teachers, who probably spend more time with these young people than anyone else outside the home, do not find it readily accessible. Irony again!

Every effort has been made to avoid technical jargon. The field of mass communications, like other areas of scholarly activitiy, has not escaped an explosion of "in" terminology. Where it is used, I have made every effort to explain what it means, as in the chapter on media effects theories. If the reader is overwhelmed by the amount of research, I apologize. There is a reason, and it goes to the nature of media research. Trying to understand the effects of the media is somewhat like trying to put together an intricate puzzle with thousands of pieces. Measuring human behavior is an inexact science. Studies are often very specific and highly focused, presenting only a small part of the picture—a piece of the puzzle. In some cases, scholars have drawn very different conclusions as they interpreted the same data! Likewise, research comes in a variety of packages. Making a case for the effects of media is much more convincing when a variety of studies, such as correlational, experimental, and content analysis, are used. In the midst of all of this research, I have looked for patterns to emerge. The reader might be surprised by some of the findings, such as the case of the relationship between television and learning.

In the middle school tradition, I have chosen to examine the media's impact on students using the rubric that educators of young adolescents use in approaching their students, i.e., that of their intellectual, social, emotional, and physical development. And so there is a chapter on each of these areas. The chapter on media myths has been written to operate on two levels. First, it provides the teacher with some valuable background information on the media. In this respect, it serves as a primer of sorts on the media for the uninitiated. It is important for teachers to understand these myths in order to impart them in one form or another to their students. The other reason this chapter is included is to help the teacher to situate him/herself within what Phelan has called "the mediaworld." Myth is not about information as much as ways of seeing and being in the world. Hopefully, then, this chapter will also give teachers a "feel" for what the media are all about. The curious reader may want to skip to this chapter and read it first.

Although computers make up a significant portion of the electronic environment of today's students, I have not included them. Computer technology has become part of the mainstream American education and is already receiving considerable attention. Similarly, pornography goes unexplored. Considerable research exists, but for reasons that are clear, it has not been conducted with students younger than college age. Therefore, while accessible to adolescents (and sometimes children), it is not included. I have included some of the research on video games where appropriate, but it does not represent a major focus in this book. As an area of scholarly inquiry, video game research is still very new.

Pungente, a leading proponent of media literacy, has observed that, to be successful, media literacy will have to be a grass roots movement among teachers who will lobby for it. It is my profoundest hope that *Educating Students in a Media-Saturated Culture* will make some small contribution to this effort.

CHAPTER 1

Towards an Understanding of the Mass Media and the Meaning of Media Literacy

We live in a world where media are omnipresent: an increasing number of people spend a great deal of time watching television, reading newspapers and magazines, playing records and listening to the radio. . . . The role of communication and media in the process of development should not be underestimated, nor the function of media as instruments for the citizen's active participation in society. Political and educational systems need to recognise their obligations to promote in their citizens a critical understanding of the phenomena of communication.

UNESCO Declaration on Media Education, 1982

WHAT ARE THE MASS MEDIA?

Today's world can truly be described as a global village. Much of what has made this possible has been technological developments, particularly in mass communications. Virtually any person or event is instantaneously accessible because of communications technology. Students in classrooms today are literally "coming of age" in the age of mass communication. This has profound implications for them today, as well as in the future. As the word suggests, the mass media make mass communications possible. Generally, the mass media can be divided into two broad categories: print media, which consist of newspapers, magazines, and books and electronic media, consisting of radio, recordings, television, video, and film. Also, any understanding of the mass media cannot be complete without mentioning advertising, which while not technically media, serves as a support system for the mass media. Without advertising, the mass media would not exist.

1

Black and Whitney (1988) explain that the mass media have four primary functions: information, entertainment, persuasion, and transmission of culture. They note that each of these functions may also have an opposing "dysfunction, such as violent entertainment contributing to aggression, too much advertising contributing to a spirit of materialism." Print media tend to be informational, while radio, television, and film are generally geared towards entertainment. The use of media to provide information and entertainment is fairly straightforward. The functions of persuasion and transmission of culture need some explanation. Persuasion is clearly a function of advertising; however, as Black and Whitney point out, this function is usually much more concealed and subtle. Sometimes advertisements themselves are subtle. Miller (1990), for example, demonstrates how films in the 1980s became still another avenue for advertising within the movies themselves. Companies now pay large fees to have their products appear in films. "Product placement" now provides a hefty increase to the bottom line of a movie. In many cases the lines between the information and persuasive functions of the media are blurred so that what passes for and is viewed as information by the media consumer represent efforts to manipulate public opinion.

The mass media perform a dual function in terms of transmission of culture. The media serve to reinforce existing cultural norms and values as seen in the persistence of gender stereotypes, which are examined later. Because the media operate within existing social, political, and economic structures to remain economically viable, they must tap into the present culture. In some cases the media use this line of reasoning to justify some of the messages that they offer society. It is very common, for example, to hear the media respond to criticisms about sex and violence with, "We are just giving audiences what they want." While the media serve to transmit the existing culture, they are tremendous shapers of culture as well. Sometimes these influences are direct and intentional; other times, cultural change is a by-product of the media. An example of a direct influence on our culture is consumerism. Few would disagree that our's has become a culture where consumerism and materialism are part of the cultural fabric. A less direct, but nonetheless powerful, influence is the contribution that the media have made to a culture of violence that is very pronounced in today's society. Only in becoming aware of what the mass media are and their functions in society can we, as educators, really appreciate how they impact on our students today and how we can teach them to understand the role of the media in their lives.

WHAT DOES THE TERM *MEDIA LITERACY* MEAN?

The term *media literacy* has been defined by different authors. A common feature they all share is the analytical nature of this kind of literacy. The earliest efforts dealt primarily with television and the development of critical viewing skills. Ploghoft and Anderson (1982) coined the term *receivership skills* to describe critical viewing. Working with several school districts in the early 1970s, Anderson and Ploghoft helped develop programs to integrate the teaching of critical television viewing skills into the curriculum. The growing use and influence of other media have broadened the scope to include critical analysis of other mass media as well. Today, there are a number of organizations and materials available that include not only television, but the other media as well in their media literacy efforts.

In *Teaching the Media* Masterman (1985) identifies the core of media education. "The first principle of media education from which all else flows, and to which teachers and students will continually return is *that the media are symbolic (or sign) systems which need to be actively read, and not unproblematic, self-explanatory reflections of external reality.* Another way," he continues, "of stating this principle is to say that television, newspapers, films, radio, advertisements and magazines are *produced.* The media, that is, are actively involved in processes of *construction* or *representing* 'reality' rather than simply transmitting or reflecting it" (p. 21).

Given this principle, Masterman identifies four areas of investigation: 1) the sources, origins, and determinants of media constructions; 2) the dominant techniques and codings employed by the media to convince us of the truth of their representations; 3) the nature of the "reality" constructed by the media, the values implicit in media representations; and 4) the ways in which media constructions are read or received by their audiences (p. 21). Each of these areas of study are critical if students are going to learn to approach the media with a critical perspective.

Not only does Masterman outline the elements for media literacy (he uses the term *media education*), but he also maintains that media literacy is essential for a number of compelling reasons:

(1) The high rate of media consumption and the saturation of contemporary societies by the media

(2) The ideological importance of the media and their influence as consciousness industries

(3) The growth in the management and manufacture of information and its dissemination by the media

(4) The increasing penetration of media into our central democratic processes

(5) The increasing importance of visual communication and information in all areas

(6) The importance of educating students to meet the demands of the future

(7) The fast-growing national and international pressures to privatize information (p. 3)

For these reasons Masterman argues that media literacy is an idea whose time has come. He notes that, "At present our schools largely continue to produce pupils who are likely to carry with them for the rest of their lives either a quite unwarranted faith in the integrity of media images and representations, or an equally dangerous, undifferentiated skepticism which sees the media as sources of evil" (p. 14).

The National Leadership Conference on Media Literacy (1992) defines a media-literate person as one who "can decode, evaluate, analyze, and produce both print and electronic media. The fundamental objective of media literacy is critical autonomy in relationship to all media" (p. 1). This definition reflects the work of Considine (1992) who has argued that educators must have a clear definition of media literacy before it can be taught. There is considerable overlap between his understanding of media literacy and that of Masterman's. He defines the term as the ability to analyze and evaluate the media in terms of content, form, impact, ownership, and production and design. Content is the story or message presented. Form is similar to what Masterman calls techniques, i.e., lighting, sound, props, camera angles. He notes that the media's impact is to be understood in terms of how messages and images influence both the individual and society. Here, there are a number of theories, and they will be briefly explored in the next chapter. It is impossible to understand the media without exploring the ownership and the corporate nature of media ownership. The media are driven by certain economic imperatives that shape literally every aspect of media production and dissemination. Finally, Considine underscores the need to explore how the media are produced and designed, that is, "designing particular messages to achieve particular goals, with particular groups." Today's media target very specific audiences, largely in an effort to deliver markets to advertisers. To accomplish this task, design becomes a very important component.

In its resource guide *Media Literacy* the Ministry of Education (1989) of Ontario, Canada, identifies eight key concepts for media literacy. What follows are excerpts from the introduction of that resource guide:

(1) All media are constructions. This is considered the most important concept in media literacy. The ministry notes that the media do not simply represent reality; rather, they present productions crafted for specific reasons. The power of these productions resides in their apparent "naturalness," and even though they appear to be natural, a great deal of thought has gone into making them appear natural for very specific reasons.

(2) The media construct reality. The resource guide notes that we all construct our picture of the world based upon our experiences and observations; however, when the media provide a significant number of these experiences and observations, then it is the media, not ourselves, that construct our reality.

(3) Audiences negotiate meaning in media. The idea is that each of us brings to our media experiences our own unique backgrounds. The meaning one person finds in the media will not necessarily be found by another. Here, the resource guide notes an important point because research shows that people clearly process meanings from the media differently. This is a point often forgotten by adults who reason that children are deriving the same meanings and understandings that they do.

(4) Media have commercial implications. It is not possible to understand the media without understanding the economic sources of the media. Virtually all of the media function to generate profit. For this reason most of the decisions made reflect the business side of media production. A show of high quality with low ratings will not last. A related issue is regarding who owns the media. The tendency for concentration of the media into the hands of fewer and

fewer media conglomerates has far-reaching implications for what media will be produced, as well as who controls the information sources in society.

(5) Media contain ideological and value messages. Media texts are not value and ideologically neutral. "All media products are advertising in some sense—for themselves, but also for values or ways of life." Sometimes these values are overt, sometimes more subtle. A later chapter on "media myths" speaks to this concept at length. For now, a good example to illustrate this ideological/value nature of the media can be found in the consumer mentality that the media promote. Therefore, a media literacy program must teach students how to decode these messages.

(6) Media have social and political implications. It would not be an exaggeration to say that society has been profoundly altered by the mass media. As this work will point out, it is not possible to understand socialization without understanding the role that the media play. From a political standpoint the media have literally changed the way politics are conducted. Image often wins out over substance. The ministry also notes that, because the media are so widespread, we can be aware of events across the globe, and, more importantly, this awareness carries with it the potential to be drawn into those events. One might say that we now live in a global village whether we like it or not, and because there is now only one village, there is no place to move!

(7) Form and content are closely related, the resource guide notes, and students need to understand this relationship. The ministry reaffirms McLuhan's thesis that each media has its own grammar and codifies reality in a different way. "Thus, different media will report the same event but create different impressions and different messages."

(8) Each medium has a unique aesthetic form. The media have the power to make us feel good—they have an artistic dimension that allows us to enjoy them. By exploring this dimension of the media, students can come to enjoy and appreciate them more.

The Ontario Ministry of Education concludes:

When all these concepts have been understood and validated by practical, creative, or production experiences, students should be able to apply their skills and general awareness to any specific media product they encounter. This process enables students to establish and maintain the kind of critical distance on their culture that makes possible critical autonomy: the ability to decode, encode, and evaluate the symbol systems that dominate their world. (p. 10)

Still another approach comes from the Center for Media Literacy. Borrowing from the Brazilian educator Paulo Freire's educational model, the Center encourages a four-step process for developing media awareness. This approach contains an invaluable component in that it requires the student to translate what has been learned into some kind of action. The Center's framework begins with developing the student's level of awareness regarding a particular topic or theme related to the media. Topical questions are raised. The next step is analysis. Curriculum materials developed by the Center provide support information with which to analyze the media topic. The third step within this framework is to get students to reflect on what they have learned. Finally, students are encouraged to follow up with some kind of action. This action component might entail a letter writing campaign, a stereotype alert, or creating a mini-documentary. The Center for Media Literacy has used this model very effectively in developing some of the best media literacy educational materials presently available.

If media literacy is to successfully become a component of American education as it has in other countries, it must be a literacy that flows from a proactive stance. The Report of the National Conference on Media Literacy demonstrates that, until now, much of the media activism has come from a "protectionist model." This model is based upon the assumption shared by most Americans that the media have long-term effects and that most of those effects are negative. Thus, media activism has centered around protecting young people as if they were being given some sort of vaccine. While this dimension is important, the report notes that this approach conceives of the viewer as if he or she were passive. What is needed, the Leadership Conference argues, is an approach to media literacy that assumes that media consumption is an active experience and one that is based upon an inquiry model of pedagogy.

CHAPTER 2

The Omnipotent Media?
Understanding Media Effects Theories

> There are many conflicting views of media effects. We researchers get rewarded in various ways for saying the media are totally ineffective and we get rewarded—sometimes even by the same people—for saying that the media are omnipotent, they're to blame for everything.
>
> Elihu Katz, "On Conceptualizing Media Effects: Another Look," 1988

Katz's observation underscores the wide diversity of opinion on the question of media effects research, as well as the reactions among media producers and users in terms of researchers' conclusions concerning the media's impact. Concerns in the educational community today are by no means new. These same concerns in the past among teachers and administrators constitute the source of modern theories and research on media effects. "For many educators, the development of movies and radio represented a major challenge to the supremacy of public schools as an influence on the minds of children and as a source of common culture and shared values. Educators were quick to criticize the impact of these new forms of mass media on national culture and children" (Spring, 1990, p. 284). What emerged Spring has referred to as a battle of control of the minds of children and national culture.

As early as 1914, representatives of the film industry were addressing the National Education Association (NEA). This debate led to a series of research studies, conducted by educators and social scientists, called the Payne Studies. The negative conclusions on the impact of movies led to the creation of a "photoplay appreciation" course in high schools throughout the country. The National Council of Teachers of English

9

(NCTE) provided much of the impetus for these early attempts at some form of media literacy, just as it still does today. The Payne Studies are significant for more than historical reasons. This approach to media effects influenced research for the next three decades. Still another impetus for media research came with World War II. The government sponsored communication research to study the effectiveness of film and other media in terms of persuading audiences.

Buckingham (1991) writes that there are three general responses arising over concerns about media effects. The first he calls "moral panics." Overwhelmingly negative in its approach to media effects, this approach sees the media as responsible for many of the ills that plague our society, in particular, violence. Based on this approach, much of the erosion of values taking place in this country and others can be attributed to the mass media. Buckingham points out that the problem with this response is that it may deflect attention away from other causes of social problems, and it fails to take into account the complexity of the media experience.

The second approach Buckingham calls "the plug-in-drug," a term he borrows from Winn's (1977) book which bears a similar title. Here, the emphasis is placed on the passivity of the media experience. He notes Postman's *The Disappearance of Childhood* (1982) as another example.

> Thus we are told that watching television retards the development of the brain, blunts the senses and encourages mental laziness. It impairs children's sense of their own identity, their linguistic abilities and their attention span. Furthermore, because of their addiction to television, children are deprived of play and of the opportunity to participate in the interpersonal rituals of family life. The metaphor of television-as-a-drug recurs throughout Winn's book: TV is "insidious nartcotic," children are "TV zombies" who watch in a "trance-like state" which "blots out" the real world, and parents are urged to help their children "kick the TV habit." (p. 15)

Another shortcoming Buckingham finds with these kinds of approaches to television is that they fail to take into consideration the pleasures that children derive in watching television.

Finally, Buckingham is critical of a third understanding of media effects based on the work of Masterman (1985). Masterman conceives of the media in terms of "Consciousness Industries which provide not simply information about the world, but ways of seeing and understanding it" (Masterman, p. 4). He argues that those who control the media have the power not only to construct their own versions of reality, but to make them appear natural and authentic—an observation that has been made by the semiotician Roland Barthes as well. Buckingham is critical of this kind of response for the same reasons as he is of the other two approaches. "There is little sense that children may compare their experience of television with their experience of the social world, or that they may question or distance themselves from the representations it provides" (p. 17).

All three approaches, he maintains, provide a simplistic understanding of children and television, which makes these approaches attractive. The media get blamed for everything. The emphasis in each is also on the passivity of the media user. Media studies, then, become analogous to inoculation, to use Buckingham's term, in which students are armed with the skills necessary to resist the media's negative effects. Having thus said this, he argues that using the media is about "meaning making" and realizing that users of the media, even children, are actively involved in constructing meanings of their own.

Because more television is consumed than all of the other media combined, much of the attention concerning media effects has centered around this medium. While there is disagreement on how television affects viewers, few, if any, individuals would deny that this medium has some impact. This fact is clearly understood when one considers the results of a study conducted by Bybee, Robinson, and Turow [cited in Comstock (1989), pp. 198–199] in which they surveyed about 500 communications professors and scholars. Respondents rated television effects as "the cause," "an important cause," "a somewhat important cause," and "not at all a cause." They asked those surveyed to rate eighteen possible television effects. Comstock provides the top ten, along with the percentage of responses that designated television as a cause to some degree. The results showed that 91% believed that television increased world knowledge. Over 80% indicated that television increased buying behavior, decreased physical activity, increased social value reinforcement, and decreased reading. When asked if television increased the desire for immediate gratification, 76% responded that this medium had some effect. Respondents also indicated that television increased curiosity (70%). Of the remaining three effects, 66% believed that television increased violent behavior, increased ethnic stereotyping, and increased verbal ability.

Since the Payne Studies several different schools of research regarding media effects have developed: the "hypodermic needle theory" (sometimes also referred to as the "magic bullet theory"), the social learning theory, cultivation analysis, the "uses and gratifications" approach, the "drench hypothesis," and the application of semiotics to media research. Moreover, media effects theory is an ongoing enterprise. Developments in the social sciences, particularly the behavioral disciplines such as cognitive social psychology, continue to make contributions to our understanding of the mass media. In addition, the growing interest in popular culture as a serious scholarly pursuit over the last two decades has made a significant contribution towards an understanding of how the media influence their audiences.

A brief overview of the mainline media effects theories follows. The "hypodermic needle theory" operates on the assumption that the media message had a direct effect on media consumers. This theory likens media messages to being directly injected into the media users, much like receiving a shot from a hypodermic needle. According to this theory, a passive media audience absorbs messages uncritically. This perspective guided much of the media research until the 1950s. New developments in research, theory, and findings proved that this theory was too simplistic to explain how the media affected individuals. Nevertheless, some variation of this theory can be found in popular literature and seems to be widely held by a significant portion of the American public. For example, much of the public concern about violence in television and music has its origins in this approach. Recently, Gantz (1993) has suggested that, during periods of crisis, such as the Gulf War, in which the public is dependent upon media for its information, the direct effects model may be operative.

The "social learning theory" of Bandura, developed in the 1960s, highlights the role that modeling plays in the social development of children (Bandura & Walters, 1963). In his early experiments (referred to as the Bobo doll studies) Bandura and his colleagues showed children films projected onto a simulated television set. In one film an adult struck a plastic doll in several different manners, for example, punching, using a plastic mallet, and throwing rubber balls. One group of children viewed the film in which the adult aggressor was rewarded. In a different film he was chastised verbally and spanked. A third group of children watched a film that stopped after the model's aggressive behavior, with no sequence of reward or punishment. Children were then left alone individually to play in a room with a plastic doll, as well as the same sort of toys the adult used in the film to strike the doll. The children had the option of imitating the aggressive behavior or playing with other toys in the playroom. Bandura found a strong tendency among the children to imitate the aggression they witnessed in the film in which the aggressor was rewarded, as well as in the film that included neither reward or punishment. This was not the case for the children who had seen the adult punished. Bandura held that these children had learned the aggressive behavior. To test his theory a person entered the room and provided treats for each reponse that a child could remember. A large number of children from all three film groups reproduced the adult's responses.

The Cultural Indicators Project started by Gerbner at the Annenberg School of Communcations led the development of the "cultivation theory." This theory has been explored primarily in the world of television because it is based upon the type of long-term media exposure that this medium provides. "The basic hypothesis of cultivation analysis is that the more time one spends living in the world of television, the more likely one is to report conceptions of social reality that can be traced to television portrayals" (Gross & Morgan, 1985, p. 226). This research found that heavy viewers of television see the world as a "mean world," that is, they feel at higher personal risk and are more mistrustful and suspicious than lighter viewers. This view of the world held up even when sex, age, education, income, newspaper reading, and church attendance were controlled for (Gerbner et al., 1977). Another concept of enculturation theory is that a viewer develops knowledge about the real world using the reality television presents. Thus, for example, though not always consciously, a person learns about the world of police work or medicine based upon these types of television dramas (Gerbner & Gross, 1976).

Drawing on research three decades earlier, a new paradigm for media research, called the "uses and gratifications" approach, was developed in the 1970s. Unlike the hypodermic needle concept, uses and gratifications scholars recognized that media consumers are not passive; rather, each brings a personal agenda to media consumption because of social and psychological needs. Katz, Blumler, and Gurevitch summarized this approach as one concerned with: "(1) the social and psychological origins of (2) needs, which generate (3) expectations of (4) the mass media or other sources which lead to (5) differential patterns of media exposure (or engagement in other activies), resulting in (6) need gratifications and (7) other consequences, perhaps mostly unintended ones" [cited in Rosengren, Wenner, & Palmgreen (1985), p. 14]. Thus, the media can fill a wide variety of gratifications, depending upon the needs of the individual. Employing this approach to media research means that the concept of a "mass audience" has little value. An example of this type of research is the study of uses of music by adolescents. Music and other media are used at all stages of life to satisfy wants and to gratify the needs of people who use them. Some of the motivations for using the media are trivial, while others are profoundly psychological and social (Lull, 1985). The adolescent might, for example, listen to the radio to simply "pass time," but on the other hand, he or she might listen to a particular song or music groups because it resonates deeply with a strong emotional feeling.

An alternative explanation of media effects is the "drench hypothesis" formulated by Greenberg (1988). "On occasion, and perhaps more occasions than we acknowledge, certain role portrayals may generate a drench effect." Greenberg continues, "Some series, or miniseries, or single programs may be so forceful as to account for a significant portion of the role images we maintain" (p. 97). His theory takes a different approach than media effect theories, which presume a cumulative effect over time. Greenberg also notes that the drench hypothesis provides an alternative to one of the main lines of media research, that is, content analysis. "One woman is not *every* other woman on television; one act of violence is not every other act, one minority character is not to be equated with every other minority character" (p. 98). Thus, Greenberg maintains, content analysis fails to consider "individual differences in the power of performance." Because this hypothesis is relatively new, a strong research base is lacking; however, there is reason to believe that it is credible. It is generally recognized that quality miniseries like *Roots* and *Holocaust,* which drew record-breaking audiences, not only increased viewers' levels of awareness, but affected attitudes as well.

Most recently, the field of semiotics has focused on media research. Semiotics is the study of signs, that is, "the smallest unit of meaning," and explores "the way signs communicate and the rules that govern their use" (Seiter, 1987). The world of the media is replete with signs, many of them symbolic. Beyond language, which is one type of sign system, there are a host of other symbolic signs. Semiotic analysis of the media is an attempt to become conscious of and to understand the world of signs, whether they are visual images, sounds, or words. From a media effects perspective semiotics provides another avenue from which to understand how the powerfully symbolic world of the media might affect us. Because television is so "real," a viewer often takes a sign at its face value, without fully sounding its meaning. As a result, the viewer accepts what comes across the television screen without exploring the real meaning of a particular sign.

Seiter uses the example of the camera. The accepted image ("the camera never lies") is presented as objective, that is, telling the viewer how things are. In his study of local news, entitled *Creating Reality,* Altheide (1974) demonstrates how reporters use the camera to present a distorted view. Because local news operates on a tight budget, the person behind the camera is not able to shoot enough film to provide an optimum presentation. He notes that it is the cameraperson's job to shoot an "editable version of reality." Therefore, the cameraperson approaches a news event with an eye towards editing. Similarly, skillful editing of visual images can collapse time. Finally, Altheide demonstrates how news stations approach a story with an "angle" that may or may not communicate what has really occurred. It is the cameraperson's responsibility to help bring this angle to life.

The power of the symbolic nature of the media is brought home in the work of Real (1977). His exploration of mass-mediated culture and the human ecosystem identifies three subsystems: the symbolic, the material, and communication (including mass communication). Communication represents the nexus between making these two other subsystems. "The manner in which a given society *symbolically* represents itself, for example in popular culture and media, is part and parcel of the manner in which that society *materially* organizes itself. They are dialectically related so that if one changes, the other must change; if one remains unchanged, the other cannot change." Real continues, "Distortions in the structural distribution of income, property, energy, food, and other items in the material subsystem are both cause and effect of distortions in the symbolic subsystem" (Real, pp. 31–32).

Two areas of interest have tended to dominate media effects research. The first is the influence of the media on education, both achievement and cognitive development and, secondly, the potential for media violence to cause similar behavior in the media user. Both areas have received considerable discussion in both scholarly and lay circles, even in the media themselves. Many of the concerns about media effects on behavior and learning represent a combination of research and conventional wisdom. Anderson and Collins (1988) have identified numerous common theories about televison effects on cognitive development. The research basis for several of these ideas are explored in the chapter on media and intellectual development. For now, they are listed briefly to familiarize the reader with the scope of these theories and hypotheses. No doubt, the reader will recognize several of them from educational publications.

> These assertions are: 1) Television has mesmerizing powers over children's attention; this power is exerted by the movement, color, and visual changes typical of television. 2) Children's comprehension of television is extremely poor; they remember only disconnected images. 3) Children do not think about television programs, that is, they do not engage in inferential and reflective thought while television viewing. 4) Children get overstimulated by television; by some accounts this leads to hyperactivity, and by other accounts leads to passivity. 5) Television viewing displaces valuable cognitive activities, especially reading and homework. 6) Attention span is shortened, probably because of the rapidly paced visual images. 7) Creativity and imagination are reduced; in general, the child becomes cognitively passive. 8) Reading achievement is reduced. 9) The development of the left hemisphere of the brain is deleteriously affected because television viewing activates the visual, spatially oriented right hemisphere. (p. 3)

There are additional explanations for television's influence on learning, which are addressed in a later chapter.

Just as there are a number of what might be termed "subtheories" on the media and education, so too there are additional theories for explaining the aggressive effects as well. Generally, these theories fall under one of three categories. The first is that media aggression and violence actually *reduce* aggression. A second group of theories are based on the assumption that there is a link between mediated violence and behavior. Finally, some researchers postulate that the experience of media violence has *no* effect on aggressive behavior.

The "reduction" school offers two different explanations for the position that experiencing media violence can actually reduce or forestall aggressive behavior. The catharsis hypothesis is founded on the assumption that seeing another engaged in aggressive behavior diminishes one's desire to behave in an aggressive manner by way of some sort of emotional release. This theory is widely mentioned but has few subscribers. Feshbach's (1961) early study stimulated this hypothesis. One problem with the catharsis theory as it relates to the mass media is that catharsis requires intense emotional experiences, which are not found in most television viewing experiences (Murray, 1980). Few subsequent studies have provided much support for this position, and like many other studies on media violence, Feshbach's has received considerable criticism. The empathy hypothesis is grounded on the assumption that encounters with media violence are distasteful. There is limited support for this hypothesis in the research. It may, in fact, explain some viewers' reactions to violence. While it is not clearly understood why, media experiences can, in some cases, reduce violence. van der Voort (1986) notes, for example, if viewers experience what they see as frightening, this can reduce aggression. He also cites Leyens' work, which demonstrated that humor may also reduce aggression by changing the meaning of the program content.

There are several theories that postulate a linkage between experiencing media violence and behavior. The social learning theory, one of the most prevalent, based on Bandura's work, was noted above because it has been applied to numerous other areas of media effect research besides violence, for example, gender socialization. Considerable research by Zillman and his colleagues has been conducted on the arousal hypothesis. Some of this research has been criticized because it has involved pornography viewed by college students. The arousal theory is physiologically, as well as content, driven. In other words, the experience of media violence generates a physiological response, which, in turn, encourages aggression. Aggression generated by physiological arousal need not be media violence. Other types of content are believed to create arousal as well. Unexpected experimental research findings have led to refinements and variations in the arousal theory, some of which are very complex and beyond the scope of this work. The theory remains viable today. A new direction currently being examined is whether the formal aspect of the media themselves, regardless of content, might induce arousal.

Two theories have been advanced based upon the psychological principle of conditioning. According to the desensitization hypothesis, repeated exposure to media violence can reduce one's aversion to violence. Desensitization has been used as a therapeutic process to help individuals overcome phobias and irrational fears, which indicates the existence of some kind of psychological mechanism at work. The individual is reconditioned, as it were, over time not to react to violent content. The other theory applies the principle of classical conditioning to mediated violence. Berkowitz, classical conditioning's leading proponent, argues that aggressive behavior can become a conditioned response to certain cues elicited by violent media content.

Research supporting the contention that violence has no effects is scanty. One of its strongest supporters is Milavsky. He and his colleagues conducted an extensive longitudinal study on television violence and concluded that either no effect existed, or if it did, it was minimal (Milavsky et al., 1982). As further evidence he suggests that, as media violence has increased, society should have experienced a considerable increase in violent crimes. "We have to wonder why, if such fare does affect people, we don't have 'Apocalypse Now' or at least some real-world signs" (Milavsky, 1988, p. 167). Somewhat related to the no-effect school is a small group of scholars who seriously question the methodologies and interpretations of studies to date linking media violence to aggressive behavior. They do not dismiss a connection but, rather, suggest that the present state of research does not establish such a conclusion (Freedman, 1984, 1988).

There are a number of different ways to approach media effects. A fuller understanding of this impact of the media can be developed by exploring five basic dimensions of media effects, as outlined by McLeod and Reeves (1980): 1) micro versus macro, 2) direct versus conditional, 3) content-specific versus general-diffuse, 4) attitudinal versus behavioral versus cognitive, and 5) alteration versus stabilization. A brief explanation of each of these dimensions highlights the complexity of media effects research, as well as the difficulties of conducting this type of experimentation. McLeod and Reeves note that most studies are conducted with very restricted audiences. What happens is that this micro data is often generalized to a much larger audience. "For example, if some members of the audience are found to become more informed by using media content, it is sometimes assumed that such information gains must be functional for the society" (p. 18). At other times macro research may be assumed to have broad applications without reference to smaller audience groups. McLeod and Reeves cite the example of the growth of media monopolies and the impact that this trend has had on news coverage.

Direct versus conditional media effects call into play the hypodermic needle theory, an approach that is still very popular today. As noted above the direct effects theory assumes that media consumers are passive and that the media message generates an immediate response in the individual. Research today tries to take into account the many conditions and intervening variables that may affect the way the media impact audiences. McLeod and Reeves cite the "perceived reality" of television by viewers as a mitigating factor in television effects.

The content-specific versus general-diffuse dimension is best understood by two examples. Content-specific effects research looks at one particular area in the media and examines whether a one-to-one relationship exists between very specific content and an expected effect. Does violence in the media, for example, lead to aggressive or violent behavior? On the other hand, general-diffuse effects do not relate to specific content but, rather, the dynamics of viewing or listening that generate effects. Many media have an arousal function that may have certain effects, irrespective of the content, and many television studies have focused on the activity of watching television and the effects it might have in terms of displacing other activities.

In their discussion of the attidudinal versus behavioral versus cognitive dimension, McLeod and Reeves (1980) point out that the history of media effects research is nearly synonymous with the history of attitude change research. They note the absence of a strong research link between learning (cognitive gain) affecting attitudes, which, in turn, should affect behavior. Much research has been conducted since McLeod and Reeves's observation. Basically, any socialization process, whether it be gender, consumer, or political, involves all three of these components. An additional dimension is the learning of values. Since McLeod and Reeves's assertion, considerable research on the media and various types of socialization has been done. Media and communications scholars have come to borrow heavily upon developments in the social sciences, for example, cognitive social psychology, and grafted insights from these disciplines onto media research. There is evidence to suggest that there is a linkage between the media and learning, attitudes, and behaviors.

One of the ironies is that the media have been variously criticized for simply reinforcing prevailing mores and values. Borrowing from other media theorists, Williams and Frith (1993) have developed a typology that provides a framework for approaching media effects in this regard. *Interdependence* indicates that media and society are interactive and mutually impact on one another. *Idealism* holds to the proposition that the media mold society. Often a popular position, its proponents tend to shift much of the blame for social problems, for example, education, on the media. The third descriptor of this typology Williams and Frith refer to as *materialism,* meaning that the media are dependent on society and are a reflection of it. A more common term in the media literature used to describe this concept of media effects is the *reflection hypothesis* and represents still another attempt at addressing the media effects issue. Proponents of the reflection hypothesis hold that the media have little real impact in terms of creating culture; rather, they simply reflect the existing culture as it is. A final avenue for conceptualizing media effects is *autonomy.* According to this position, media and society vary independently. The alteration versus stabilization dimension addresses this question. Clearly, the variety of theories and ways to approach the study of media effects reveals how complicated this dimension of the media can be. As noted previously, a number of developments in the social sciences have influenced media research and will continue to do so in the future. Moreover, the study of the impact of violence in the media has generated several theories in addition to the social learning theory of Bandura. For example, the catharsis hypothesis holds that exposure to media violence has a cathartic effect, such that it reduces the tendency to be aggressive. In other words, by experiencing violence vicariously, one "gets it out of one's system."

With so many different notions of how the media affect children and adolescents, one wonders if it is possible to arrive at a clear understanding of the dynamics of experiencing the media. There is, however, a large body of media research, several thousand studies at least, that offer compelling evidence that young people do not simply walk away from the media experience exactly as they were.

Comstock (1989) has identified four "meta-factors" that need to be considered when exploring television's effect (although he believes that they have application for the other media as well).

Efficacy—the portrayal of behavior as leading to reward or the avoidance of punishment, particularly in regard to achievement and social goals, such as money and friends.

Normativeness—the portrayal of behavior as accepted or widely engaged in, within the boundaries of the commonplace, and not leading to ostracism, criticism, or loss of social standing.

Pertinence—the portrayal of behavior as particularly relevant to the circumstances being experienced by the viewer, through overlaps between the portrayal and real world cues, participants, and motives.

Susceptibility—the degree to which viewers are in a state in which the media may exercise influence, such as anger or need for the solution to a problem. (p. 195)

One final question that relates to media effects and is frequently dealt with is the question of television addiction. Several popular books on television have examined this issue, of which the most notable are Mander's (1978) *Four Arguments for the Elimination of Television* and Winn's (1977) *The Plug-in Drug,* thus contributing to the notion that television can be addictive. Winick (1988) conducted a study with over 1600 people over a six-year period, exploring what happened to them when they lost their television sets either through malfunctions or thefts. He classified the effects in four ways: extreme disruption, significant disruption, moderate disruption, and little disruption. He found that nearly one-fourth of the interviewees experienced extreme disruption and discomfort similar to the reaction of mourning over a loved one's death or apathy and lack of responsiveness to stimuli in their enviroments. Of those experiencing such discomfort, a third reported a high level of depression or melancholia. Of those studied, 39% experienced substantial disruption, that is, anxiety and unhappiness. Another 29% experienced moderate disruption, with only 8% unaffected.

Smith (1986) conducted a study on this topic and did not find strong supportive evidence. Because television addiction is a prevalent belief, even among teachers, Smith's study is worth examining in some detail. In order to develop a profile for the potential television addict, Smith conducted a literature search and compiled a list of twelve characteristics and behaviors by self-described television addicts or those who had written on the topic. Using the characteristics as a guide, she then designed a questionnaire with twenty-seven items, of which eighteen would indicate addictive behavior and nine would be considered normal behavior. Of the 981 adults mailed the questionnaire, 491 responded. Among some of the items Smith included were: "I feel depressed when I can't watch TV," "I can't walk away from the TV once it's on," "I lose track of time when I watch TV," "I cancel plans in order to watch TV," "I feel guilty about how much TV I watch," and "I feel nervous after I watch TV." Using sophisticated statistical analyses, Smith was unable to find evidence to support her hypothesis for television based on the criteria for addiction that she formulated. Nevertheless, 65% of those surveyed believed that television is addictive, and eleven of the questionnaire respondents called themselves television addicts. She concluded, "Television addiction exists as a popular concept and as a self-label for heavy viewers, but it was not possible to document its existence in this sample as a behavioral syndrome such as that described in the popular literature" (p. 125).

Kubey and Csikszentmihalyi (1990) argue that, at the very least, television can become habitual and may be addictive. They note that it depends upon how one defines addiction. In their study of the impact of television on everyday life, Kubey and Csikszentmihalyi used an experience sampling method in which subjects were randomly beeped. Once notified, they filled out an information form in which they indicated what activity they were involved in at the time, as well as their physical and emotional states. This method provided data within a very natural setting. Data from this study indicated that television addiction may occur. Unlike other types of addiction, television is very inexpensive and easily accessible. Some of their conclusions about individuals' use of television are indicative of addictive characteristics. Kubey and Csikszentmihalyi found that viewers tend to feel passive and less alert after viewing. Television viewing is often driven by the need to escape or avoid negative affective states. They also found a difference between the affective states of heavy and light viewers, with heavy viewers feeling worse than light viewers generally, and particularly when alone or during unstructured time.

> It could be argued that indiscriminate viewers also get what they want, even if they do not consider each time whether to watch TV or not. Their habit may represent a decision, made years earlier, that television watching is among the best and most enjoyable ways to spend time. However, that may not be the whole story. A long-held habit becomes so ingrained that it borders on addiction. The person may no longer be watching television because of simple want, but because he or she virtually has to. Other alternatives may seem to become progressively more remote. What might have been a choice years earlier is now a necessity. (p. 213)

Whether television addiction exists or not is not easily determined. Some people, however, clearly organize a substantial part of their lives around television and find its absence disconcerting.

A POSTSCRIPT TO MEDIA EFFECTS THEORIES

Commenting on research, someone once remarked that "if you torture the data long enough, you can get any results you want." Nowhere does this seem more apropos than with media effects research. Media effects studies will continue, but it is unlikely that any study will ever provide "clean" results. Despite great strides in statistical analysis and quantitative research, it will always be difficult to "isolate" media effects, given the fact that the mass media operate within a very complex environment. While scholars can control for a number of variables in the search for more accurate findings, they will never be able to garner the definitive data. In some cases, the same data may be interpreted differently. This is nothing new for those who engage in literary criticism. Great works of literature have been variously interpreted by equally gifted scholars. Social scientists should take note. Where does that leave the lay person, the educator, the intended audience of this book? Despite numerous theories and sometimes ambiguous findings, patterns do emerge. The purpose of this book is to allow those patterns to manifest themselves and to lay open their implications for education today.

CHAPTER 3

Coming of Age in a Media Culture

Children today live in a multimedia world. It is a world composed of media forms that are now part of the total culture in which a child is born, grows, and develops into an adult. It is also a world in which the United States is well on its way to being truly universal in its cultural diversity. Against the backdrop of the media explosion and changing cultural landscape in the country, television and other electronic media are becoming more important than ever as a type of noncertified teacher of children.

Gordon L. Berry and Joy Keiko Asamen in *Children & Television: Images in a Changing Sociocultural World,* 1993

It is nearly axiomatic to say that today's students are growing up in a media world. Ellis (1983) notes that, within the context of an electronic environment, adolescents seem to be located at the center of a technological revolution. Young people's exposure to and use of the mass media is so widespread because it is so accessible. *The Wired Bedroom* (Office of the Superintendent of Schools, 1989), a media consumption survey conducted by one California school district, revealed the following: nearly 90% of seventh- through twelfth-grade students have radios; over 60% have stereos; and 50% have televisions in their own rooms. About 18% of the students report having their own VCRs (see Figure 3.1). Greenberg, Ku, and Li (1989) found that over 80% of the sixth and tenth graders they surveyed had their own audiocassette players. They also found that 69% of the sixth graders and 73% of the tenth graders in their study reported having their own television sets. Beyond their bedrooms young people come into contact with some form of mass media virtually all day long. This chapter explores the

25

The Wired Bedroom

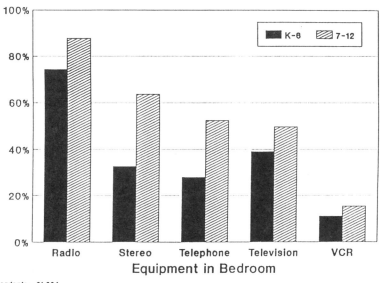

Respondents: 21,364

Media Consumption Survey, May 1, 1989

Figure 3.1 Easily Accessible Media. From The Wired Bedroom *(Office of the Superintendent of Schools, 1989). (Permission to reprint granted by the Santa Barbara County Education Office.)*

consumption of those media that are most popular with young adolescents: television, films, popular music, and magazines. Media consumption starts even before the school day for most young people. Greenberg, Ku, and Li found that sixth graders spend nearly two hours, primarily with television, radio, and audiotapes before they even leave for school. Tenth graders spend about one and a half hours with the same media in the morning.

TELEVISION

Comstock et al. (1978) found that time spent watching television steadily increases during childhood (see Figure 3.2). These numbers have remained relatively constant over time. Although hard data are not available, Hollenbeck and Slaby (1979) maintain that, given the number of hours that television is on in the average American home, children begin watching television well before their preschool years.

Likona [cited in DeGaetano (1993), p. 1] estimates that by kindergarten age the average child will have spent more time watching television than a college student has spent in four years of classes. Anderson and Levin (1976) estimate that infants watch one to two hours of television per day by age one. By age four children watch two hours a day. By age eight the average number of hours of viewing is two and a half. By age ten this time is increased to about three and a half hours per day. Abelman (1992) notes that four- and five-year-old gifted children watch more television than their peers, but the amount of television viewing decreases rapidly as these youngsters enter elementary school (see Figure 3.3). Emotionally disturbed and learning disabled children tend to watch more television than nondisabled children (Sprafkin, Gadnow, & Abelman, 1992). Viewing peaks during early adolescence at nearly four hours per day and then begins to decline. Hollenbeck and Slaby (1979) found that watching television begins as early as six months of age, and Huston et al. (1992) note that children become regular television viewers around age three. Wartella et al. (1990) found that children five years of age and under with cable access watch about three more hours of television per week than those without cable. One can see why

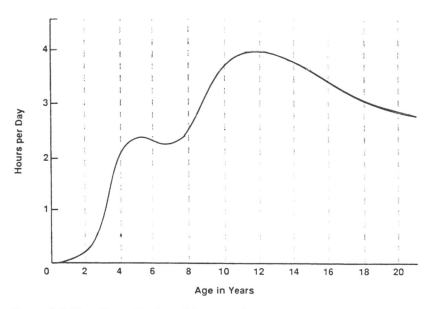

Figure 3.2 Time Spent Watching Television. From Comstock et al. (1978), p. 178, ©*RAND. (Reprinted by permission.)*

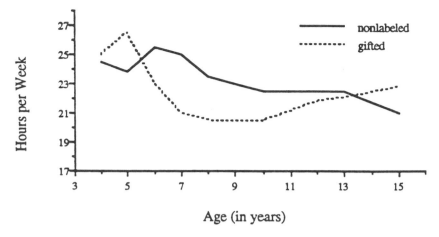

Figure 3.3 Gifted Children's Time Spent Watching Television Compared to Peers. [Reproduced with permission of the National Research Center for Gifted and Talented (Albelman, 1992).]

when the numbers for a cable channel such as Nickelodeon (a network "kids can call their own") are examined. This channel is available in 56 million homes and is viewed by an average of 6 million children per hour (Laybourne, 1993). This channel even features its own version of the Academy Awards, where the children pick their favorite programs. Wartella et al. also found that 59% of younger children report their favorite programs are found on public television. Part of this decline in viewing can be attributed to a growing interest in popular music and movies. Larson and Kubey (1983) note that another reason viewing declines is because television is targeted at the largest possible audience. As a result teenagers may become disaffected by the mainstream focus of this appeal. Still another factor may be that teenagers are both underrepresented (Signorielli, 1987) and often portrayed stereotypically on television (Peck, 1982).

The nine- to thirteen-year-old age group watches more television than any other segment of the population except the elderly. Timmer, Eccles, and O'Brien [cited in Carnegie Council on Adolescent Development (1993)] report that young adolescents (ages nine to fourteen) spend 20.7% of their time watching television. About 8 million students watch television every day in school. Over 12,000 schools are subscribers to Channel One. About one-quarter of all adolescents are heavy viewers; that is, they watch more than five hours of television on weekdays. Adolescents from single-parent families or where both parents work watch more television (Brown et al., 1990). Early adolescents from minority populations, as well as those from lower socioeconomic and lesser educated families, watch more television. Both elementary and middle and high school students watch adult programming with little parental influence on what they watch.

Adolescents prefer movies and situation comedies most of all when they watch television, followed by action-adventure and variety shows. Boys prefer action-adventure, westerns, and sports, while girls have a preference for variety, game and talk shows, soaps, movies, and children's shows (Greenberg, Ku, & Li, 1989). Approximately 10% of the 30 million daily soap opera viewers are adolescents [Cantor & Pingree, cited in Alexander (1985)].

Medrich et al. (1982) studied the lives of 764 sixth graders from Oakland, California. To insure a representative cross section of the community, they included students from public schools in twenty neighborhoods. The purpose of the study was to examine the lives of children outside of school. The study is significant in that it reveals the television habits of sixth graders. Mcdrich and his colleagues did not collect data on daily viewing patterns. Students were divided into light, medium, and heavy viewers based upon parent responses to the question: "On school days, about how much time does your child watch television?" They found that 40% of the sixth graders they studied were heavy viewers, that is, watching three or more hours per day. Minority status represented one of the biggest predictors of heavier television viewing. Parents of the black children and nearly half of the other non-Asian minority children reported that their children watched three or more hours of television per day. Students from non-Asian minority groups also indicated less selectivity in what they watched, and children from single-parent homes also tended to be heavier viewers.

Medrich et al. examined two other dimensions that might affect television viewing: family income and mothers' educational attainment. Generally, the percentage of heavier viewers declined as family income increased. The same was found to be true in regard to mothers' educational level as well, although the relationship was stronger for white children. The reason sixth graders gave for watching television was also of interest in this study: 82% indicated that they watched television because there was nothing else to do. The number of respondents indicating they could watch as much television as they wanted remained equally high. Only 35% responded that their parents did not allow them to watch some programs. This finding supports the work of Lyle and Hoffman (1972) a decade earlier, who noted that parents exercise little influence over what their children watch, and Busch (1978), who found that this pattern continues during early adolescence. Blacks and other non-Asian minorities revealed less selectivity in what they watched, with 61% of blacks and 66% of non-Asian minorities replying that they watched whatever was on television. Only 33% of whites and 33% of Asians responded this way.

Generally, girls probably watch more television than boys. Gross and Jeffries-Fox (1978) examined the viewing habits of sixth to ninth grade students by grade and sex. At each grade level the mean reported hours of daily television viewing was higher for girls than boys. Sixth grade boys reported watching 4.6 hours, while girls watched 5.2 hours per day. By ninth grade viewing patterns evened out, with each sex watching a little over three hours per day.

There are gender differences in viewing styles. In her study of adolescent and adult cable viewers, Heeter (1988) found that females are more likely to watch the same program on a daily or weekly basis and to check the program guides to see what programs are available. They are more likely to watch a show from start to finish. Males check more channels and change channels more often. They tend to watch more than one show at a time and to shift channels to see what else is on.

Why do adolescents watch television? Greenberg, Ku, and Li (1989) examined the media uses and gratifications of 476 adolescents in grades six and ten and asked them this question. Thirty-four percent and 20% of sixth and tenth graders, respectively, indicated that they did so to relax. Over 30% of each grade did so because they wanted company, excitement, or to pass time. Television is also watched for news. Over 50% of the sixth graders and 60% of the tenth graders watched television for the day's news. Drew and Reeves (1980) also found that a substantial number of students in their study of third through seventh graders watched television news in formats designed for both adults and children. These adolescents (sixth and tenth graders) also reported they used televiewing for guidance (Greenburg, Ku, & Li, 1989). Over a third of each of the respondents from both grades watch television to learn about life. Twenty-one percent watch to learn how to handle problems in the sixth grade and 17% of tenth graders watch for this reason.

The percentages are very similar when these students are asked if they use television to learn about themselves. Again, over 30% from each grade watched television for this reason. Television also serves as a distractor, particularly for younger adolescents. A third reported watching television for this reason, while nearly a quarter of the older adolescents watched television of this reason. As expected, a significant number of adolescents turn on the television for entertainment (50% of sixth graders and 42% of tenth graders).

MOVIES

As movies became popular in the 1920s, they attracted large audiences that included children and adolescents. Dale's 1935 study, *Children's Attendance at Motion Pictures*, highlighted this fact. He found that early elementary school children attended the movies, on average, approximately once every two weeks. Students in grades four through twelve went to the movies, on average, about once a week. So popular were movies, as well as concerns about young people seeing movies, that by the 1930s many high schools offered movie appreciation courses, which were designed to help students become critical viewers. During the 1950s the film industry discovered the "teen pic," and a whole new movie genre came into existence. Cheap to produce and popular with young people, these movies quickly became a staple in Hollywood. Today, this adolescent market has been responsible for the tremendous growth in the popularity of horror and slasher films. Little wonder then that, in a recent Gallup survey, teenagers reported that their favorite pastimes are going out with friends, watching television, and going to the movies [Bezilla, cited in Schultze et al. (1991), p. 59]. One of the major target populations for the movie industry is the male ten-to-fifteen-years-old. This accounts for the blockbuster success of recent movies and their sequels like *Batman, Terminator*, and *Wayne's World*. Young adolescents also watch films for older audiences. A media use survey by Ellis (1983) found that over 66% of them had watched an R-rated movie the month preceding the survey. The youth market is also one of the driving economic forces in the film industry. In 1989 summer hit films accounted for 40% of the $5 billion moviegoers paid to go to the movies that year (Greenwald, 1990). Children and adolescents are the major targeted audience. In many cases film executives count on young adolescents to be repeat viewers in order to insure a film's economic success.

About 18% of the students surveyed in *The Wired Bedroom* (Office of the Superintendent of Schools, 1989) indicated that they went to the theater on a weekly basis. A study conducted for the Motion Picture Association of America [cited in Greenberg (1988), p. 52] illustrates the appeal of film to teenagers. Two age groups, twelve-to-fifteen-year-olds and sixteen-to-twenty-year-olds, accounted for a third of the total admissions to movies from 1985 through 1987. The VCR has changed early adolescents' movie viewing habits by extending the possibilities for movies, as well as other visual media consumption, among this segment of the population. With three out of four households owning a VCR, over 40% of seventh through twelfth graders reported renting a movie on a weekly basis (*The Wired Bedroom*). Adolescents with access to VCRs attend fewer movies in theaters, and boys show a greater preference for watching movies than girls. While girls do watch movies, they also prefer viewing taped television programs more than boys (Hughes & Dobrow, 1988). Among adolescents, horror and comedies are the most preferred film genres. This is true for both males and females (Greenberg, Ku, & Li, 1989). Greenberg, Siemicki, et al. (1993) conducted a survey among ninth and tenth graders to see how often they viewed R-rated films with sexual content. He and his colleagues selected forty-five films, with thirty having an R rating. The results indicated that these students regularly viewed these types of movies. Greenberg and Heeter (1987) found that adolescents reported being able to watch more R-rated movies by VCR with little guidance or intervention from their parents. Roe (1989), who has conducted extensive research on Swedish adolescents and VCR usage, found that those experiencing self-esteem problems used VCRs more often. In addition, adolescents who do not find experiences in school that promote self-esteem watch more violent, horror, and pornographic movies.

The VCR is popular with children as well. Krendl et al. (1993) studied preschoolers' use and understanding of VCRs. Using a sample of fifty children (predominately four and five year olds), Krendl and her colleagues found that 64% indicated that they knew how to use a VCR, although many were vague in their responses when asked what a VCR does. Almost half of the sample could put a tape in the machine. If children are developing competency with media technology at an early age, their access to VHS programs is limited. In their study of video media for children in one community, Wartella et al. (1990) found that, aside from Disney movies and old cartoons, children's tapes consisted of television-oriented products dominated by toy-related programming. Educational tapes were television-related as well, such as *Sesame Street* and *The Muppets*.

POPULAR MUSIC

While music is generally associated with older children and adolescents, younger children have considerable access to music as well. Wartella et al. (1990) found that 35% of children aged zero to five had their own radios, with nearly 26% having their own stereos. These percentages increase to 65.5% and 44.5%, respectively, for children aged six to twelve. Popular music is easily shared, and taping music from the stereo or a peer's recording is relatively easy. Music is used to relax, escape, affect mood, and express healthy rebellion. It provides a source of commonality within the peer group. With advances in audio technology, adolescents can take their music with them virtually anywhere. Lull (1992) writes, "Popular musicians are loved, even worshiped, not only for their abilities to write songs and perform them publicly, but for their ability to 'speak' to their audiences." Moreover, "Even an artist whose only contact with the audience is through the sale of millions of compact discs and tapes communicates 'personally' with each listener" (Lull, p. 2).

Christenson and Roberts (1990) found that seventh graders listen to about two and a half hours of music per day, while ninth graders reported listening to about three and a half hours per day. Popular music may in fact be the most accessible media to the middle school students because it is so inexpensive. Recall that 90% of seventh through twelfth graders have radios in their rooms, while 60% have their own bedroom stereos. Brown, Campbell, and Fischer's (1986) study of twelve to fourteen year olds found that they reported listening to the radio an average of twenty-two and a half hours per week, with girls listening about six more hours per week than boys. Wells and Hakanen (1991) and Carroll et al. (1993) reported greater use of the radio by girls than boys, a finding supported by Greenberg, Ku, and Li (1989). The dominant radio content preferences for adolescents are rock music and black music, followed by sports and the weather (Greenberg, Ku, & Li, 1989).

MUSIC VIDEOS

Since its inception in 1981, MTV has transformed the way popular music is viewed. Music television has created a whole new dimension for media as popular culture. MTV is the fastest growing channel in cable history. Its popularity can be attributed to a number of factors, not the least of which is that it combines several entertainment media already attractive to adolescents., that is, television, rock music, and film.

In interviews of 100 fourth through sixth graders, Christenson, Begert, and Gunther (1989) found that these students, while very aware of music videos, were more attracted to popular music. While the study did not measure the amount of music television these students watched, 69% reported that they had not watched any the day before the interview, and the total mean time was only .34 of an hour. Therefore, while most of these young people watched music television, they did so only occasionally. Christenson and his colleagues (1989) suggest two reasons why popular music and regular television have more appeal than music videos to nine-to-twelve-year-olds: the sexual content of music videos and difficulty in trying to interpret them. When asked what they should not see in music videos, 34% mentioned sexual content. When asked what they did not like about music videos, 15% mentioned sexual images and references to sex. The authors of this study concluded that these young people perceive that music videos contain imagery considered taboo for children. Similarly, 14% indicated confusion and disorientation as a reason they did not like music videos. Viewing increases with age. Nearly 35% of the adolescents surveyed by Brown, Cramond, and Wilde (1974) reported watching music videos every day. Sun and Lull (1986), in their study of 600 ninth through twelfth graders, found that they watched an average of just over two hours per day. Boys and girls watched about the same amount of MTV during the week, with girls watching more than boys on weekends. Sherman [cited in Gelman et al. (1985), p. 55] reported that those adolescents who watched more MTV tended to be better students. Adolescents in this study provided a number of reasons for watching MTV; the reason most often given related specifically to the music, whether it was to see a particular performer and/or music. The second most frequently given reason for viewing was for enjoyment/entertainment. A third reason given related to the visual aspects of MTV.

Finally, Sun and Lull found these high school students used MTV to pass the time, either because television has nothing else to offer them, for companionship, or out of habit.

Walker (1987) examined the relationship of watching MTV with the use of other entertainment media, that is, television, radio, recordings, and movies among seventh graders and juniors in high school. As expected, he found that watching MTV positively correlated to listening to recordings of rock music, as well as rock format radio stations. Walker notes that adolescents who watch MTV do not seem to be substituting viewing for listening to other sources of rock music. He found some evidence that music video watching is related to attending movies. He found a positive relationship between seventh graders' attendance at romantic comedies and teen appeal motion pictures. Among high school juniors he found a positive correlation for total motion picture attendance. Walker speculates that the frequent use of rock music by film makers, particularly those produced for adolescent populations, may explain part of this relationship. Walker's point is a good one when one considers that motion picture soundtracks often prove more profitable than box office receipts. Within specific media genres Walker found MTV watching was positively related to exposure to two types of romantic fantasy genres, that is, daytime soap operas for juniors and romantic comedy films for seventh graders. An interesting negative correlation emerged in Walker's findings, in which MTV watchers evidenced a negative correlation between music television and action/adventure programs, which typically contain high levels of violence. Walker observes that, given the levels of violence on MTV, watchers may be substituting one kind of media violence for another.

Brown, Campbell, and Fischer (1986) explored this theme as well. They found that adolescents watched rock videos primarily for diversion; that is, "the videos are exciting, they're a good thing to do when alone and they get the adolescents in a mood they like to be in." A significant number of adolescents watch music videos to divert their attention away from worries as well. Respondents in their study also reported they like music videos because they are better than simply listening to songs and because they teach the viewer how to dance. Brown, Campbell, and Fischer's study is important because it also points to the differences, both ethnic and gender, in both the uses and responses among adolescents. This may have implications in terms of how different groups may be affected. One of the focuses in their study was music videos as a "school of life." This area consisted of three items: "remind me of things happening in my own life"; "they show how other people deal with the same problems I have"; and "they help me learn things about myself."

Blacks who reported watching music videos "a lot" differed significantly from whites (23% versus 17%). Blacks also reported using these videos for "trend surveillance," that is, to learn how to dance and what the latest fashions are, much more often than whites. Again, for those adolescents in this study who reported watching music videos "a lot" for this kind of information, 55% of blacks reported doing so as opposed to 29% of whites. This is an interesting finding, given the fact that the world of music videos is overwhelmingly a white world. Blacks are much more likely to use music videos as a "social stimulus." Items measuring this dimension included: "it's something I can do with friends"; "music videos fill the silence when I'm with other people and no one is talking"; and "to have something to talk about with my friends." Again, for those that responded that they watched music videos "a lot" for these reasons, blacks far outnumbered whites (41% and 33%, respectively). Heavy black music video viewers also wished they were like the characters in the videos more often than their white counterparts. While 35% of the blacks expressed this wish, only 22% of the whites did so. Female viewers watch music videos more often than males (82.7% and 76.2%, respectively), and they indicated that they watch videos "every day" more than males (37.2% versus 31.9%).

Paugh's (1988) study, which included older adolescents, found that heavy MTV viewers watched MTV with more companions. These viewers reported greater participation in music interests. They purchased more recordings, spent more time reading rock magazines, watched more television, and attended more movies.

If factors such as gender and race affect the use of the music videos, they are important to interpretation as well. Brown and Schulze (1990) examined the way older adolescent blacks and whites interpreted the music video by Madonna entitled *Papa Don't Preach*. Students viewed the video in an undergraduate communications class. Brown and Schulze found considerable differences between the way the different races and genders understood the video. While 97% of the white females mentioned pregnancy in their interpretation of the video, 73% of the black females noted this element. The differences between black and white males is more striking. Among black males only 43% mentioned pregnancy, compared to 85% of white males. There are racial differences in interpretations of the primary theme of the video that are very significant. The most prevalent response among blacks regarding the theme was that the video is about a father-daughter relationship (43% males and 50% females). Only about a quarter of the whites interpreted the video in this manner (22% males and 25% females). Considerably more males than females identified a boy-girl relationship as the primary theme. The most common primary theme identified among whites was that the video is about teenage pregnancy.

PRINT MEDIA

Print media are popular with both elementary and high school students. In this section magazines (including comic books) and newspapers will be examined. With over 12,000 magazines in circulation today, there are more magazines designed to appeal to the youth market than ever before.

Children are not without their own magazines. Wartella et al. (1990) found that over 43% of the children aged five and under had their own magazine subscriptions. This percentage increased considerably in the six- to twelve-year-old category, with nearly 62% of these children being magazine subscribers. Over 20% of both of the age groups maintained memberships in book clubs. The Newspaper Readership Project (1980) study indicated that two-thirds of the children between the ages of six and seventeen read magazines. Avery (1979) notes that adolescents not only read magazines aimed at them, but also those designed for adults as well. Trends in the magazine industry as a whole are also reflected in the teenage market. Unlike general interest magazines of the past, today's special interest magazines help create and reinforce various subcultures (Snow, 1983). One of the best examples of this is a publication like *Screamer*, which is designed to catch the attention of predominately male, early adolescent, heavy metal music fans who refer to themselves as "headbangers." "Fanzines," magazines devoted to individual adolescent media personalities, are quite popular. Humor magazines such as *Mad* and *Cracked* are also aimed at middle school–aged males who appreciate sarcasm. Comic books have experienced a resurgence in recent years, largely due to their popularity with early adolescent males. Superhero comic books, which constitute about 80% of the industry, generate sales of $96 million annually

(Pecora, 1992). A third of the sixth graders in Greenberg, Ku, and Li's study (1989) indicated that they have their own collection of comic books. Children are being introduced to comic books at an increasingly younger age. To appeal to younger readers, comic book heros are now being used in children's books. These "comic book readers" are designed for incremental reading levels so that the same story line can be upgraded as the child's reading level advances. Like other types of children's books, vocabulary lists are included.

The early adolescent girls' magazine market also thrives. When surveyed about what magazines they read most often, teenage magazines topped the list for female adolescents, followed by fashion magazines. On newsstands one can find *Seventeen*, as well as similarly titled magazines like *Fifteen* and *Fourteen*. Most recently, *New Moon*, a new magazine, has entered the market. Unlike the typical adolescent girl magazines that focus on fashion, makeup, and boys, this new publication is designed to build self-esteem among young girls as they move into their adolescent years. The periodical market provides an avenue for creating media personalities who often become heroes and role models for early adolescents as they consider identity issues. Another print medium popular with adolescent girls is the teenage romance novel. Like comic books, this fiction is now becoming part of the educational publishing world. Christian-Smith (1991) observes that publishers are attracting new readers with teenage romance fiction. These works now regularly appear in book clubs such as Scholastic Inc., a leader in the elementary and high school market. More specifically, Christian-Smith points out that these novels are becoming an important segment of the educational publishing industry in the Hi-low market. Hi-low books combine high interest content with easy readability aimed at students who are "reluctant readers."

Schramm, Lyle, and Parker (1961), in their study of children's patterns of newspaper readership, found that not until around eighth grade did the newspaper become that important on a daily basis. Drew and Reeves's (1980) investigation of elementary school children indicated that they may read the newspaper more often than they are given credit for. Their sample of 435 third through seventh graders revealed that a third reported reading the newspaper "almost every day," while another 28% reported reading it "sometimes." However, only 19% reported reading the front page. Comics are the most popular (60%), with sports being the second most given reason (22%) for reading the paper.

In the Newspaper Readership Project (1980) the Newspaper Advertising Bureau sponsored a major study of media usage in the United States. Interviews with mothers indicated that 54% of the children in the 817 households surveyed read the newspaper. As children grow older, these percentages increase. For example, the mothers of these children indicated that 34% of children aged six to eight read the newspaper. For fifteen-to-seventeen-year-olds this percentage climbs to 72%. Children's self-reports were higher. The best predictors of newspaper reading were availability on a regular basis and parental readership.

Cobb (1986) conducted an extensive study of newspaper readership among 1355 high school juniors and seniors. She found that these students read the newspaper for very specific kinds of information. They read the front page, television schedules, and the amusement pages most often. Her findings support other studies that show that adolescents prefer to get their news from television. Despite availability in 80% of the homes in the study, only 34% read the newspaper as a matter of habit. Cobb categorized the students as heavy readers, sporadic readers, scanners, and apathetic readers. Heavy readers read the newspaper four to six times per week and spend anywhere from sixteen minutes to over two hours with the newspaper on an average daily basis. This group, Cobb noted, is the most likely to believe that television news does not provide enough depth and represents the second largest group of readers. Their parents tend to be heavier readers as well. Sporadic readers (the third largest group) average one to three weekday newspapers per week and spend over fifteen minutes in reading time. They also spend more time than any of the other groups with other media. They are generally satisfied getting most of their news from television. Of the four groups they are the most likely to read the advertisements, and their parents are strong newspaper readers as well. Scanners read the newspaper four to six times per week, but for fifteen minutes or less. They regularly read the front page and the comic sections. Apathetic readers read, on average, one to three newspapers per week for fifteen minutes or less per day. They represent the largest group of readers. Their parents are not particularly serious newspaper readers. Two factors affecting readership are lack of time to devote to reading the newspaper and the ability to get news from other sources. The best predictors of adolescent newspaper readership, according to Cobb, are the perception of time to read the newspaper, availability in the home, and usage of other media. Given the data, Cobb concluded that "virtually half of the sampled high school juniors and seniors represent only fair prospects for developing a newspaper reading habit" (p. 324).

Greenberg, Ku, and Li (1989) found that the most read sections of the newspaper for males were sports, comics, television, and movie listings. Girls turned to newspapers most often for the comics and movie listings. Supporting the findings of Cobb, neither gender nor grade level used the newspaper for national news, international news, or editorials.

RULES GOVERNING MEDIA USE

An issue raised with some regularity is what rules today's students have regarding media use. Generally, it can be stated that young people have access to various media, both qualitatively as well as quantitatively, that they are not supposed to have. Industry rating systems provide an indirect set of rules by restricting the availability of certain types of media content. Their effectiveness is questionable. Studies consistently indicate that adolescents under seventeen clearly view films with violent and sexual content that carry an R rating (Ellis, 1983; Greenberg & Heeter, 1987; Greenberg, Siemicki, et al., 1993; Greenberg, Linsangan, et al., 1993; Buerkel-Rothfuss et al., 1993). Schultze et al. (1991) point out that, following the release of the first *Rambo* film, this Stallone character became a major hero for young adolescents, even though the film carried a rating that should have precluded them from seeing it. Record label warnings championed by Tipper Gore and the Parents Music Resource Center have met with mixed success. Only fear of government regulation seems to prompt action by the recording industry.

When Krendl et al. (1993) examined parental rules governing preschoolers' VCR and television use, they found that parents clearly have rules limiting both what is viewed and how much programming and tapes are viewed. Krendl et al. also found that these rules are "often unspoken and invoked arbitrarily." The enforcement of these rules fell to the mother. One can generalize as well that, as children grow older, parental control over the media declines. The Newspaper Readership Project study found parental control and guidance of children's television viewing is governed by two variables: the age of the child and the family's social economic status (SES). The age group for which more guidance and control are exercised is for children aged six to eight. This study found that 72% of the children have rules about what kinds of television they can watch, and 66% of them are encouraged to watch certain programs. By the time these children become adolescents, these percentages have dropped to 29% and 42% respectively. Whites exercised significantly more control and guidance than nonwhites. The more educated the mother, the higher was the input on television viewing as well.

Greenberg, Ku, and Li (1989), in their study of sixth and tenth graders, found that parents' mediation of media experiences is stronger for younger adolescents. They also found that mediation is slightly stronger for females than males. The results reported here are based on the Likert scale with 1 = never and 4 = very often. Televiewing is still a family activity although more so for sixth graders (3.0 for sixth graders and 2.7 for tenth graders). Moreover, the respondents in this study indicated that their parents know what they watch fairly often. Extrapolating from this data, one can say parents don't typically discuss what their children watch, nor do they suggest programming. Parents offer rules about the number of hours television can be watched sometimes, more so for school days than on weekends. Regarding movies, parents have a pretty good idea of what their children are watching (2.8 for both grades) but, again, don't discuss them much.

Rules governing VCR usage among adolescents are in evidence, but these rules are not particularly strong. Respondents to Greenberg, Ku, and Li's (1989) survey reported that rules sometimes existed in their homes regarding videotape content and how late they could stay up and watch. These sixth and tenth graders indicated that a more frequent rule controlled how often the VCR could be used, more so with the sixth graders. Nearly a quarter of those surveyed reported that their parents used the VCR as a reward, but rarely as a punishment. Neither did they indicate that their parents told them what not to watch or that they watch videotapes too much.

CONCLUSION

Media use constitutes one of the major activities of children and adolescents outside of the classroom. When one combines time spent with television, music, and printed materials, today's student spends several hours a day with media (as many as eight hours per day). While much of this media usage is for entertainment purposes, the research suggests that young people are learning (often informally) and that they are being affected by the media in both their form and content.

CHAPTER 4

Mind over Media?

All television is education television. The only question is, What is it teaching?

Nicholas Johnson, former U.S. Federal Communications Commissioner

I believe that one reason why it is hard to interest some children in school today is that their minds have been filled and their imagination thrilled with too vivid motion pictures, and, when these children come to school, they are disappointed because the teacher cannot make the subject as interesting as a motion picture.

Peter Olesen, school superintendent, addressing
the National Education Association, 1914

The impact of the mass media upon the intellectual development of today's students has created tremendous controversy. Nor is it new as Olesen's eighty-year-old address testifies. Regarding television, Comstock et al. (1978) have observed, "The least contestable generalization about the effects of television on young persons is that they learn from the medium." In fact, children may have an inclination to believe that the medium is a teacher. Dorr (1980) notes that comments from children in her research often indicate that they believe amusing programs are also made to teach them. This may be true of commercials as well. Meyer, Donohue, and Henke [cited in Graves (1982), p. 53] found that five- to twelve-year-old black children believed that commercials are designed to teach people, not to sell a product. Because time spent watching television is greater than time spent using all of the other media combined, most of the research has looked at television.

In this chapter the focus is on cognitive development and academic achievement. Other chapters explore what children and adolescents learn in terms of social behaviors, as well as information, such as sexual and political, that is relevant to them. Here, two areas will be explored: the effect of media consumption upon academic achievement and the learning process itself.

EDUCATIONAL TELEVISION

Considerable debate has surrounded the efficacy of educational programming. While the case can be made that all television is educational television, here, educational television refers to those kinds of programs that are designed to teach skills and information that traditionally fall under the rubric of school curriculum. To provide a fuller picture it is important to mention some of the early research history on educational programming. Since its inception *Sesame Street* has been widely acclaimed for its educational value. It has also been blamed for "the death of reading." The flagship of educational television, *Sesame Street* began as a program to provide disadvantaged preschool children who remained at home with the kind of experiences provided in school by Head Start or similar educational programs. Nearly half of the preschool children in this country watch it weekly, and over 5.8 million children between the ages of two and five watch an average of three episodes per week (Healy, 1990). Initially, expectations for *Sesame Street* were high. Lesser (1974) noted: "Here is *Sesame Street*'s main lesson: it deliberately uses television to teach without hiding its educational intentions and yet attracts a large and devoted audience of young children from all parts of the country" (p. 234). And so it did. Early expectations of the numbers of viewers proved to be greatly underestimated. Not only did television represent an opportunity to provide an educational experience for millions of viewers, but also to turn every home into a special kind of classroom. Again from Lesser: "Television does not hover over children with demands and expectations. They can watch without being tested, graded, reprimanded or even observed by others. They are saved from the threat of humiliation or riducule for not living up to what is expected of them" (p. 246).

Tremendous planning by a team of teachers, educational psychologists, and television professionals preceded the program. Ball and Bogatz (1972) summarized how broad the scope of this project was.

This planning team developed an ambitious set of goals. These goals fell into four categories: 1) symbolic representation, that is, letters, numbers, geometric forms; 2) cognitive processes (perceptual discrimination, relationship concepts, classification, ordering; 3) physical environment; and 4) social environment. All told, these goals numbered over sixty and were couched in behavioral terms and represented considerable organization and planning by a team of professionals.

The early evaluations of *Sesame Street* proved positive. In their extensive studies Ball and Bogatz (Ball & Bogatz, 1970; Bogatz & Ball, 1972) administered tests to *Sesame Street* viewers, consisting of a battery of over 200 items, which required two hours of testing. Testing took place in several different cities. Controlling for maturational effects, IQ, previous attainments, and home background constant, Ball and Bogatz found that frequent viewers made relatively large and significant gains. Moreover, they found evidence to suggest that three and four year olds could learn skills traditionally reserved for five year olds! Disadvantaged children who were frequent viewers did better on the measures of the show's goals than middle-class children who rarely or never watched *Sesame Street* (Ball & Bogatz, 1972).

In *Sesame Street Revisited* Cook et al. (1975) evaluated Ball and Bogat's findings. They argued that Ball and Bogat's research contained a number of methodological flaws. The one that has received attention in popular works critical of *Sesame Street,* such as Winn's (1977) *The Plug-in Drug* is that some of the children, particularly those who were disadvantaged, watched the program with encouragement from parents, thus inflating test results and tainting the data. Because the program was not expected to be popular, some of the children in the research population were encouraged on a regular basis to watch the program through home visits and telephone calls from those conducting the research. These visitors and callers prompted parents to encourage their children to view as well. Cook et al. noted:

> Encouragement-to-view "Sesame Street" had more desirable consequences than viewing "Sesame Street." One reason for this is probably that encouragement increased viewing among disadvantaged children almost to the level of advantaged children in Philadelphia. But, since encouragement probably had effects over and above those directly attributable to viewing, it is possible that the encouraged children were especially conscious of being in a research study, or that the testers behaved differently with encouraged children, or that the parents of

encouraged children interacted more with the child in ways relevant to "Sesame Street." (p. 24)

Cook et al. also noted that the positive publicity surrounding the program might also have contributed to an overestimation of its effects. Nevertheless, other studies have demonstrated that children do learn from *Sesame Street* (Huston et al., 1992).

In their survey of research on a number of educational programs, Bryant, Alexander, and Brown (1983) found evidence that some of these programs are effective. Ball and Bogatz (1972) found that *Electric Co.* had significant positive effects on reading, especially among first graders. *Freestyle,* a program that will be treated in more depth in a later chapter, achieved some of its goals in terms of challenging gender stereotypes. Similarly, *Big Blue Marble,* designed to break down cultural barriers, reported very positive results. Summarizing the research on children's educational programs, Bryant, Alexander, and Brown concluded that "the dominant generalization to be drawn from analyzing these outstanding programs is that viewers can and do learn from educational television" (p. 26).

A few years ago, a new kind of educational programming became available. Since its introduction in 1990, Channel One (Whittle Communications) has stirred considerable and often heated debate. The question of what students learn from the ten minutes of educational programming has partially been eclipsed by the issue of commercialization of the classroom with the two minutes of commercials that accompany each program. Nevertheless, with several million students watching on a daily basis, the question of whether students are learning from this "new educational genre" (DeVaney, 1994) is an important one. Johnston and his colleagues at the Institute for Social Research have conducted an ongoing study on Channel One since its introduction. Most recently, they examined the use of Channel One to improve civic discourse in the classroom (Johnston et al., 1994). In 1992–1993 Channel One created a series of segments entitled *You Decide* as part of the programming. These fourteen segments, consisting of selected news events centered around public issues, were similar in format to the public issue pamphlets developed at the Harvard Social Studies project recognizing that one of the important goals of the social studies is to prepare future citizens to engage in critical discourse about public affairs. Over the course of the broadcast season, Channel One broadcast fourteen segments of *You Decide.* Students watched segments on such issues as public funding for education of children in public schools, capital punishment, and immigration policy (see Table 4.1). Eight teachers received training in the use of public issues discussion strategies to prepare them to lead students in discussions based on the *You Decide* segments. As Johnson et al. noted, "The ultimate goal of this experiment was to teach students how to discuss controversial issues using oral strategies designed to facilitate thorough exploration of an issue in an atmosphere of calm deliberation" (p. 13).

Table 4.1.   You Decide *Segments from 1992–1993.*

Public Issue	Date of Broadcast
Should public funds be used to educate children in nonpublic schools	November?
Does the government have the right to execute a citizen for certain crimes?	November
Is there a place for prayer in public schools?	December
Does the government have the right to impose curfews for teenagers?	January
Should gays be allowed to serve in the U.S. military?	January
Should the U.S. military intervene in Bosnia-Herzegovina?	February
Should doctor-assisted suicide be legal?	February
Should males and females be integrated on high school football teams?	February
Should a five-day waiting period be imposed for the purchase of guns?	March
Should the United States continue to trade with China while China continues to violate human rights?	March
Should major league baseball be exempt from antitrust laws?	April
Should workers continue to pay into the social security system, even though the money may soon be used up?	April
Is the U.S. policy toward Haitian refugees fair?	April
Should women be allowed to fight on the front lines of our nation's wars?	May

To measure the effectiveness of viewing and discussion, Johnston et al. employed several different measures with two groups of students. One group watched *You Decide,* followed by teacher-led discussion. Another group of students simply watched the programs. Measures included current events knowledge tests, critical analysis by students of excerpts of transcripts of public issues discussions, and analysis of videotapes made of small groups of students discussing the *You Decide* programs. In terms of oral discourse skills, Johnston and his colleagues wanted to see if the combination of viewing and discussion would improve not only the *substantive* aspects of oral discourse, but the *procedural* ones as well. The substantive dimension included styles of argument that facilitate a thorough examination of a person's point of view, as well as the reasoning behind it. The procedural aspects included elements such as summarizing another's points, encouraging participation by all, and negative elements such as personal attacks and monopolizing discussion.

Students' skills for discussing issues did not noticeably improve. Students in the experimental group did, however, demonstrate that they could identify some of the characteristics of effective discussion, even though they had trouble applying them on their own. These students scored significantly higher on the Public Issues Analysis Test (PIAT). Students who participated in the discussions also developed an appreciation of the complexity of issues and stated that they enjoyed discussing them. Students in the experimental group also scored higher on the current events test. They averaged 74% versus 67% by the control group. Moreover, grade-point average in this study proved to be a weak predictor of performance on the test. The difference between "A" viewers and "C" viewers in the control group was only 5%. However, in a much larger study, which measured the current events knowledge of Channel One viewers, the difference between high and average achieving students was twelve percentage points. These findings would seem to indicate that those students with lower grade-point averages benefitted more from the discussions following the *You Decide* segments.

One of the problems identified in this study relates to the amount of information provided in the *You Decide* segments. Each segment lasted up to six minutes. This length imposed serious limitations on the amount of information that could be provided. Nevertheless, Johnston et al. (1994) concluded:

The *You Decide* segments advance the potential of school-based news broadcasts by setting the agenda and triggering debate, and perhaps making the very activity they describe—classroom-based citizen debate—more intriguing to social studies teachers around the country. Previous efforts to infuse this type of activity in the social studies curriculum have not resulted in large-scale adoption. The regular appearance of *You Decide* features in 12,000 schools may be the very catalyst for change that is needed. (pp. 28–29)

In another series of studies [summarized in Johnston, Brezezinski, & Anderman (1994)], Johnston and his colleagues examined the impact of Channel One over three years in terms of students' short- and long-term learning after viewing the program. They also examined students' and teachers' assessments of Channel One. Separate studies were conducted for each of three years, beginning with 1990. Over the three years two factors had an effect on their findings. The first represented an evolution in content and format. The introduction of *You Decide* as a feature represented one change. In another change during the 1992–1993 season, Whittle expanded its treatment of "hard news" and put less emphasis on teen issues (see Figure 4.1). During that season Channel One also featured fewer public service announcements as well. A second factor that impacted findings was the isolation of certain segments in the research populations. In the second year (1991–1992 school year) of research, Johnston and Anderman identified two

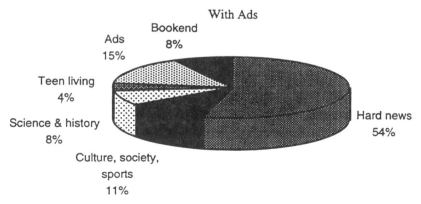

Figure 4.1 *Distribution of Topics by Time, Fall '92 and Winter '93. [Reproduced with permission of the authors, J. Johnston, Evelyn J. Brzezinski, & E. M. Anderman. (1994). Taking the Measure of Channel One: A Three Year Perspective. Institute for Social Research, University of Michigan.]*

schools involved in the study as "exemplary." In these exemplary schools both teachers and students valued current events as a topic for school learning. That year also included middle school populations in the study.

Experiments on short-term learning employed students from both public and parochial high schools. Using a true-false testing format on major facts from three news broadcasts, it was found that students who viewed Channel One scored 3%, 8%, and 7% higher, yielding an average score that was 6% higher than the control group, which had not viewed Channel One. A study on long-term learning (over a period of twelve weeks) in 1990–1991 yielded an average advantage of 3.3% for Channel One viewers. This study employed student populations from eleven schools. While a gain of a little more than three percentage points was rather small, these researchers found wide variation between schools. Some schools reported no differences in scores, while others reported advantages ranging from 6–9%. Despite the relatively small gains in scores for Channel One viewers, teachers gave the program ratings averaging from A− to B+. Moreover, when asked if they would recommend Channel One to other schools and teachers, 60% of the teachers surveyed reported that they would recommend it "strongly" or "very strongly."

A study the following year revealed the reason for the wide range of differences among scores found in the previous study. Upon closer examination those schools that reported higher scores in 1990–1991 valued a place for current events in the curriculum. Therefore, many of the teachers routinely discussed the content of the Channel One programs. Overall, high school test results showed only a 3.6% increase in scores that measured long-term learning. Factoring out scores from the exemplary schools, this percentage dropped to 3%. Middle schools reported even lower scores than the high schools. Students who watched Channel One at this level demonstrated only an average 2.25% increase over nonviewers. The following year, Whittle Communications altered the content of Channel One and replaced features on teen living and entertainment with more hard news, thus increasing the time for news from an average of three to six minutes. In addition, fewer stories and topics were featured, but those that aired were treated in more depth. In the third year of the study, test results on long-term learning reflected both a change in content and in data from a group consisting of the "best" Channel One schools. The criteria for being selected as one of the best schools included the value both students and teacher placed on learning about current events, attention to broadcasts by teachers and students, discussion of the news segments, and flexibility to deviate from the day's planned activities on occasion to discuss an important news story. Departing from earlier research, Johnston and Anderman tested for a broad understanding of events rather than for highly specific details.

In this third year study high school students who watched Channel One scored an average of 5% higher than those who did not. Middle school viewers scored approximately 7% higher than their nonviewing counterparts. Although not originally designed for middle school students, Johnston and Anderman concluded that Channel One seems to work equally well for both levels in terms of student learning. Several factors were predictors of how much students learned. Generally, students with higher grade-point averages (GPAs) scored higher on the measures. Thus, "A" students did better than "B" students, and "C" students averaged only .81% better than those "C" students who did not watch Channel One. Male viewers scored higher than female viewers in both the high school and the middle school (4.6% and 2%, respectively). Grade level was also a factor with eleventh graders performing the best. This third year study also explored whether watching news in school might have a "priming effect" that leads students to seek opportunities outside of school in terms of pursuing news stories; however, no data emerged to support this hypothesis.

Given the findings from the third year study, Johnston and Anderman addressed the question of how improvements in learning based on watching Channel One compared to other innovative curricula. Using statistical computations they arrived at an effect size. Johnston and Anderman compared the effect size of Channel One with those from other innovative curricula. They concluded that the effect size from the Channel One study of exemplary schools is "moderate to large." These findings clearly suggest that this programming has educational merit.

Two other studies have looked at the impact of Channel One on student learning. Tiene (1993) conducted a study in four Midwestern junior high schools. After two weeks of viewing, Tiene gave students a twenty-seven–item quiz based upon the material presented in the broadcasts. Students who watched Channel One scored an average of 60% correct on the quiz, while nonviewers averaged a score of 52%. Tiene concluded that Channel One held considerable promise if schools chose to take advantage of the opportunity. Knupfer and Hayes (1994) reported very different findings in their study of the effects of Channel One on students' knowledge of current events. They conducted their study using junior and senior high school students. Knupfer and Hayes looked at overall current events knowledge and students' recall of specific news and advertising. To test general current events knowledge they administered five standardized current events tests developed by *US News and World Report.* They found no significant difference between the control and experimental group. The mean scores were nearly identical. While the senior high school students scored higher than the junior high students, this proved the case for both viewers and nonviewers alike. To measure knowledge and recall of Channel One, some viewers took a pop quiz immediately following viewing, while others took a quiz twenty-four hours later. Each question about the news had three parts. The first required students to simply recall the topic of the news stories. The second asked them to explain something about the news stories, and the third required the students to explain the relevance or implications of the story. While most of the students could answer the first part of the question, fewer could explain what the stories were about. Only one student in the entire sample could relate the implications or importance of the news stories. Perhaps one of the most interesting findings in this study was that students remembered the advertisements better than the news stories. This finding is discussed in a later chapter. Knupfer and Hayes also included a qualitative component in their study. In their classroom observations of students viewing Channel One, Knupfer and Hayes found little preparation for or follow-up to the program. Most teachers did not watch the newscast; rather, they did paperwork or lesson preparation while the program aired. Student attention varied. Some watched the entire program, while other students paid attention part of the time. Still others paid little or no attention to Channel One, preferring to read or do paperwork.

Given the available research to date, how is Channel One impacting on student learning? Given its current level of implementation, the results indicate that students are learning, although it would appear to be less than original expectations. The most positive results arise from Johnston and Anderman's (1993) study with schools where the program is integrated into instruction and not simply broadcast. Regarding how much attention students give Channel One, the survey reponses from students and teachers in the studies conducted by the Institute for

Social Research are somewhat more positive than those found by the unannounced visits reported in the Knupfer and Hayes study. Similarly, Robinson (1994) found no more than a third of the students watching during her classroom visits. Generally, then, it cannot be said that large numbers of students are giving their full attention throughout the program. This likely accounts for the inability of Channel One to meet its original expectations. It would be premature to make a final judgment on the impact of this innovative programming at present. Tiene's observation that Channel One has yet to be fully taken advantage of merits consideration. What we do know, however, is that simply turning Channel One on and letting students watch (if they want to) will not make any substantive difference in their learning about what is going on in their world. Still another factor may well be the use of what is primarily an entertainment medium for educational purposes. De Vaney noted that the Channel One format is very similar to MTV. "Such is the drawback of trying to teach with television. If a program incorporates the codes of MTV, it most likely encourages a predisposition for entertainment in the classroom" (p. 13). Her observation accords with the research by Salomon, which is explored below.

Because the use of Channel One has become so widespread, it is likely to remain a point on the educational horizon for some time. For teachers to provide the kind of learning Tiene believes is possible with Channel One may require a media literacy of sorts for teachers. Part of this teacher training would enable them to help students make the transition from an entertainment to a formal learning medium. At present this is lacking.

> It is important for educators to recognize that all learning experiences delivered through a medium that is also used as a popular entertainment form, provide an aesthetic experience as parts of their motive for viewing, and draw on cultural expectations to communicate. Because most teachers are inadequately prepared to evaluate anything but the educational subject of media programs designed for education, how the formal and stylistic qualities within educational media interact to determine the type of instruction available to students and teachers is, unfortunately, rarely examined. (Erdman, 1994, p. 154)

Erdman argues that teachers must analyze both the content and the aesthetic design of educational programming, such as Channel One, in order to find out how knowledge is constructed and what kinds of educational experiences might be forthcoming. If Erdman is correct, considerably more work is to be done to recognize Channel One's full potential.

THEORIES ON THE MEDIA AND LEARNING

Hornick (1981) has summarized the major hypotheses regarding the impact of television on schooling. The first, the "displacement" hypothesis, argues that time spent watching television takes away time from other activities, like reading, that affect school achievement such as reading and homework. The idea of displacement has been generalized to other media, particularly electronic media, including video games as well.

In discussing what Hornick calls displacement, Phillips (1989) offers some interesting insights. According to him, the single most important variable concerning whether a student learns anything is whether the information is related to the student's life experiences. Phillips believes that television diminishes social interaction and other important activities so that today's student brings fewer experiences to the classroom. Emotion is the missing ingredient in education, he contends. The successful teacher engages the student's limbic brain (the sensory portion of the brain) to activate long-term memory. Relating a lesson to life experiences activates the sensory-emotional dimension. "Emotion is the vehicle, learning the passenger," according to Phillips. He uses the analogy of a movie to describe learning. The student learns little he or she hears or reads unless the mind creates a movie. These mental movies are created by using real or imagined life experiences. When television replaces life experiences, learning is adversely affecterd.

A second hypothesis regarding television and learning Hornick terms the "development of an intolerance for the pace of schooling" hypothesis. This theory can be found in both academic and lay circles and can be expanded to include other media, such as music videos. Here, the often fast-paced flow of visual media with quick cuts, repeated commercial interruptions, and effortless viewing are believed to be injurious to learning because, in the classroom, learning often requires sustained attention and hard work. "Extended exposure to television, it is feared, might lead to a lowered tolerance for the pace of the classroom. Students in the classroom are quick to 'change the channel,' that is, to turn their attention away from their studies if instruction is inadequately entertaining" (p. 194). In this vein Postman (1985) faults television with creating the expectation among viewers that learning and entertainment are equivalent.

A corollary to the "pace of schooling" hypothesis is the belief that television viewing contributes to the development of a shortened attention span. Speaking before a group of educators, Robert MacNeil (1983), executive editor and co-anchor of the *MacNeil/Leher Report,* observed, "The safest technique to guarantee mass attention is to keep everything brief, not strain the attention of anyone, but instead to provide constant stimulation through variety, novelty, action and movement. You are required," he continues, "in much popular TV fare, to pay attention to no concept, no situation, no scene, no character, and no problem for more than a few seconds at a time. In brief, TV operates on the short attention span" (p. 2). MacNeil's comments underscore another concern over the impact of television. Here, the focus is on the medium's *form,* rather than content. Again, as MacNeil suggests, to hold the viewer's attention, television depends upon "perceptual salience," employing scenes that change quickly, rapid cuts and action, zooms, pans, camera angles, special effects, and sound effects. This argument can be extended to other visual media similar to television, such as rock videos or commercials.

A third hypothesis, the "interest stimulation" hypothesis, accentuates the positive role of television on learning. Proponents of this idea maintain, that, when children see some types of programs on television, they are likely to transfer this interest to more school-related topics. For example, they might watch a program or movie on television and be more inclined to read a book upon which the program or movie was based. Proponents of the "learning of school-equivalent" hypothesis believe that students can learn some of the same things from television that they do in the classroom. By viewing a television documentary on the Vietnam War or watching a political convention, for example, students can learn about history or civics. Indeed, in her essay on filmic representations of Vietnam, Aufderheide (1990) observes that movies and television programs are the "avenues through which history becomes part of popular consciousness" (pp. 81–82).

Still a fourth hypothesis, which Hornick (1981) terms the "learning of new cognitive skills" hypothesis, is rooted in the formal features of television. The argument is that students can learn skills that allow them to process the unique symbol system of television in terms of its formal features such as zooms and rapid cuts. These cognitive skills are very different from those required in traditional learning, such as reading, and are part of developing a *visual* literacy to supplement the traditional concept of literacy based upon the written word.

Finally, Hornick identifies the "learning of instrumental information" hypothesis:

> There are a very large number of understandings about school and how it operates which a student develops in order to make it through the day. The expectations of one's mathematic teacher, how kindergarten is organized, how one's peers will act when the football team loses, all must be learned. They are not schooling's ends, but information instrumental to those ends. The question . . . is whether television teaches such instrumental information and whether it affects one's understanding of and expectations for schooling. (p. 206)

Instrumental information may be garnered from media other than television. For example, the depiction of educators in films popular with teenagers may affect their attitudes towards their teachers.

An additional hypothesis not mentioned by Hornick is the "threshold hypothesis." The idea behind this theory is that the relationship between television viewing and school achievement may not be a linear one. Rather, it may be curvilinear, in that a certain amount of viewing may positively affect school achievement but that there may be a threshold beyond which the relationship becomes negative and learning is adversely affected.

The only area to receive more research attention than the impact of the media on learning has been the relationship between the media and violence/aggression. Two general trends have emerged in this area of research. Initially, most of the research centered around media content with an underlying assumption that the viewer was passive. Beginning in the 1970s, however, a second trend in research began to focus on the possible effects of the "formal features" [a term coined by Huston and Wright (1983)] of television on learning. During this decade media research also began to reflect the developmental nature of learning using the Piagetian theory of cognitive development. Some of the research represented a shift away from the notion of a passive viewer to one actively engaged in televiewing. This approach to understanding media use accompanied the interest in the formal aspects of television. Today, we have a much more sophisticated concept of the young viewer, and we realize that the impact of the media upon learning varies according to age, ability, and social background. Young people respond differently to the content of television programs because they process this content differently based upon these variables (Collins, 1982).

RESEARCH FINDINGS: THE IMPACT OF MEDIA ON LEARNING

Television

Burton, Calonico, and McSeveney (1979) examined the amount of television viewing of preschoolers and found that those who were heavier viewers had lower grades in the first grade. They also found that heavier viewers tended to have friends who spent similar amounts of time watching television. Childers and Ross (1973) studied 100 elementary school children and found a slightly negative relationship between viewing and GPA. A study of middle-class first graders by Gadberry (1980) suggested that restricting television viewing enhanced IQ scores, encouraged more reading time, and promoted greater reflectivity, as measured by the Matching Familiar Figures Test. This study also provides support for the displacement hypothesis. Slater's (1965) study of third graders revealed a significant correlation between amount of viewing time and school achievement, particularly in reading and spelling. Slater also found a negative correlation between IQ and viewing. In one of the earliest studies on television and learning, Greenstein (1954) studied third, fourth, and fifth graders and found the data inconclusive. Nonowners of television sets in his study were consistently higher achievers than television owners, but not significantly so.

Because television ownership is almost universal in this country, it is difficult to compare viewing and nonviewing groups of students. The introduction of television into a small Canadian town in the 1970s provided an opportunity for one of the few natural experiments on the impact of television ever conducted. Researchers conducted pretests on fourth and seventh graders in three towns referred to as Notel (which had no television), Unitel (which had only one television station), and Multitel (a town with regular commercial programming). Before the introduction of television into Notel, researchers examined all aspects of life, including leisure time and aggression in Notel, as well as in the two control towns of Unitel and Multitel. The research team then returned two years later to study the possible effects of the introduction of television on life in Notel. Contrary to their hypothesis, Harrison and Williams (1986) did not find support that television viewing affected vocabulary development positively. On the other hand, creativity seemed to be adversely affected, while no relationship between television viewing and spatial ability emerged. Corteen and Williams (1986) also looked at the effects of the introduction of television on reading skills and concluded that "television may have a negative effect on reading competence" (p. 69). They suggested that those most likely affected are children who are slower to develop reading fluency and, therefore, may turn to television because it is a more attractive way to spend leisure time. Corteen and Williams also noted that other aspects of the Notel study, such as the impact of television on leisure time, led them to suspect that the introduction of television may have displaced reading as a leisure activity.

Initial exposure to television seems to enhance achievement in some middle school students (Hornick, 1978; Busch, 1978), which calls into question the displacement hypothesis. For reasons that are not clear, however, during the elementary and middle school years students with lower academic and reading abilities tend to become heavier viewers. It is difficult to determine whether television viewing contributes to lower achievement or vice versa. In his longitudinal study involving seventh through ninth graders in El Salvador, Hornick found that television viewing had no short-term effect on school achievement. Over time it did, however, have a negative effect on reading improvement in all the subjects and a significant negative impact on general ability growth on some students. Busch reported that low-ability seventh and eighth graders continued to watch more television, while television watching for middle- and high-ability seventh-grade students began to wane. High-ability students were not as well informed as their high-ability counterparts who were heavy readers. Busch also found that 95% of the low-ability seventh and eighth graders in her study received a "great bulk of their information from television." She notes, "To the student who cannot read well and receives 95% of his information through a form other than print, the standardized achievement tests are a confusing and frustrating puzzle" (p. 670). Conversely, all of the high-ability seventh-grade respondents to her survey indicated that a television program had led them to read a book to gather additional information on a topic. This lends some support to the interest stimulation hypothesis mentioned above.

In his study of 10,000 sixth graders, Fetler (1984) found that those students who viewed moderate amounts of television scored higher on achievement tests than those who reported watching less. He speculates that television contains some information relevant to success in school. The study also found that heavy viewers watched less public television and tended to do homework in front of the television set. Like Busch, Morgan (1980) found that television may have a positive impact on time spent reading. In his longitudinal study of sixth through ninth graders, he discovered that heavy viewers' reading increased, while reading activity of light viewers' decreased. The study revealed noticeable differences, however, in *choice* of reading materials. Heavy viewers chose materials reflective of television programming, for example, love stories and true stories about celebrities. Controlling for demographic variables, IQ, and socioeconomic status among fourth through sixth graders, Neuman (1982) did not find that television was a significant predictor of reading achievement scores. She did find, however, that students who were both very heavy television viewers and light readers tended to choose books of lower quality than those who fell into other viewer/reader categories such as those who were heavy television viewers and heavy readers or light television viewers and light readers.

Jönsson's (1986) research with Dutch six- through twelve-year-olds underscores some of the *positive* aspects of television learning. Her research supports the interest stimulation, as well as the learning of school equivalent, hypotheses. She notes that television provides an opportunity to help young people become familiar with the outside world and situations that cannot be recreated in school. Jönsson found evidence that, when children are trained to view television for cognitive stimulus and to look for information, television can be a complement to school. Children who watched educational programming during the preschool years did better in sixth grade. Conversely, heavy viewing of children's programming by fifth graders negatively influenced school performance during the sixth grade. Here, she suggests a displacement explanation, that is, television watching displaces more cognitively stimulating activities. Jönsson's research is significant for two reasons: it points to the importance of teaching media literacy skills early on, as well as the value of educational programming.

Williams et al. (1982) suggested a threshold hypothesis. They performed a meta-analysis of twenty-three research studies, which examined the impact of leisure time television viewing on student achievement in kindergarten through twelfth grade. The results suggested that television viewing effects on student achievement depended upon how much television is consumed. They found a slightly positive effect for up to ten hours of viewing per week. Beyond ten hours the effects are negative and increasingly more deleterious up to thirty-five and forty hours. Beyond forty hours there is little additional negative impact. Those most adversely affected were girls and those with high IQs.

Other researchers question the link between television viewing and academic achievement. In his review of the research, Hornick (1981) found no correlation between viewing and student achievement, with the exception of reading, with an impact he described as slight. When Ritchie, Price, and Roberts (1987) applied sophisticated analytic techniques to negative correlations between television viewing and reading achievement, the relationship became considerably weaker. Hornick, as well as Ritchie and his colleagues, noted the need for additional study and research methodologies.

Morgan and Gross (1982) have suggested three reasons why studies exploring the relationship between achievement and television viewing have found relatively small correlations: 1) these modes of correlation may, in fact, be accurate; 2) they might be masking a nonlinear association; and 3) larger effects may be occurring among "highly susceptible subgroups" but are not being manifested because they are included in larger research population results. Here, the effect is the same as if one averaged a few larger numbers with a series of smaller numbers. By looking only at the average, the large numbers are obscured. They point to four major studies involving statewide testing projects (Texas, Pennsylvania, Rhode Island, and Connecticut) that came up with very similar findings. Younger students who watched only an hour or two of television a day scored higher on reading achievement tests than those who watched less. At the next level of viewing, scores began to decline and they dropped substantially among the heaviest viewers.

Morgan and Gross (1980) conducted cross-sectional analyses of over 600 sixth through ninth graders, which lend support to their third explanation. They found that low-IQ girls showed a significant positive correlation between viewing and reading comprehension. Among the high-IQ group, on the other hand, they found strong negative associations between viewing and achievement, even after other factors are controlled for. Television viewing, then, may make a contribution to learning for lower-ability students but adversely affects brighter students. In the case of Morgan and Gross's study, those students with lower IQs might be learning vocabulary from television that they would not learn otherwise.

Considerable research has been conducted on how learning takes place with different media. Again, because of its pervasiveness, television has received most of the attention. Research revolves around questions of whether certain media affect creativity or imagination more or less than others. Might how students learn from one media carry over to another? An interesting series of experiments conducted by Salomon (1983) addresses this question in terms of television and print media. The research of Meringoff et al. (1983) indicates that learning varies from medium to medium. She and her colleagues argue that television delivers to child audiences messages that are qualitatively different from other media because television is a very distinctive medium, for example, types of programming, combination of pictures, print, sound, sound effects, and music.

A prerequisite for the media to affect learning is that the viewer/listener pay attention to the particular medium. Again, most of the research centers around televiewing. Two general approaches have dominated this research. The first might be termed "what the television does to the viewer" approach. The second is "what the viewer does with television." The former emphasizes *passivity,* with the viewer reacting to what is seen and heard. The latter places the viewer in a *proactive* posture.

Both of these approaches have paid particular attention to the formal features of television, which are the visual and auditory production techniques such as cuts, pans, zooms, sound effects, and voice characterizations (Fitch, Huston, & Wright, 1993). An area of particular concern to researchers is "perceptual salience." This term refers to those features of television usually employed as attention getting devices. For example, television is characterized by rapid cuts, with scenes often lasting only a few seconds, or fast-paced action. Because so much of the attention has focused on the formal aspect of television, it is worth exploring briefly. Wright and Huston (1983) note that what separates television from other media are its forms, not its content.

Healy (1990) is one of the most recent critics of television, as well as video games, and their impact upon learning. She reasons from the assumption that many of the formal features of these two media negatively impact learning on young children. In her chapter *"Sesame Street* and the Death of Reading" she refers to this program as a "peripatetic carnival" that does little to teach the habits of the mind necessary to be a good reader: language, active reflection, persistence, and internal control. Encouraging preschoolers to watch *Sesame Street* programs them to "enjoy—and perhaps even need—overstimulation, manipulation, and neural habits that are antagonistic to academic learning" (p. 221). She provides ten reasons why *Sesame Street* is detrimental to reading. Because Healy's book has been so widely received, particularly among teachers, it is worth briefly reviewing each of these reasons:

(1) *Sesame Street* pushes reading skills before children have completed certain developmental tasks. She notes that most preschoolers are not ready to connect written symbols to sound.

(2) The program overemphasizes letters and numbers at the expense of language and thinking skills. This is an implicit message to children that the alphabet letters are the major key to reading when it should be searching for meaning. She cites an example of when researchers ask poor readers what reading is all about, they reply something to the effect that it is "sounding out words." Conversely, good readers respond that it is "understanding what the words and sentences say."

(3) Healy argues that *Sesame Street* sends the wrong message about how print behaves. Technically termed *metalinguistic awareness,* this awareness includes the understanding that letters make up words and that words are linked together to create meaningful sentences. Another aspect of this awareness is understanding what a word is.

(4) *Sesame Street* treats the viewer to "bites" of information, but not "big bites of meaning." The rapid change in images makes it difficult for viewers to be able to reflect and to be able to see relationships, to understand the sequence of cause and effect, or to maintain a train of thought.

(5) Because it is a visual program, *Sesame Street* places a premium

on looking versus listening. Healy uses phonics as an example, which is an *ear* skill, not an *eye* skill. She also correctly notes that research shows that children process information differently, depending upon whether they hear it or see it.

(6) The pace of educational programming is such that, instead of practicing *perceptual organization,* the viewer must practice *perceptual defense* "simply as a matter of neural self-protection."

(7) Again, because of the formal features of *Sesame Street,* comprehension is difficult. Healy argues that, over time, the inability to comprehend (a sign that the brain is being active) conditions the brain to become passive.

(8) Healy notes that good readers learn to remember, but passive brains "retain sensations, not information." Because comprehension, a prerequisite for understanding, is lacking in *Sesame Street,* strategies for remembering are not activated.

(9) Good readers pay attention, Healy asserts. Attention to *Sesame Street* does not represent sustained voluntary attention. She writes, "When you hear that children 'actively' watch programs like *Sesame Street* you should know that this really means that the viewer is frequently tuning out, looking away from the screen, playing, eating, or doing other things." Healy continues, "The average look at the screen is actually less than five seconds in duration. The truth is that the viewer may indeed be active, but the viewing is not" (p. 231). Healy dismisses this kind of attention as *involuntary attention* as opposed to *voluntary attention,* the kind of attention needed for reading.

(10) Because television is visual, this precludes providing children with the opportunity to create pictures in their own minds, which is a critical skill for reading.

For these reasons Healy dismisses *Sesame Street* as "sensory hucksterism" and notes that its popularity explains the decline in reading and learning skills. In her criticisms Healy has clearly placed herself in the "what television does to the viewer" position. A number of her arguments are flawed and are not borne out by research. For example, she maintains that the young viewers must practice "perceptual defense" for their own neural self-protection, given the pace of educational programming. In fact, there are differences between the pacing of educational and commercial programming. Moreover, there is considerable research to suggest that children selectively attend to educational television and that the formal features of this medium cue them to segments of programs that are of interest or comprehensible to them.

Much of Healy's approach to educational television and this medium in general is rooted in the research on the formal features of television, which began in the 1970s. Some of the pioneering research in this area has been conducted by Singer and Singer (1983) at the Yale University Family Television Research and Consultation Center. Their work with television developed as a collateral interest growing out of their research on children's make-believe play and social influences on the emergence of fantasy. In conducting their studies they found that children consistently exhibited heavy exposure to television in their fantasy activities like when they used television characters or plots during play.

Schramm, Lyle, and Parker (1961), in one of the most comprehensive studies of television to date, noted that television provided a rich course of fantasy material for children. Singer (1982) notes that children get their ideas of play from their immediate environment, and, increasingly, one of these sources is television. How does this impact upon children?

> Here, then, we confront the major question about this medium. A cognitive analysis suggests that because cognitive processing takes place over time, effective learning and storage of material presented requires some mental replaying and rehearsal with an occasional opportunity to shift one's attention away from the set and reflect on what was seen. If new material is piled on top of other material, particularly irrelevant contents, can one really intelligently sit and reexamine information? (Singer & Singer, 1983, p. 827)

Singer and Singer (1981a) conducted an extensive longitudinal field study of preschoolers, exploring the relationship between television viewing and imagination and aggression. Some of their findings, taken together with results of other studies, leads them to question whether television content enriches a child's imaginative capacities. For example, in an early study they examined three to four year olds' responses to *Mister Rogers' Neighborhood*. One group watched the program by itself, while another group watched the program with an adult mediator. A third group did not watch *Mister Rogers' Neighborhood* at all. Singer and Singer (1976) found increases in imagination for those children who viewed with an adult mediator, while those who viewed the program alone showed only a slight increase. The group that did not watch the program, but played fantasy games instead, showed significant increases in imagination. The Singers also believe the cognitive properties of television may result in a shortened attention span and lack of reflectiveness, an idea shared by Moody (1980), who maintains that the perceptual salience of television with its rapid cuts, special effects, and high action conditions the brain to change at the expense of continuity and concentration of thought.

The power of formal features has not been lost on broadcasters and advertisers. Wright and Huston (1983) point out that these two groups combine perceptually exciting characteristics such as rapid pace and electronic embellishments with violence and refer to it as "action." Together with their colleagues at the Center for Research on the Influences of Television on Children (CRITIC), they have demonstrated that perceptual salience will hold attention independent of content. Because television viewing begins so early, Wright and Huston speculate that this kind of attention may become a pattern by third or fourth grade. Children become very savvy and use the formal features to direct their attention such as when a laugh track cues them to the fact that something humorous is taking place.

Children use these formal features not only for attention, but as a guide to comprehension as well. In their summary of the research with children, Huston and Wright highlight several ways in which the formal features of television can aid in comprehension. First, visual and auditory cues help children to attend selectively to important information. Formal features may create interest and motivation to understand. This is a lesson that educational programming has learned from commercial children's shows. Formal features can convey "processing requirements," signalling to the viewer "where uncertainties to resolve are located, and the options a viewer may reasonably choose among in order to comprehend" (p. 839). They use an example from *Sesame Street*. When the song "One of These Things Is Not Like the Others" is played, a child is cued that a sorting problem will be presented. Formal features may play a similar role for content as well. In some cases these cues may encourage a child to try to figure out something that is not immediately comprehensible. Wright and Huston give the example of a laugh track, which signals that something funny has occurred. In signalling the type of content, the viewer might try to figure out what is amusing, even though he or she does not immediately understand the joke.

Formal features can convey connotative meanings as well. For example, soft fuzzy images and background music have a feminine association. High action, quick cuts, sound effects, and loud music carry a masculine connotation. Advertisers play upon these cues and frequently associate their products with one gender or the other using these techniques. Television forms and formats can serve as a visual model of a mental activity. By manipulating a formal feature a viewer can literally "see" a cognitive skill. When children experienced difficulty in understanding the part-to-whole ratio when the picture cut to a close-up, Salomon (1979) modeled this concept by using a slow zoom to make the transition from larger picture to the details contained in the close-up. Children then understood. Wright and Huston (1983) point to some of the studies at CRITIC, in which it was shown that children learned Piagetian number tasks using animated television sequences. Finally, formal features can assist viewers in encoding content in ways in which the print media cannot. They point to catch phrases, songs, rhymes, and jingles on television, which can enhance memorability. Similarly, "repeated stereotypic visual sequences, such as when Bugs Bunny hands someone a bomb with a lit fuse or an actor's classic double take can serve as a mnemonic shorthand and provide directly the vivid images appropriate for iconic representation" (p. 840).

Research within the last decade or so has taken a different approach to visual attention to television and has called into question many of the assumptions directing research. Anderson and Lorch (1983) have developed an alternative theory for explaining how the viewer visually attends to this medium. They believe that, far from being passive, the viewer controls his/her own attention, guided by efforts to "understand the television program and to deploy attention efficiently between the television and the other aspects of the viewing environment." Their theory is significant because it questions some of the basic assumptions of educational television. As noted above, the reactive passive viewing experience is believed to hold its greatest sway among younger viewers. According to Anderson and Lorch (1983) viewers develop schema with which they approach television. These schema are developed through a combination of viewing and life experiences. The viewer then approaches the television experience with certain expectations "about the temporal and conceptual flow of normal television programs." This alternative explanation is critical because it has a different set of implications for the cognitive effects of television upon viewers, particularly children.

Anderson and Lorch advance four premises for a theory of visual attention, which they have tested and for which they have found support in their research. These premises provide the foundation for what has been termed the "comprehensibility-attention" hypothesis, which is based upon Anderson's research. First, visual attention to television is contingent upon the kind of environment in which viewing takes place. Other activities may be available within this environment, such as toys to play with or another person with whom to converse. Second, maintenance of visual attention is guided in part by viewer ability and the need to answer "questions" posed by comprehension schemata. In their research Anderson and Lorch have discovered evidence of a third principle—that the viewer moves through periods of visual attention and inattention. They cite some of their research with their colleagues, which indicates that, in an hour of viewing, a child will look at and away from the television screen about 150 times [Alwitt et al. and Anderson & Levine cited in Anderson & Lorch (1982), pp. 10–11]. During periods of inattention, the viewer will engage in an alternative activity. These shifts from the latter to the former occur through a use of information cues that are primarily auditory. Finally, these researchers posit a theory of what is termed "attentional inertia," which aids the viewer in maintaining "cognitive involvement" across breaks in comprehension and content changes. In explaining the seeming contradiction between a reactive approach to viewing and attentional inertia, which suggests passivity, they write:

> Attentional inertia, we believe, provides the means by which attention is maintained to a source of information even across breaks in the continuity of the information. Rather than the television-viewing child being a victim of attentional inertia, we see it as an essential weapon in the child's cognitive arsenal. Attentional inertia allows the child to keep processing a stimulus even when it is currently not understandable. Attentional inertia thus sometimes produces a dynamic tension with program comprehensibility. Although in general the young child stops paying attention when the program becomes incomprehensible, attentional inertia serves to maintain attention further than it might otherwise go.

As such attentional inertia may be part of the means by which the child comes to process a stimulus that is poorly understood. This enforced, nonstrategic, attention may occasionally provide the child the means by which he or she ventures into unknown cognitive territory, occasionally leading to new cognitive discoveries. (Anderson & Lorch, 1983, p. 25)

In a study testing the relationship between comprehension and visual attention, Lorch, Anderson, and Levine (1979) divided five-year-olds into two groups. One group watched *Sesame Street* in a room with toys. The other group watched the same forty-minute program in the same viewing environment but without toys. Although the no-toy group's attention was nearly twice that of the toy group, there was nearly no difference between the groups in comprehension. Their results did show a relationship between attention and comprehension, however. The children's attention was higher for portions of the program that they comprehended better. Those portions of the program that the children least understood received relatively less attention.

Collins's (1982) work, based on some of Anderson's research, provides a much different tack to the idea that the televiewing experience of children is essentially passive and that television holds their attention through its perceptually salient features. Contrary to this passivity, he argues that children actively respond to these formal features of television because they have come to learn that formal features will often accompany content that is important to their understanding of the program.

This study and others by Collins and his colleagues have helped them develop a catalog of visual and auditory cues for maintaining or terminating attention. For example, an auditory cue that maintains attention is children's voices, while men's voices terminate attention. Cuts and motion maintain attention, while visual cues such as still photos and long camera pans are visual cues that foreclose attention.

The work of Anderson and Lorch (1982) points to the highly complex nature of television research and a fuller explanation of how children interact with television. Their work has found support in other research as well. Krull and Husson (1979) have found "cycles of anticipation" in viewing among young school-age children, which also points to the active nature of the viewing process.

The growing body of research on how and what children learn from television has also explored how children interpret and make inferences about what they see. Clearly, the ability to make inferences is contingent upon age and cognitive development. One can add to this list prior social knowledge. Collins (1983) points out that comprehension of dramatic programs requires that the viewer be able to selectively attend to central program events, orderly organization of program events, and *temporal integration,* which he describes as the ability to make inferences about implicit relations between explicit scenes (p. 131). It is this third cognitive skill that he and his colleagues have researched extensively. Young children often do not understand motives for characters' actions. The temporal separation between when an action takes place and the actual consequences that occur later are difficult to connect. In an experiment involving kindergartners and second-grade students who watched an action-adventure program, these children had difficulty remembering the relations of the motives and the consequences that involved aggressive actions (Collins, 1973; Collins, Berndt, & Hess, 1974). Clearly, the intervening extraneous material in the program made this connection difficult. In a subsequent experiment, however, when children were shown a similar action-adventure program with part of the intervening material edited out, the children immediately saw the relationships [Purdie, Collins, & Westby, cited in Collins (1983)]. The implications for understanding television among young children are important. Collins notes that "TV should be viewed as a source of general social information, rather than as a mere purveyor of certain highly salient images, such as violence" (p. 144).

Another researcher who has emphasized the active nature of television viewing is Salomon (1983). He borrows from the field of cognitive social psychology with its emphasis on how people actively affect their environment (including television) through their personal and socially shared perceptions. The assumption here is that people affect and are, in turn, affected by their environment; thus, the "child is perceived not only as a responder, but also as a potential determiner of the television experience." In language reminiscent of Anderson and Lorch's discussion of schemata, Salomon makes a similar argument. "The child does not always or necessarily respond to the 'real' attributes of the medium but applies to it his or her often culturally shared perceptions and attributions (themselves the partial results of prior exposure to the media), which in turn affect the kind of experiences he or she encounters." He continues, "Thus seen from one point of view, what the child brings to the screen is taken to set the limits to what and to how television elicits from him or her; seen from the other point of view, what the child brings to the screen—in terms of perceptions and expectation—is taken to influence what the medium experience is to be" (Salomon, 1983, pp. 183–184).

Salomon notes that these two perspectives are complimentary and points to the work of Huston and Wright and their colleagues on the variations between the way children of different ages attend to television. Their research indicates that younger children attend more to the formal features of television and less to the informative features. In older children this is just the reverse, with more attention paid to information and less to the salient features.

Salomon's work is important not only for what it tells us about the active nature of viewing, but also for the potential for insights into differences in how the various media are processed, as well as the potential crossover effect. Specifically, how does the experience and expectations of one medium affect experience with another medium? He has developed the concept of AIME—"the amount of invested mental effort in nonautomatic elaboration of material" (p. 186). Salomon reasons that we approach different media and potential learning situations with different sets of expectations. The amount of AIME invested in a situation depends upon whether an individual feels that there is much or little to be gained from the material in the medium. AIME is also contingent upon how the individual views the material that is to be encountered. Is it difficult or easy? Novel or old hat? Again, the key here is that each individual approaches a medium with his/her preconceptions and schemata. Salomon and Leigh (1984) assume that there is a "pool" of available mental effort that can be allocated to tasks. When a task requires mental effort, this pool can be tapped into.

What does this mean for learning and media? In one study Salomon measured sixth-grade students' perceptions of television and print in terms of understanding each. He also examined the extent to which these sixth graders believed that AIME affected their learning, as well as whether AIME as self-reported depended upon their preconceptions. "As expected, we found that television is perceived to be a much 'easier' and a more lifelike medium, demanding far less effort for comprehension than printed material of the same content. Children," Salomon continues, "also expressed more self-efficacy with television than with print. Although failure to comprehend print was attributed to 'dumbness.' On the other hand, success with print was attributed to 'smartness' and with television to its ease" (p. 189). Salomon found correlations between the way students perceived a medium and their investment of mental effort in processing the information from the medium, which, in turn, related to how much they actually learned from it. In one study Salomon and Leigh (1984) compared high- and low-ability students using print and television to tell a story. High-ability sixth graders who performed well on the print story did relatively poorly with the comparable television story. Salomon and Leigh attribute this to the students' not mobilizing mental abilities. In fact, the high-ability students performed even more poorly than the low-ability students exposed to the same television story.

The implications of Salomon's research for learning are important. First, his conclusions suggest that young people can be taught how to attend to television differently, thus increasing AIME and, consequently, learning. The ability to increase one's AIME may be pertinent to the classroom teacher employing television as an instructional medium. If students have a preconceived notion about television viewing, that it is easier and requires less AIME, then they may be learning less. Secondly, he also speculates that individuals may bring preconceptions that are successfully applied to television to other kinds of media. He notes research that suggests that heavy viewers tend to read materials that reflect television programming (Morgan, 1980) and to write narratives in a different style than light television viewers. Salomon's research may help explain the limited knowledge gains by students who watch Channel One as well. It is very possible that viewers are predisposed to television as an entertainment medium and, therefore, attend less to educational programs such as Channel One because they are investing less mental effort.

Given the research to date, the evidence does not point to limited television viewing as having an adverse effect upon school achievement. More sophisticated data collection and analysis techniques call into question conclusions of earlier research. No doubt, criticisms of television as a medium that adversely affects learning will continue. However, television as a learning culprit is largely not borne out when one controls for intelligence, environment, or socioeconomic status. And the image of the student glued to the television set in a passive zombie-like state does not present an accurate picture of how children attend to this medium. This is not to suggest that the relationship of television to learning should not be a concern. There is some evidence to suggest that the television displaces learning activities such as reading, but not to the degree that many critics argue. Students who are at most risk of being *adversely* affected tend to be heavy viewers. Finally, there are a number of other issues related to learning and the media, which are explored in other chapters, such as what students learn about their world and that of others around them.

Any examination of the impact of the media on learning should include some exploration of media use and creativity and imagination. Anderson and Collins (1988) have identified a number of different arguments regarding the impact of television on these two areas. In general, the perception is that there is a negative relationship. Meline (1976) found that students gave more creative responses when a problem was presented in the written or audio form, rather than on television. In the Notel experiment Harrison and Williams (1986) found that the children in Notel, which had no television, scored higher on ideational fluency tests than children in Unitel and Multitel. Two years later, however, the scores for Notel children had fallen, and scores among the three towns did not differ. In her study of adolescents, Wade (1971) found a negative relationship between hours spent watching television and performance on creativity tasks. And as noted above, the Singers' research on television arose from their interest in imaginative play and how often children used television as a referent in such play. As with television and learning a number of arguments have been offered to prove that a negative relationship between television and imagination and creativity exists. Anderson and Collins (1988) summarize these arguments. One of the most popular conceptions is that the visual nature of television reduces the need for children to spontaneously produce their own representations as they would if the medium required only listening or reading. From a more positive perspective it can be argued that television provides a storehouse of images that can be drawn upon later for imaginative enterprises. A third criticism [as noted in Healy (1990)] is that the continuous images one receives from televiewing do not allow time for reflection or to ask the question "What comes next?" "Alternatively, it is argued that the mind's eye of the child is not inactivated by the TV; rather, children often use the most observed content on television as a point of departure for fantasy play in the presence of the TV set" (p. 54). Anderson and Collins identify two additional hypotheses regarding the indirect effects of television upon creativity and imagination. Both of these arguments can be extended to the other mass media as well. The first relates to the notion that television has a homogenizing effect on culture, thus creating a common culture that reduces the diversity of ideas. The second, related to the displacement hypothesis, is that the easy availability of television leads children to spend time watching television instead of other activities. This curtails their experiences and knowledge, which, in turn, reduces the potential for creativity. Summarizing the research, Anderson and Collins write:

> What can we conclude about television's effects on imaginative capacities and creativity? Television may require less productive use of imaginative capacities than listening to a story. However, it has not been demonstrated that over time this experience diminishes imaginative capacity. In addition, there is no evidence that the product of television inspired imagination is of poorer quality than that inspired by radio. In general, television does not appear to interrupt the development of fantasy play or imaginativeness. In fact, its incorporation as a common cultural experience into group play in preschool settings may be facilitative in forming friendships, promoting role-playing and adding variety to play. (p. 61)

One study [cited in Anderson & Collins (1988), p. 59] by McIlwraith and Schallow did find that children who were heavier viewers had more unpleasant fantasies.

Notwithstanding Anderson and Collins's conclusion, additional research is needed, particularly in the area of the potential cumulative effects of watching television. Again, a curvilinear explanation may prove to be more satisfactory. At present, however, many of the negative criticisms of television regarding creativity and imagination may be exaggerated.

Music

Although research on creativity and imagination and the media have focused primarily on television, Greenfield et al. (1987) conducted a series of experiments on the cognitive effects of music lyrics and music videos. One of the studies examined the impact of music videos on imagination. Greenfield et al. showed a group of fifth and sixth graders four music videos, while another group listened to the four songs on audiotape. Each student received a sheet of general questions, as well as a list of questions to answer after each song. Researchers observed the students and noted comments and reactions to the songs. To test the effects on imagination, students were asked questions such as "If you were going to make a video about the song, what would it be like?" and "If you were to add another verse, what would it be about?" Greenfield et al. measured imagination by noting if the mental representation or construction was present in the immediately preceding stimulus. Generally, the verses of the group that viewed the music videos were less imaginative than those who listened to the songs. "The video also seemed to draw mental activity away from the verbal lyrics and towards visual stimuli" (p. 322). Those who watched the video evidenced less ability to imagine other videos. Even though the students did not know the purpose of this experiment, in subsequent discussions 81% of the students indicated that the videos made them less imaginative, and all of the subjects indicated that seeing the video before hearing the song on the radio inhibited their imaginative thinking. Greenfield et al. noted with interest that students demonstrated so much self-awareness of the negative effects of the videos on imagination. Although they used a small sample population ($n = 26$), the results of this study, while preliminary, point to the need for additional research using various media.

Video Games

Finally, a medium that has generated considerable debate is that of video games. A number of the same criticisms of television have been applied to this electronic medium as well. Because of the paucity of studies, it is difficult to make many generalizations about video games. In *Endangered Minds* Healy (1990) suggests that video games are addictive and that many formal features of television that impede learning are inherent in this medium as well: "As with television viewing, human brains are easy prey for the demanding, colorful, fast-paced visual formats" (p. 207). Healy maintains that there is little evidence to suggest that certain skills learned in playing video games are transferred to school tasks. Greenfield (1984) offers a different perspective. She believes that the damaging effects of the electronic media are not intrinsic to these media; rather, these effects arise from the way they are used. Among the cognitive skills Greenfield identifies are spatial skills such as coordinating visual information coming from multiple perspectives, working with multiple interacting variables, and parallel processing. She also believes that the multiple levels of increasing difficulty, "a ladder of challenges," are a positive factor in video games and notes that work with learning-disabled children indicates that arcade games made better educational tools than conventional educational games. Greenfield acknowledges that these skills are not automatically transferred to school tasks but suggests that they can be by integrating video games into instruction. Clearly, it is difficult to assess the impact of video games on cognitive development. Learning how to play video games does require the development of some rather sophisticated skills. For these skills to be useful in school, however, would require a special effort on the part of teacher to relate these skills to what is being learned in the classroom.

WHAT DOES SCHOOL "LOOK LIKE" IN THE MEDIA?

Before leaving this chapter on the impact of the media on learning, one other related topic should be considered. What images do the media create in terms of the "world of learning"? Here, a couple of issues are significant. What are the images of teachers and educational institutions as portrayed in both entertainment and the information media? In an essay on the teacher image in mass culture, Gerbner (1973) reminds his readers of Hofstadter's observation: "The figure of the schoolteacher may well be taken as a central symbol in any culture." The question Gerbner then posed was what symbolic functions the teacher played in the "hidden curriculum." Another question he addresses is the manner in which knowledge and information, as new scientific research, are portrayed in the mass media. These questions are significant when one considers a study conducted with Canadian education majors by Travis and Violato (1981). Among the hypotheses that these researchers tested was that the mass media are more frequently perceived as being reliable and trustworthy sources of information and ideas about social, political, economic, and other world affairs than are other sources. Over 66% of these future teachers listed the mass media as reliable sources, while books and professors were listed by only 16.2% of the respondents! In his study on the symbolic functions of the teacher image in mass culture, Gerbner summarized his research findings, as well as that of others, on the image of education and teachers in the media. The research is dated but provides a point of departure for understanding that image today. Drawing upon mass media studies conducted primarily in the 1950s and 1960s, as well as his own work, he writes:

> American media scholars symbolize the promise of learning on behalf of noble and idealistic goals, and undercut the promise by being strange, weak, foolish, and generally unworthy of the support of the community. The "hidden curriculum" cultivates the illusion of social reform through education and at the same time helps pave the way for the perennial collapse of its achievement. As things work out in the symbolic realm, the bankruptcy of the school is their own fault. The invidious distinction between teaching and "doing" is maintained. The promise of a productive society to place the cultivation of a distinctly human self-consciousness highest on its scale of priorities is again betrayed. (p. 285)

It is interesting to note that Gerbner found a much more positive image of the teacher in the mass media of other countries, as in the case of Russia where media teachers appeared more "learned," "democratic," and "manly" than those in the West.

In *Images of Education: The Mass Media's Version of America's Schools* Kaplan (1992) surveys educational journalism and finds it disturbing. He notes that rarely does one find educational reporters as knowledgeable in their field as political correspondents or a sports commentator. Kaplan observes that, with 3500 employees and "hordes" of specialists, fewer than a dozen work in education on a full-time or continuing basis. Therefore, journalists lack the understanding necessary to report a story in an in-depth way. Kaplan is also critical of newscasts that look only for the "down-side" of education. "One of journalisms's favorite indoor sports is educationist-bashing. Many columnists and editorial-writers delight in targeting public school officialdom, an always-inviting victim that is usually oversized, job-secure, and rarely disposed to fight back." Kaplan adds, "When the media do praise a school official, the fortunate functionary is customarily singled out as an exception in an otherwise dreary lot" (p. 21). Moreover, the media are personality- and celebrity-driven. This does not portend well for most educators who are selling learning, not themselves and their entertainment talent. Kaplan notes a study by the Center for Media and Public Affairs, which found that, in his first year as the "Education President," the major national network evening newscasts mentioned Mr. Bush's dog Millie more than then Secretary of Education Cavazos! In the same vein, he writes that journalism's "megastars" have yet to deal with topics in education.

Kaplan (1992) is equally critical of the portrayal of education in the print media:

> In a more rational world, the publishing industry's search of high-profit products would jibe comfortably with the heightened public awareness that the schools are in trouble. . . . But the marquee names of popular non-fiction writing have steered clear of the schools. To the extent that a popular literature about them can be said to exist, it appears to consist of two categories: the dark-horse entry—usually by a university professor—E. D. Hirsch Jr.'s *Cultural Literacy* and Allan Bloom's *The Closing of the American Mind* are typical—whose central message is that our system of public education is producing uninformed airheads; or an assortment of highly critical potshots at the school and show up briefly on commercial shelves but sell poorly. (pp. 100–101)

Overall, the portrait that Kaplan paints on the state of education is highly unfavorable. He is not entirely negative, however. He provides examples of educational journalism the way it should be when he has found it. Elsewhere, he observes that television can play a very positive role in helping its audiences understand some of the new ways of teaching, instructional technology, and the role of education in the development of the child (Kaplan, 1990). Bracey (1994) echoes Kaplan's criticism of the mass media's version of American education. He notes that "an aura of failure has so come to surround the schools that even friends of education misinterpret data" (p. 80). He provides examples from educational publications that report inaccurate or misinterpreted data, further undermining the public's perception of the country's schools. The editors of *Education Week,* reporting on the decade since the publication of *A Nation at Risk,* noted a decline in the number and proportion of those scoring at or above 650 on the verbal and math sections of the Scholastic Aptitude Test (SAT). When Bracey checked the data against College Board records, he found that *Education Week* had taken only those students scoring between 650 and 690 on the SAT and omitted those students who scored between 700 and 800. In fact, the number of those scoring higher had increased from 29,000 to 32,903 on the verbal section and from 76,000 to 140,401 on the math.

In his exploration of American values as reflected in its films,

O'Brien (1990) devotes an entire chapter to teaching. Like Kaplan, O'Brien observes that, with some exceptions, such as *Stand and Deliver,* the general image of teachers is bleak. Moreover, he acknowledges the impact these films might have:

> The media, we are told by educational experts, provide a "hidden curriculum" that supersedes the learning process in school, a sad index of how educational decline had made America "a nation at risk." Sadder still are the images in this "hidden curriculum" that have so caricatured teachers as incompetent nincompoops or rigid authoritarians. It is bad enough that teachers have been *displaced* by the media, but worse that their image—in so many eighties movies—has been distorted. Scores of recent national reports on education now urge an upgrading of the image of the teaching profession, an uphill struggle given the prevalent media caricatures of educators. (p. 33)

O'Brien suggests that *Stand and Deliver, Lean on Me,* and *Dead Poets Society* provide some hope. He is particularly praiseworthy of the story of Jaime Escalante, as played by Edward James Olmos, because the film includes the act of teaching, a feat difficult to capture in a screenplay. In addition, the film presents teaching as a worthy occupation, Escalante having giving up a successful career in the computer industry.

If the image of education and educators in the media is a poor one, what about the media's reporting of knowledge? Singer and Endreny (1986) conducted a content analysis of ten news media (major print sources as well as network evening newscasts) in an effort to determine how and what social science research got reported in the news. The major areas of research centered on economics, politics, and government. Most of the social science research reported in the media consisted of public opinion polls, usually conducted internally by the news source. Singer and Endreny point out that there are considerable differences in the way this kind of research is reported to the public as opposed to social scientists. "By far the most significant difference between social science research as written for the general public and for other social scientists has to do with the way research findings are presented. In newspapers," they continue, "newsmagazines, and on television, findings resulting from one piece of research, done in a particular time and place, with a distinct sample and a specified research instrument, are often presented as if they were universal truths, holding for all people everywhere" (p. 297). The authors explore several media practices that contribute to the image of social science and contrast them with the manner in which social science is reported in scholarly journals. While the social scientist is expected to present the source for research findings, Singer and Endreny found that the media often do not provide these sources (only 40% of the time in focus stories) and are sometime inaccurate when they do. They recall Dunwoody's point (cited on p. 298) that, since the media are the major source of scientific and technical information, the media should provide this type of information to enable the reader to pick up "where the news stories leave off." Not only do references go unreported, but the identities of the researchers themselves as well are often neglected. Singer and Endreny found that in less than 25% of the stories could tbe viewer/reader tell how many people had been responsible for the research. Likewise, some explanation of thc methods used in a given study is even more difficult to locate in social science reporting. Finally, this study found that the media do a poor job of putting research findings within some context, unlike journals where the reader is given some indication as to how or if the findings accord with or depart from other studies.

Singer and Endreny's assessment of how social science research "comes off" in the media on several levels is a poor one. What is newsworthy determines what research gets reported. The reader might recall the discovery of cold fusion! Qualifications, important to social scientists, such as "these findings hold for this sample, in this place and especially under these conditions," are rarely included. Without these conditions research findings "attain universal validity." As a result they note that media audiences often encounter findings that appear to contradict earlier findings. The authors observe that the academic community may be at fault for tailoring press releases to media values and releasing findings that the media will find newsworthy. Echoing Kaplan, Singer and Endreny argue the need for reporters trained in the methods of social science.

O'Brien (1990) offers a different perspective on how interaction with the media might impact upon learning, in this case history. He notes that history teachers sometimes avail themselves of the few good historical films that are available on video. Television even provides a good historical television movie. Again, much like good education reporting, good history films are hard to find. In a culture that seeks validation through the mass media, this lack of history films may be having a more subtle impact. "For a new generation weak on 'cultural literacy,' the lack of history on screen can only intensify the decline of respect for history in the classroom. What results may be a *China Syndrome* of intellectual meltdown," he continues, "the less history in the 'hidden curriculum' in the media, the harder to teach history in class; the less history that is taught in class, the fewer history films that can hope to find an audience—or get made at all" (p. 48).

CONCLUSION

The mass media's impact on learning operates on a number of different levels. Traditionally, the media has been blamed for a number of problems in education. Everything from the displacement of time spent reading and doing homework to hindering creativity has been blamed on television. In some respects it seems like these concerns about media and learning are permanent. Olesen's comments about film and schooling in his address before the National Education Association in 1914 are repeated nearly verbatim by critics today about television. All would agree that the media most certainly have changed the way students learn. In some cases, such as educational television, these changes have been positive. The negative impact of the media on learning is less clear. As research has come to identify the complex dynamics of watching television, even among small children, some of the criticisms of television seem exaggerated. On the other hand, to suggest that the media exercise no negative influence is irresponsible. The problem in understanding how the media adversely affect learning may lay in the fact that too much of the blame for what has taken place in education has been placed on the media's shoulders. Thus, when a popular book among parents and teachers announces that *Sesame Street* is responsible for a major decline in reading and learning skills, the exaggerated claim is readily accepted. This kind of media criticism has the effect of obscuring the real influence the media has on learning by overstating its impact. The reality is that a substantial body of research supports a negative media effect on learning, but not nearly as extreme as we've been led to believe. Likewise, after years of being told that television watching is a passive activity that turns children into "zombies," research to the contrary has a hard time getting its message across. Children do become very proficient at learning to negotiate the formal features of the media, but they are still taken advantage of by advertisers who use these visual and auditory techniques very adeptly to get children to purchase their products.

In some cases the effects of the media on learning may be less direct and harder to measure, but no less real. These influences are examined elsewhere. For example, the media contribute to a culture of violence that has clearly found its way into school, as evidenced by the number of aggressive crimes perpetrated in schools. The negative stereotypes that are created by the media are pervasive. These media images that students have of other ethnic groups and places in the world are most certainly brought into geography class. The list continues. In the final analysis the question may not be mind over media, but, rather, mindfulness of the medium.

CHAPTER 5

Lessons on Life: The Media and Social Development

Television is much more than mere entertainment; it is also a major source of observational learning experiences, a setter of norms. It determined what people judge to be appropriate behavior in a variety of situations. Indeed it might be that television has become one of the most important agencies of socialization that our society possesses.

J. Philipe Rushton, *"Television and Prosocial Behavior,"* 1982

TV takes our kids across the globe before parents give them permission to cross the street.

Joshua Meyrowitz, author of *No Sense of Place: The Impact of Electronic Media on Social Behavior*

Echoing Rushton's comments, Ball, Palmer, and Millward (1986) suggest that the major educational impact of television may be in teaching children about society and themselves. In his comparative study of children, *Two Worlds of Childhood: U.S. and U.S.S.R.,* Brofenbrenner (1970) argued that television and peer groups represented the two major agents of socialization in this country. The impact of the media upon children and adolescent social development can be examined from several different perspectives. What role do the media play in the social life of young people? Are their attitudes towards other groups impacted by the mass media? This is a crtitical question as schools seek to promote multicultural understanding in education. Are there ways in which the media affect social interaction, such as promoting aggressive or prosocial behavior? Do the media have any impact on children and adolescents in terms of how they are socialized to gender roles? Might the media provide para-social relationships? What is the "social reality" of children and adolescents as portrayed in the media?

If the media contribute to various aspects of socialization, conversely, social situations may lead the media user to seek out the media to meet certain needs. Katz, Blumler, and Gurevitch (1974) suggest that a number of social factors may generate mass media–related needs. Persons may respond to social situations that produce tensions and conflicts by using the media to ease these tensions and conflicts. Social situations may create an awareness of a problem in a person for which they may look to the media for information. Individuals who are unable to have real-life experiences to satisfy certain needs may turn to the media to complement, supplement, or substitute for this dearth of real-life opportunities. Social situations may also give rise to certain values. These values may be affirmed and reinforced through media use.

SOCIALIZATION AND MEDIA USE

For younger children media consumption often occurs within the context of the family. In fact, television viewing is one of the most common family activities in our culture. As older children begin to make the transition from late childhood into early adolescence, their media habits change. The average number of hours spent watching television declines as the early adolescent matures, while those spent listening to music increase. Media consumption becomes an activity done with peers. Larson and Kubey's (1983) study of adolescent television and music usage found that adolescents experience these two media differently. Watching television is often a family activity; listening to music is done privately or with friends. Music is more engaging because it speaks to the world of youth and involves them emotionally. Adolescents who watch more television sometimes do so for family social reasons. When there is a heavy emphasis on maintaining harmony in interpersonal communication, family patterns of communication influence television viewing [McLeod & Chaffee in Faber, Brown, & McLeod (1979)]. Another social factor that can affect the amount of television viewing occurs when adolescents are not well integrated or are experiencing status frustration within their peer group. This segment of the adolescent population tends to spend more time watching television (Johnstone, 1974). Video games, another electronic medium, may serve a similar function for some adolescents, as well as serve as an "electronic friend" (Dominick, 1984; Selnow, 1984).

The media may serve children as a source of information for social learning. At a very young age children report that one of the purposes of television is to "teach" (Dorr, 1980). The media may also provide what Noble (1983) has termed *anticipatory socialization.* Some of the earliest research indicated that adolescents watch television to learn how to interact socially (Schramm, Lyle, & Parker, 1961). Similarly, Faber, Brown, and McLeod (1979) suggest that adolescents may find it easier to learn about relationships via television because it is less threatening than the peer group where there is always a risk of ridicule or ostracism when new behaviors are being "tested out." Those who are less integrated into the peer group may rely even more heavily upon television for information regarding social interaction (Morgan & Rothschild, 1983). Summarizing research on the 1970s program *Happy Days,* Noble (1975) shows the extent to which social learning can occur from a popular television series. Anaylzing responses from adolescents twelve to sixteen years old, it was found that significant numbers of respondents indicated that they learned how to ask for a date, how to be popular with people, how to behave on a date, what to do when you feel shy, and even how to behave at McDonalds.

In his study of the impact of electronic media on social behavior, Meyrowitz (1985) suggests that these media have rearranged the social landscape. These social changes have occurred on a number of different levels. Echoing the work of Postman, Mcyrowitz points to the breakdown between adulthood and childhood. Before the advent of television, the combination of parents and literacy served as a control for what and when adults wanted children to learn certain things. It was understood that there was a world of adult knowledge to which children were gradually initiated as they grew older. Sexuality is an obvious example. The electronic media, television in particular, has modified this arrangement considerably. Because the electronic media require no literacy per se, children are easily exposed to things that their parents may not want them exposed to. On another level the electronic media have contributed to a blurring between the private and public order. Traditionally, there has been the public sphere "out there" and the private realm of the family. A projectionist model of sorts operated, in which these two worlds remained separated. This situation no longer exists. The public life now makes its way into the home on a daily basis. One of the most profound effects that the electronic media have on social behavior may come from the lessons they teach about "real" life. Before the age of electronic media, schools worked in consort with parents and other community institutions to teach children about the world, first with myths and ideals, and only gradually did children learn that the social reality fell short of the ideal. Now, Meyrowitz (1985) writes:

> Through the electronic media, young children are witnesses to "facts" that contradict social myths and ideals even before they learn about the myths and ideals in school. Children see politicians disgraced, police officers and teachers on strike for higher pay, parents accused of battering their children. Through television news and entertainment, children learn too much about the nature of "real" life to believe the ideals their teachers try to teach them. The result is not only that they grow up fast, but that they grow up having an image of society and roles that differs markedly from that held by children of earlier generations.

> In the traditional, print based school system, children learned the myths and ideals before they learned about the social reality. The "truth" about society did not necessarily obliterate the myths, but rather put them in perspective. The myths and facts were two separate but equal realities. One was the embodiment of social ideals, the other, the result of observations of social reality. They were complementary: the way we would like things to be and the way things often are as a result of human frailty. The first was the invisible model for the second. Televison largely destroys this bipolar reality. (pp. 255–256)

By providing children with so much information about how the world operates, the electronic media has substantially altered both the content and the method in which the lessons of life are taught.

Luker and Johnston (1988) suggest that television may play a positive role for socially isolated or deprived adolescents. Adolescents who find themselves in this situation can watch other adolescents experience social situations and develop a repertoire of behaviors that would be rewarding if the socially isolated adolescent found himself or herself in a similar situation. Their research with adolescents provides evidence that this may be the case. Luker and Johnston have found differences in viewing preferences between adolescents in high-quality and low-quality social relationships. The latter prefer family dramas with story lines centered around family relationships, while the former prefer action series that feature action and violence and little information about personal relationships. Luker has developed a model to explain social development, which contains a media component (see Figure 5.1). Termed *instrumentality in social relationships,* Luker's model

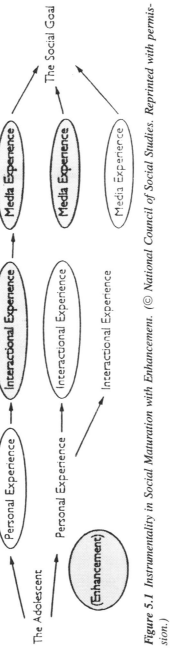

Figure 5.1 *Instrumentality in Social Maturation with Enhancement.* (© *National Council of Social Studies. Reprinted with permission.*)

contains three basic ways (or instruments) in which individuals can gain social knowledge or experience: personal experience, experience with other people, and experience through the mass media. These three instruments carry degrees of value, with personal experience being the most preferred, followed by experience with other people, and lastly the mass media. Luker points out that, while adolescents may prefer personal experience, this vehicle may not be open to them, because the information or behavior may not be accessible (the adolescent wants to start dating but his parents prohibit it) or beacuse of a lack of confidence or competence (the adolescent is allowed to date but is afraid to ask someone).

When personal experience is blocked, the young person may turn to others for information or experience. Again using the dating example, Luker argues that the adolescent who is not permitted to date or who is too shy to ask for a date may learn about dating by talking to friends about their dates or by observing his or her friends' dating behaviors. Luker notes that these interactional experiences are not as powerful as those of personal experience but are better than no access. When both of these types of experiences are blocked, the teenager can either turn to the media or simply "fail to develop the blueprint" because no other avenues are available. The media experience is not as fulfilling as the other two instruments but is better than no access at all.

> Television viewing is likely to have the greatest effect on adolescents unable to gain confidence and competence in social interaction with parents who subsequently have few or no fulfilling peer or peer-group experiences for trying out potential adult behaviors. For these adolescents the mediated images are instrumental in the development of their blueprints of adult social behaviors. To the extent that television models are representative of real life and are fulfilling, television instrumentality may not be altogether bad. (Luker & Johnston, 1988, p. 352)

These three instrumentalities are not mutually exclusive. They sometimes work in combination and may enhance one another. A teenager may be dating, and this personal experience is enhanced by sharing it with others. They may also change over time. Luker and Johnston provide the example of marriage. During adolescence learning about marriage is a vicarious experience but becomes a personal experience as teenagers become adults and actually marry. When the primary mode is the media experience, enhancement from interactional experience and personal experience are not available. If they were, the media would not be instrumental. "This suggests that, when media information is instrumental, it is quite powerful because there is no enhanced basis for comparison" (p. 352). Luker and Johnston suggest that teachers encourage their students to watch the kinds of programs that depict relationships and then to explore them in the classroom.

In a similar vein Ellis, Streeter, and Englebrecht (1983) hypothesize that media personalities, particularly those on television, may function as significant others and allow viewers to take on other roles vicariously. As a result, the electronic environment becomes a symbolic reference group. They offer several propositions, including viewers evaluating their behavior from the imagined perspective of a television character or vicariously taking the roles of selected television characters from the perspective of other television characters.

MEDIA KIDS

The "social reality" of children and adolescents in the media is frequently neither positive nor accurate. Children are often presented as very sophisticated and smarter than their adult parents. Minority children are underrepresented and, when they are portrayed, are done so in a stereotypical fashion. In her study Hamamoto (1993) examined the "controlling image" (she prefers this term description over the word *stereotype*) of Asian American children on television. She argues that these children are exploited for ideological reasons. Hamamota cites the case of tremendous television coverage of Asian war orphans, which she believes deflects attention away from America's responsibility for their condition to begin with. Schultze et al. (1991) point out that teen films are primarily about white adolescents, with ethnic minorities being unfairly represented or unrealistically portrayed. In her study of how children and adolescents are depicted on television, Signorielli (1987) found that, in relation to their proportion of the total population, early adolescents were consistently underrepresented in prime-time television. Moreover, children and adolescents were much more likely to be victimized than older television characters. For every ten early adolescent girls who committed violence on weekend daytime programs, twenty-six became victims. Boys on prime-time were victimized twenty-three times for every ten who committed violence.

Signorielli concluded that "the portrayal of children and adolescents on TV does little to enhance self-esteem and to instill visions of childhood as a good time of life" (p. 267). Describing television teenagers, Peck (1982) notes that they play supporting roles or they are portrayed with social and psychological problems that are either narcotic, sexual, or racial. "The young are played for laughs, kept subordinate to adult roles, or cast as victims—three states they are anxious to avoid in their own lives" (p. 63).

MEDIA VIOLENCE AND AGGRESSION

The issue of media violence spans the social and emotional dimensions of development. For the purposes of this book, however, it will be explored in this section on social development. A previous chapter examined some of the theories explaining the impact of violence and aggression in the media upon users. Media effects regarding violence may be explained by observational learning, attitude changes, the arousal process, or an information-processing model (Huesmann & Eron, 1986). The American Psychological Association Commission on Youth and Violence's (1993) recent report *Violence & Youth* represents still one more acknowledgement of the link between media violence and aggression. In 1972 the Surgeon General issued his report on the effects of television. An entire volume of the report dealt with televised violence and its effects on adolescents. Conflicting research results and politics resulted in an ambiguous summary, despite the fact that researchers found a causal relationship between viewing television violence and aggression.

A decade later the National Institute of Mental Health (Pearl, Bouthelet, & Lazar, 1982) published a report summarizing another decade of research on television effects. Regarding violence on television, the report stated:

> After ten more years of research, the consensus among most of the research community is that violence on television does lead to aggressive behavior by children and teenagers who watch the programs. This conclusion is based on laboratory experiments and on field studies. Not all children become aggressive, of course, but the correlations between violence and aggression are positive. In magnitude, TV violence is as strongly correlated with aggressive behavior as any other behavioral variable that has been measured. The research question has

moved from asking whether or not there is an effect to seeking explanation for the effect. (p. 6)

Children and Mediated Violence

Preschool children have been the subject of several studies. Steuer, Applefield, and Smith [cited in Liebert & Sprafkin (1988)] working with a small sample of ten children, examined the effects of aggressive and neutral television programs on their aggressive behavior. Using a matched pairs study design, they paired students on the basis of how much television they watched. They collected baseline data over ten observations, tallying the number of incidents of aggressive behavior. Steuer and her colleagues used a very stringent definition for aggressive behavior, that is, hitting, pushing, or throwing an object at another. They then modified the television diets of each pair. One child from each pair viewed an aggressive program taken directly from Saturday morning programming, while the other child watched a nonaggression program. Viewing occurred on eleven different days. Ongoing observations took place measuring aggressive behaviors by each child. When the televiewing was completed, the difference between the aggressive behavior for each pair was evident. The children who had watched the violent programming behaved in a more aggressive manner than their counterparts who had viewed neutral programming.

Studies with very young children have also been conducted by Singer and Singer (1981a) and Singer, Singer, and Rapaczynski (1984). Both studies found a correlation between the amount of television viewed and aggressive behavior. In the first study Singer and Singer conducted a one-year longitudinal study with three and four year olds. They monitored the children's viewing habits periodically for twelve months, examining the amount, as well as the content, of the programming the children watched. They based their measurement on observation of spontaneous play at their respective preschools. In their results Singer and Singer noted that "none of our children were 'monsters' or presented major examples of serious violence. But the link of heavy viewing to attacking other children or property as a consistent pattern cannot be denied. Frankly, we had not anticipated as clear a result as we obtained" (p. 153). Their data also indicated a relationship between aggressive behavior and program content. Singer and Singer found that action shows provided a model for violence and proved to be the most discriminating predictor of a child's aggression.

In a later study conducted with Rapaczynski, the Singers (1984) began to track four-year-old girls and boys over a five-year period. Again, they collected data periodically on television viewing habits, aggressiveness, restlessness, and self-restraint. Borrowing from cultivation analysis, Singer, Singer, and Rapaczynski also attempted to measure children's beliefs about the degree to which they thought that theirs was a "mean, scary world." Again, these researchers found at age nine that those children who watched the most television as preschoolers were the most aggressive five years later. Additionally, this relationship held, even after controlling for the pretest levels of aggressiveness. Moreover, those children who watched more television, especially violent programming, evidenced higher levels of restlessness and less self-restraint.

In another study involving preschoolers, Stein and Friedrich [cited in Murray (1980)] exposed children to three types of programming, that is, "antisocial, prosocial, or neutral." One group watched twelve episodes of *Batman* and *Superman* cartoons. The children exposed to prosocial programming watched twelve episodes of *Mister Rogers' Neighborhood*. The neutral programming consisted of children's travelogue films. The children were observed for three weeks to gather baseline data, followed by four weeks of program viewing, with two weeks of follow-up observations. All of the observations were conducted in a naturalistic setting. Observers coded all behaviors that fell into a prosocial or anitsocial category. Children who were considered more aggressive based upon the baseline data and who watched the *Batman* and *Superman* cartoons became significantly more aggressive, while the children who watched *Mister Rogers' Neighborhood* demonstrated higher levels of cooperation and willingness to share.

As part of the Notel naturalistic field study, Joy, Kimball, and Zabrack (1986) examined levels of aggressiveness of children in grades one to five *before* the introduction to television. In all three towns researchers collected data on verbal and physical aggression. As measures they used observations of children during play, teachers' reports, and students' ratings of their classmates' aggressiveness. Observers used a checklist of fourteen physical and nine verbal aggressive behaviors. Behaviors indicating physical aggression included hitting, pushing, and chasing. Verbally aggressive behaviors included threatening, arguing, and insulting others. To insure consistency the same researchers measured the behaviors in all three towns. Two years after the introduction of television into Notel, these researchers found a significant increase in the levels of aggression among the children there. Joy, Kimball, and Zabrack found no differences in either physical or verbal aggression due to grade level. They note that this is significant because it allowed them to eliminate maturation as an explanation for any increase in aggressive behavior. In addition, like van der Voort's study (1986, cited below), the data indicated that both boys and girls were affected. This study also provided mild evidence that aggressive children tend to watch more television. Joy, Kimball, and Zabrack found no increase in aggression levels among children in Unitel and Multitel. The findings of this study are all the more significant because they represent long-term effects.

Huesmann and Eron (1986) participated in a cross-national study, which involved examining the impact of television on aggression in six countries. The sample population in the United States consisted of first and third graders, and the research took place over two years, providing a span of six to eleven years. Unlike other studies, Huesmann and Eron found a strong correlation between television violence viewing and aggression for both boys and girls. Violence televiewing was not only predictive of concurrent aggression, but future aggression as well. They also found evidence that aggression and the viewing of television aggression are reciprocal. Huesmann and Eron note, however, that no single factor can make a child aggressive. A number of conditions make a contribution as well, such as belief that television violence shows violence "just like it is," identification with aggressive characters in programs, and frequent aggressive fantasies.

van der Voort (1986) conducted a study with third through sixth graders in the Netherlands from a different perspective. His study concerned how these children *perceived* violent content in commercial programming. As he noted, he was "not concerned with what violent programs bring to children, but rather with what children bring to violent television programming," noting that many studies on violence assume that children see what adults see (p. 23). Thus, his study was not an effects study, but, rather, a perception study. He hypothesized that children's perceptions of violent programs would be factored into the relationship between watching violent television and aggression. Although conducted in Europe, the study employed American programming. van der Voort's findings supported his hypothesis. The students viewed the more realistic programs as more violent. Moreover, he found that the more realistic the children perceived the program to be, the more involved they were when they watched it.

Because of the complexity of van der Voort's study, he provides insights into the heavy television viewer. He notes that they view television violence differently. They are more accepting of violence on television; they enjoy it more and are more inclined to regard violent behavior as justified. van der Voort also found differences in the way boys and girls view violence on television. His data illustrates that girls do not enjoy watching violence as much as boys and are less likely to approve of violent behavior.

Media Violence and Adolescents

Adolescents have been the subject of numerous studies exploring the relationship between media violence and behaviors (McLeod, Atkin, & Chaffee, 1972a, 1972b; McIntyre & Teevan, 1972; Leifer & Roberts, 1972; Atkin, 1983; Huesmann & Eron, 1986; Joy, Kimball, & Zabrack, 1986). Similarly, adolescents have been involved in studies focusing on attitudinal changes towards aggression and violence based upon television exposure. Using fourth through sixth grade boys, Dominick and Greenberg (1972) found those who experienced a higher exposure to televised violence more willing to use it. In studies on social class and racial differences in children's perceptions of violence on television, Greenberg and Gordon (1972) used fifth and eighth graders. Those from lower socioeconomic backgrounds rated violent behavior more acceptable, life-like, and enjoyable. Rabinovitch et al. (1972) found that sixth graders who watched a violent program, as opposed to those who watched a nonviolent one, seemed, if only temporarily, to be desensitized to violence.

In their survey of violence research, Liebert and Sprafkin (1988) demonstrate how the networks can selectively attend to findings, even when they themselves sponsor them. In their description of a CBS commissioned study, they write:

> In a large-scale study conducted for CBS, Belson (1978) collected information about television viewing, aggressive behavior, and other personal characteristics of more than 1,500 male adolescents in London.

After equating for a variety of variables related to aggressive behavior, the extent of aggressive behavior of the heavy and light TV viewers was compared. Belson concluded that the evidence "is strongly supportive of the hypothesis that high exposure to television violence increases the degree to which boys engage in serious violence" (p. 15). (The antisocial behaviors included deeds that were serious enough to be labeled juvenile delinquency such as inflicting bodily harm to others and damage to property.) CBS chose to view the finds as inconclusive, and the study did not receive much publicity. (Just as a note of interest, this study took 8 years to complete and cost CBS $300,000.) (p. 147)

This response contrasts sharply with that from a longitudinal study by NBC on the same subject (Milavsky et al., 1982). The authors of this three-year study, which employed 3200 youngsters seven through sixteen years old, concluded that any effect of watching television on aggressive behavior was small, if not nonexistent. Because the effect size was so small, the researchers could not provide a definitive interpretation; however, their "judgment was that it was somewhat more likely that the effect was zero than that it was small" (Milavsky, 1988, p. 165).

A different perspective on media violence comes from Miedzian, a philosopher, who has situated this issue within the larger context of the concept of masculinity in our society. In *Boys Will Be Boys: Breaking the Link between Masculinity and Violence,* Miedzian (1991) argues that the media represent but one of several factors in our society that have created a link between our images of masculinity and violence. In her introduction she argues that "many of the values of the masculine mystique, such as toughness, dominance, repression of empathy, extreme competitiveness, play a major role in criminal and domestic violence and underlie the thinking and policy decisions of many of our political leaders" (p. xiii). Miedzian believes that one of the ways in which the early relationship between violence and gender is seen is through toys. She provides several reasons that violent toys aggravate this situation. Some are clearly media-related. The encouragement of children to play with violent toys is reinforced by violent heroes and scenarios that television, VCRs, and films provide as models. Toy advertisers not only sell violent toys, but a violent story line to accompany them.

The Rambo 81 mm Mortar Thunder-Tube Assault, which is recommended for five and up, comes with a detailed scenario: "The S.A.V.A.G.E. Army will stop at nothing in their attempt to control the world!" the box cover explains. "Their weapons, mostly stolen from the free world's ammo dumps, see a lot of action against Rambo and the Force of Freedom." Boys are also provided the factual information about the real weapons that the toy is based on: "The 81 mm mortar is used to lob ammo over hills and fortifications, and is effective because of its large bursting radius. It is currently used by U.S. Forces, Australia, Austria, and Italy." (p. 268)

Miedzian adds that many of the video games on today's market have violent themes and are dominated by males.

Many of Miedzian's arguments regarding the media are not new, some are clearly reminiscent of Gore's (1987) book *Raising PG Kids in an X-Rated Society.* She is correct in her assertion that not only is there more violence in the entertainment media, but that it is more realistic as well. Miedzian notes Comstock's work in which he conducted an analysis of over 250 television and film studies. Based on his findings, Comstock concluded that the following characteristics are most inclined to influence young people regarding violence: graphic depictions of violence, the absence of punishment for violent acts, and the absence of serious emotional or physical consequences [Comstock, cited in Miedzian (1991)].

A film genre that has generated considerable debate is "slasher films." These films, popular with adolescents (despite their R ratings), contain explicit violence. Critics point to these films as an example of a trend in which more and more media violence is directed against women. Molitor and Sapolsky (1993) credited Siskel and Ebert with this association when these film critics created the term "women in danger" films. A few years later, Linz, Donnerstein, and Penrod (1984) suggested that these films added another dimension: the association between sex and violence. Content analyses by Cowan and O'Brien (1990) and Molitor and Sapolsky challenge these two assumptions somewhat. Neither of these two studies found women to be victims more often than men. In fact, Molitor and Sapolsky found that a significant number of males died more often. Cowan and O'Brien found the ratio of deaths to be about equal. Molitor and Sapolsky did not find a link between sex and violence as is commonly assumed. Their analysis did show, however, that females are shown in fear for longer periods of time. Their research also pointed to a greater number of incidents of violence in films since 1989 than in previous years for which films were analyzed.

Another theme that Miedzian takes up is that of violent lyrics in music, particularly rap and heavy metal. At times her conclusions are tenuous. Of particular interest, however, is her treatment of the debate over how much adolescents understand of music lyrics. She cites a research study conducted with junior high and high school students, which found that HSS (homicide, satanism, and suicide) rock fans listen to music more. Moreover, compared to the rest of the rock fans in the study, a higher proportion of HSS fans understood the lyrics of the songs.

There is not total agreement regarding the media and violence, however. Milgram and Shotland (1973) did not find a link between television and anti-social behavior, nor did the Milavsky et al. (1982) study cited previously. Freedman (1984, 1988) and Cook, Kendzierski, and Thomas (1983) have criticized studies linking television violence to aggression. Nevertheless, Jeffres (1986) notes that: "There is simply too much evidence from a variety of research methodologies to reach any conclusion other than one favoring television effects" (p. 225). And the Commission on Youth and Violence of the American Psychology Association stated unequivocally: "There is absolutely no doubt that higher levels of viewing violence on television are correlated with increased acceptance of aggressive attitudes and increased aggressive behavior" (American Psychological Association, 1993, p. 33).

In addition to television, the Commission on Youth and Violence draws several other conclusions regarding violence in the media. It charges film and television with exacerbating violence against women and ethnic minorities. The report is critical of the growing association between violence and sexuality, noting that this linkage "appears to affect the attitudes of adolescents about rape and violence towards women." Much of this violence can be found in videotapes easily accessible to teenagers. The Commission notes that the effects of violence can be mitigated. Among one of the strategies offered by this group to deal with this problem is teaching critical viewing skills.

Video games represent still another electronic medium that has been criticized for its violent themes. Initial concerns about video arcades contributing to delinquency proved unfounded (Ellis, 1984). The combination of advances in technology and the popularity of games that require aggressive strategies have carried the industry a long way since

Space Invaders. The tremendous popularity of *Mortal Kombat,* in which the loser has his head torn off and spinal cord ripped out, has sparked another round of debate regarding violence in the media. To date, findings are sketchy. Summarizing the research, and there is not a great deal, Provenzo (1991) notes that it appears that there is a relationship between aggressive behavior and playing video games. In a preliminary study, however, Dominick (1984) did not find a relationship between video game playing and aggression among teenagers.

PROSOCIAL BEHAVIOR

Because much of the attention surrounding the media has focused on negative aspects such as violence, the research on the prosocial impact of the media is often overlooked. Following the publication of the Surgeon General's report in 1972 on the prosocial effects of the media, television, in particular, grew tremendously. Much of this research has been conducted with children and educational programming such as *Sesame Street* and *Mister Rogers' Neighborhood.* These programs intentionally contain positive social messages for young viewers. Commercial programs such as *The Waltons* and *Fat Albert and the Cosby Kids* have also evidenced prosocial effects. Pearl, Bouthelet, and Lazar (1982) define prosocial as "that which is socially desirable and which in some ways benefits another person or society" (p. 48). They divide prosocial behavior into three types: altruism, friendly behavior, and self-control. A fourth type of prosocial behavior added by Rushton (1982) is coping with fears. If children and adolescents can learn aggressive behaviors from viewing media violence, then young people can use the media to develop positive social behaviors as well. Surveying the evidence from television, Rushton notes that the content of programs dictates what viewers learn. "If on the one hand, prosocial helping and kindness make up the content of television programming, then this is what will be learned by viewers as appropriate, normative behavior." Conversely, if "antisocial behaviors and uncontrolled aggression are shown, then these are what viewers will learn to be the norm" (p. 255). As Johnston and Ettema (1982) point out, however, most of the research in this area has examined short-term effects. An exception to this rule is *Freestyle,* a program created to counter gender stereotypes, which showed persistence of effects over an extended period of time.

Because of the attention given to negative behaviors depicted on commercial television, prosocial behaviors are often overlooked. In her study of prosocial content on prime-time television, Lee (1988) found abundant evidence of positive behaviors. Surveying 235 programs coders found over 1000 prosocial incidents. Nearly every program analyzed (97%) contained at least one example of prosocial behavior. In a related study Selnow (1990) examined television for values incidents, many of which relate to prosocial behaviors. Of the over 1100 values incidents rated by coders, 471 were instances of "compassion for others," clearly prosocial behaviors.

GENDER SOCIALIZATION

A key component in the social development of children and adolescents is the development of a gender identity. After violence and school achievement, the impact of the media upon gender socialization has probably received the most attention. Clearly, children begin learning gender roles at an early age. The changes brought on by puberty and the increased interaction between the sexes lead adolescents to explore this issue in a new way. The question of media effects can be explored at a number of levels. How are gender roles portrayed in the media? What do young people learn from media portrayals? Can the media be used to change sex-role stereotyping, both in the home and in the workplace? Because gender equity has become such a compelling issue in education today (Sadker & Sadker, 1994; Grossman & Grossman, 1994), this topic will be explored in some detail.

Studies on Media Content and Gender Portrayals

Despite advances in the portrayal of the genders in the media, females are still poorly represented, as well as underrepresented. In his study of children's programming, Barcus (1983) examined 235 program segments and over 1100 characters. Analyzing forty-nine hours of programming recorded over a weekend and several afternoons, Barcus found that males clearly dominated. Only 20% of the characters were female, while a little more than three-quarters were male. Of the programs that included only one gender, 35% contained male characters and only 2% contained only female characters. Comparatively, women were younger, more likely to be married or widowed, and found in traditional family roles. When employed, they held less prestigious jobs.

Males frequently appeared in single-sex groups interacting. Women rarely appeared in single-sex groups and seldom appeared without men.

Gender role stereotyping has been found in virtually all of the popular media. Brabant (1976) found sex role stereotyping in family oriented Sunday comics. In a follow-up study ten years later, little significant change occurred (Brabent & Mooney, 1986). Male cartoon characters outnumber females, and some cartoons have no females at all, according to Mayes and Valentine (1979). While primarily entertainment, they believe that cartoons have the ability to teach social behavior. Mayes and Valentine examined cartoons based on Nadelson's contention that the primary function of children's entertainment is to provide a fantasy setting in which children can "try on" a variety of roles. In a similar study of main characters in Saturday cartoons, McArthur and Eisen (1976) found a three to one ratio of males to females. In addition, the commercial announcements accompanying these cartoon programs were overwhelmingly male (80% of the central figures were male). Moreover, males appeared more often as authorities than females (55% versus 32% for females). Females, however, appeared 24% more often as product users than males. In their analysis of July Fourth political cartoons over the last 100 years, Meyer et al. (1980) found changes in the way women are depicted but noted a decline in the number of women represented, as well as more subtle indications of subordination.

Berger (1972), Goffman (1977a), Betterton (1987), Barthel (1988), and Kilbourne (1989) have explored the way advertising constructs gender roles, particularly for women. These constructions are based upon content as well as the formal features of commericals. Goffman notes, for example, that, when a man and woman appear in the same advertisement, the woman is frequently placed in a subservient position, such as behind or below the man. Barthel and Kilbourne highlight how advertisers try to make beauty and glamour indispensable elements of the feminine image. In some cases this is done by creating a sense of inferiority and inadequacy that can only be remedied by the right beauty products. Betterton notes that women have little control of the feminine image in today's society. In Lovdal's (1989) study of sex role messages in television commercials, she found that little had changed in the ten-year period between 1978 and 1988. Lovdal notes that men were portrayed in three times the variety of occupations as women. The majority of commericals contained male voice-overs that, she adds, provide an "authoritative tone" and give the ideas that men are more convincing, credible, and knowledgeable.

Similarly, a study of MTV commercials revealed these commercials are heavily gender stereotyped. Almost three-quarters of the men who apeared in commercials had average bodies, while more than three-quarters of the women had very fit or beautiful bodies. The study revealed MTV showed twice as many commercials with men only than commercials with women only. Products for men tended to be entertainment related. Commercials targeted at women consisted of products to improve or enhance physical attractiveness. Only 19% of the commercials presented males as objects of another character's admiring gaze, as opposed to 60% of women. The authors concluded that "the portrayals in these commercials reveal a disturbing message: The primary purpose of women's effort is to 'look good': and to be the object of the visual attention of others" (Signorielli, McLeod, & Healy, 1994). These findings echo Adler and Faber's analysis [cited in Downs & Harrison (1985)] that children and adults see over 5260 attractiveness messages per year, of which 1850 deal directly with beauty. In their study of television commercials, Downs and Harrison (1985) examined the use of physical attractiveness stereotyping as an instrument of sexism. They note that there is good reason to suspect that television commercials provide an important medium for attractiveness stereotyping for three reasons: billions of advertising dollars are spent on products related to attractiveness (e.g., cosmetics, physical fitness, and weight reduction programs), appearance-related commercials seem to be effective, and television stereotyping has been well documented in the literature. They examined nearly 4300 network commercials. Not only did Downs and Harrison find high rates for attractiveness messages on appearance-related commercials, but also on nonappearance-related products as well. They argue that there is a link, at least implicitly, between women and attractiveness. They conclude that their findings "strongly indicate that beauty sells and that virtually any product associated with beauty attainment is more likely to sell. More important, however," they continue, "is the implication that attractiveness stereotypes have permeated virtually the entire television advertising market making television commercials powerful sources of attractiveness stereotypes" (p. 17).

Seidman (1992) conducted a content analysis of a random sample of 182 music videos, examining the sex role stereotyping and occupational roles of music video characters. He concluded that males are depicted as more adventuresome, domineering, aggressive, violent, and victimized than female characters. Females appeared more affectionate, dependent, nurturing, and fearful than males. Moreover, Seidman found significant differences in the way the sexes dressed. A third of the women wore revealing clothing compared to 4% of the men. Women appeared more sexual than men in terms of initiating and receiving sexual advances. Stereotyping by gender and occupation held as well. Women appeared in very high percentages as hair stylists, dancers, fashion models, and telephone operators. All of the scientists, politicans, business executives, and managers were male, as well as the vast majority of other occupations such as athletes, police, and soldiers.

The world of technology has not escaped gender stereotyping either. In their study of sex role messages and microcomputers, Ware and Stuck (1985) surveyed popular computer magazines. Men appeared twice as often as women. They found women overrepresented as clerical workers and sex objects. These magazines overrepresented men as managers, experts, and repair technicians. In mixed sex illustrations men were most often shown in the positioin of authority. Only women appeared rejecting a computer. While 82.8% of the males portrayed actively used a computer, only 55.7% of women did so.

Schwartz and Markham (1985) argue that the sex typing of toys contributes to sex role socialization. They studied the sex typing of toys in children's toy advertisements. Their research indicates that toys that are moderately sex typed become strongly stereotyped in the advertisements. Summarizing the research in this area, they noted that, by age four, children clearly have sex-typed toy preferences and that media models are an important source in the development of toy sex typing. Welch et al. (1979), using a different approach, looked at the formal aspects of children's commercials and noted that the advertising industry uses subtle messages. Looking at the formal features of these commercials, they noted that "distinctively masculine" messages are conveyed through high rates of action, aggression, variation, and quick shifts from one scene to another and through jazzed up sound tracks.

Signorielli (1989) points out that the sex role images on prime-time television have remained quite stable over the last ten to fifteen years. Generalizing on the status of women on television, Huston et al. (1992) observed that males still outnumbered females. Males are three times as likely to appear as major characters than females on prime-time television. This ratio increases to six to one in action-adventure shows.

Women are also more likely to appear as victims than men. Feshbach, Dillman, and Jordan (1979) described the model female on television as a "young adult, beautiful, dependent, helpless, passive, concerned with interpersonal relations, warm, and valued for her appearance rather than for her capabilities and competencies, personal and professional" (p. 376). The National Commission on Working Women (Steenland, 1986) found that the vast majority of women on television are wealthy or comfortable with portrayals of working class and poor women virtually nonexistent. Minority women are vastly underrepresented, and when they appear on television, it is usually on a sitcom. In his analysis of prime-time television, Davis (1990) maintains that few changes have occurred in the portrayal of women in terms of observable demographic characteristics. Summarizing women's occupational status on television, Vande Berg and Streckfuss (1992) maintain that relatively little has changed over forty years. "Television's working women continue to be portrayed significantly less often than working men as decision maker, as assertive corporate politicians, and as socially and economically productive working persons" (p. 205). Studies by Dohrmann (1975) and Matelski (1985) indicate that even public television does not provide accurate gender ratios.

In her study of the treatment of women in film, Haskell (1973) demonstrated how the stereotypical woman has endured throughout the cinema's short history. Slasher films, quite popular with teenagers, present still another portrait of females, in this case, usually adolescent girls. As noted above, Cowan and O'Brien (1990) found no evidence associating gender and survival in slasher films. They did find sexiness paired with nonsurvival of female victims, however. They concluded that, in these kinds of films, "the message appears to be that sexual women get killed and only the pure women survive. This message that the good woman is asexual and the bad (and therefore dead) woman is sexual, however, may be almost as pernicious as the message conveyed in pornography that violence can be fun for women" (p. 195). In a medium that has come to dominate adolescent interest, that is, rock music videos, the difference in the depiction of the two sexes is evident. Jhally's (1991) documentary *Dreamworlds* reveals a world in which women exist primarily as sex objects for men. He argues that one of the reasons for music videos is to create a fantasy world for young males.

Magazines popular with middle and high school girls represent still another source of socialization. Peirce (1990) conducted a content analysis of *Seventeen* magazine over three decades. She concluded that data suggest that teenage girls are concerned primarily with appearance, household activities, and romance and dating. Peirce concluded: "*Seventeen* is only a small part of the huge entity called media and a small part of the socialization of a teenage girl, but in conjunction with those other parts, it can be a powerful reinforcer of the traditional ideology of womanhood" (p. 499).

Another print medium that carries specific gender messages is that of adolescent romantic fiction. As noted earlier, this literary genre is becoming a lucrative segment of the educational publishing industry. Christian-Smith (1991) argues that teen romance fiction helps shape girls' understandings of themselves and their place in the world. "Teen romance fiction articulates the longstanding fears and resentments of segments of society regarding feminism and women's growing independence. Teen romance reading involves the shaping of consciousness as well as the occasion for young women to reflect on their fears, hopes, and dreams." Christian-Smith adds, "For women throughout teen romance fiction's saga of hearts and flowers is the discourse that a woman is incomplete without a man, that motherhood is someone's destiny, and that women's rightful place is in the home" (p. 192). In her study of the impact of this genre, Christian-Smith explored their use by twenty-nine young adolescent girls. Students read these novels at home and in school and averaged six novels per month. Christian-Smith found that these adolescents read romance novels for the same reasons that adults do: escape, better reading than dreary textbooks, enjoyment and pleasure, and a way to learn about romance and dating. The adolescent girls in this study employed novels in ways to counteract school-releated perceptions. Christian-Smith discovered that reading during school (usually during independent study) provided an enjoyable experience in what was usually a tedious day at school. These readers, who demonstrated an awareness of their teachers' low estimation of them, clearly identified with the heroines in these novels who were "smart, funny and resourceful."

"Sometimes the way guys are in the books helps us girls understand them a lot better," is how one thirteen-year-old summed up some of these young adolescents' use of romance fiction to learn about the other sex. Christian-Smith also found that readers of teen romance fiction have very definite ideas about what makes a good romance novel. It should be easy to read, move along and not drag, and have a happy ending. The heroine and hero are attractive, popular, friendly, and persons of means. The heroine is strong and gets the best of boys. These students translated these texts into real life, particularly regarding the heroines and real life. "All the young women believed that 'pretty girls' get 'nice boy friends.' Although having a nice personality was equally important, attractiveness was 'something that a girl could not do without.' These beliefs were validated in their everyday lives: the prettiest, most popular young women at their schools also had their pick of the boys." Christian-Smith also found that "these descriptions of feminine popularity in everyday life were reminiscent of romance-fiction heroines. The linking of beauty with romance not only motivated the young women's consumption, but also provided the reason for working for pay" (p. 205).

Kane and Greendorfer (1994) document how the media contribute to female stereotypes in the world of sports. Despite strides made by women in the world of sports, they are still vastly underrepresented. Borrowing Tuchman's concept of symbolic annihilation, they cite several studies exploring this phenomenon. Of particular note is a study conducted on race and gender in *Sports Illustrated*. Lumpkin and Williams (1991) found that, in 3723 feature articles in this magazine over two decades, nearly 91% of the articles concerned males. Only sixteen of the articles concerned black females! When females receive media coverage, Kane and Greendorfer pointed out that they are "consistently trivialized or marginalized." Again, they note that a substantial body of research suggests "that visual production techniques, language, terminology and commentary applied to women's sport are selectively imposed by the media to provide a highly stereotypical feminized view—one that tends to sexualize, commodify, trivialize and devalue (through marginalization) women's sporting accomplishments" (p. 36). Kane and Greendorfer point to the difference between the coverage of a men's and women's basketball game. One is couched in epic proportions, while the other is "given the feel of a neighborhood pickup game." Finally, they maintain that media coverage of women's sports is characterized by ambivalence. An example of this ambivalence occurs when visuals provide one image, while the narrative provides another. For example, when the camera focused on the female winner of the New York City Marathon, the commentator was commenting on who had finished third in the men's race.

Research on the Influence of the Media on Gender Socialization

Pingree and Hawkins (1980) highlight three reasons for conducting sex role research with children. First, sex role learning begins in early childhood. A second reason is that young children are open to new information and influences during these formative years. This openness can be viewed as a time of special risk or special opportunity. Finally, if the media affect sex roles, it makes sense to look for these effects where researchers have the best chance of finding them. Childhood is an impressionable period, and, therefore, media effects should manifest themselves most clearly among children. Busby (1985) believes that media content is not the only, nor necessarily the primary, factor for learning sex role stereotypes. She also points out that stereotypes may be easier to remember because they are learned at an earlier age. Tuchman (1981) notes research on gender can be guided by two concepts. The reflection hypothesis is based on the assumption that the "media reflect dominant social values," and the corporate character of the media is such that, to attract the largest audiences, the media simply reflect American values. The second concept, that of symbolic annihilation, pioneered by Tuchman, is grounded in the idea that through either condemnation, trivialization, or absence, a group such as women is annihilated, albeit symbolically. She points to numerous studies, and there have been many since she first advanced this theory, that show that women are consistently underrepresented in the media. From a different perspective, however, Davidson and Lytle (1986), in their study of images of women in the mass media during the 1950s, have posed the question: "How is it that hundreds of thousands of girls who watched themselves be symbolically annihilated during the 1950s supplied so many converts to the women's movement of the sixties?" (p. 391).

Schramm, Lyle, and Parker (1961) observed that girls early on begin watching television programs that relate to the responsibilities that they assume during adolescence and adult life. Boys, on the other hand, selected action-adventure types of shows. Moreover, the evidence suggests that males and females tend to identify with their own gender when it is portrayed in the media. Schramm, Lyle, and Parker found this to be the case with preschool children. Miller and Reeves [cited in Busby (1985)] found boys named television characters as models for their own behavior more than girls. In their study no boys named girls as models, while 27% of the girls nominated male characters. To test the possible effects of nontraditional same-sex role models upon preschoolers (aged thirty-five to sixty-six months), McArthur and Eisen (1976) used televised models. A concern for cartoon character stereotypes occasioned their research. They found that the boys recalled and reproduced more of the activities of the same-sex models even when the televised model exhibited "sex-inappropriate behavior," for example, nurturance, domesticity, and artistic behaviors. At the same time, when the same-sex model performed activities consistent with gender stereotyped roles, the boys exhibited these types of behaviors as well. Beuf (1974) interviewed sixty-three boys and girls between the ages of three and six. Children's responses indicated that television viewing was related to career choices. Heavier viewers chose stereotyped career choices more often than moderate viewers (67% and 50%, respectively). Beuf noted that her findings reveal that children as young as four and five hold the same kind of sex-typed career stereotypes as the rest of society. Pingree (1978) showed third and eighth graders commercials with women portrayed stereotypically, as well as in a nontraditional fashion. She designed her research to study the effects of perceptions of reality upon attitudes towards women. Pingree told one group that the people in the commercials were real, doing all the things they really do and that they were not acting (reality set). A second group was told just the opposite about the people in the commercial (acting set). A third group was given no instructions. Despite variations in findings, the overall test results indicated that the children who saw women in nontraditional roles had significantly less traditional attitudes about women than those who saw the traditional commercial.

Davidson, Yasuna, and Tower (1979) studied the effects of television cartoons on the stereotyping of young girls (five- and six-year-olds). The girls viewed one of three types of cartoons: one depicting a highly stereotyped sex role, a neutral cartoon, or a cartoon relating nontraditional sex roles. The girls who saw the low stereotyped cartoon reported significantly lower sex role stereotype scores than the girls who saw the high and neutral cartoons.

Miller and Reeves [cited in Feshbach et al. (1979)] set out to test three hypotheses regarding third through sixth graders' reactions to television stereotypes. They hypothesized that boys would nominate more television characters as behavior models than girls and that boys would nominate more same-sex television characters as behavior models than girls. They also wanted to study the reaction of children to women in counterstereotypic occupations; that is, would they see them as more appropriate in real life? Miller and Reeves's interviews with 200 children provided support data for all three hypotheses. Of interest was one of their findings regarding their third hypothesis. Children who correctly identified the role of a counterstereotypic character, such as a policewoman, were more likely to transfer the appropriateness to real life.

Kimball (1986) conducted a study of television and sex role attitudes as part of the larger Notel experiment. She hypothesized that the children living in Notel would have less traditional sex role attitudes than students living in Unitel and Multitel. After two years of television, she reasoned that the children living in Notel would be more stereotyped in their attitudes, while the children living in the towns that already had television would not evidence any change. Researchers administered the Sex Role Differentiation (SRD) scale to sixth and ninth graders in all three towns. This scale has two sections. The Peer Scales ask respondents to rate how frequent and appropriate certain behaviors are for boys and girls their own age. The Parent Scales require children to rate how frequently their mothers and fathers do certain tasks. Two years later, Kimball and her colleagues administered the scale again. The data supported both hypotheses on the Peer Scales, with girls holding less strongly sex-typed attitudes.

McGhee and Frueh (1980) studied the relationship between television viewing and knowledge of adult sex role stereotypes among first, third, and seventh graders. Their study is significant because it provides a research population that spans several years, an important developmental consideration. They divided viewers between light viewers (who watched ten hours or less of television weekly) and heavy viewers (who watched twenty-five hours or more of television per week). Their findings revealed significant differences between heavy and light viewers, as well as between male and female viewers. Both heavy and light viewers provided stereotypical responses at grade one. Among low viewers the perception of male stereotypes decreased with increasing age. Heavy viewers provided stereotypical responses with increasing age. Their data also suggest a ceiling effect. Stereotypical responses among heavy male viewers became increasingly pronounced between grades one and five and then leveled off. Girls responded differently. Both heavy and light viewers had similar levels of stereo-typical responses from grades one to three. Between grades three and seven, however, heavy viewing females continued to hold stereotypes, while light viewers became progressively less stereotyped.

In the naturalistic Notel experiment conducted on the impact of the introduction of television in a community that had almost no access at all, Kimball (1986) studied students in grades four through seven and then again two years later when they were in grades six through nine. The experiment measured sex role perceptions of students using two scales. The first scale asked students to measure how appropriate or frequent certain behaviors are for boys and girls their age. The second scale, a parent scale, asked the students to rate how frequently their mothers and fathers performed certain tasks. Kimball and her colleagues hypothesized that the children from the town with no television would have less traditional sex role attitudes than the control populations. They also hypothesized that, after two years of television, the young people would have developed more traditional sex role stereotypes. Overall, the post-test data supported both of these hypotheses. There were some anomalies, however, and boys were found to hold greater sex-typed attitudes than the girls. The introduction of television did not change attitudes towards parents.

Morgan and Rothschild (1983) examined cable television viewing, peer affiliation, and sex role stereotypes among eighth graders. They hypothesized that those who were less integrated into the peer groups would have stronger sex role stereotypes based upon the assumption that they would be more reliant upon the media as a source of information. They based their hypothesis upon earlier work by Rothschild (cited in Morgan & Rothschild), in which she found that third and fifth grade children who were more integrated into the peer group showed weaker associations between television and sex role images. Morgan and Rothschild surveyed evening cable viewing and administered a seven-item scale of sex role stereotypes. Sociometric mappings provided information on peer group integration. Their data results indicated that lesser involvement with peers heightens the consequences of exposure to television. Moreover, they found stronger sexism among those who viewed cable instead of network television. They concluded that "the new electronic environment will not ensure diversity, but, like its predecessors, will monopolize the message systems by further standardization and homogenization of this culture's most common social myths" (p. 48).

While much of the research on sex role stereotyping has been conducted with younger children, there are some studies that include adolescent populations. Tan (1979) studied the effects of television beauty commercials on high school students' (sixteen- through eighteen-year-olds) perceptions of the importance of beauty, sex appeal, and youth in various "real-life" roles. She asked subjects what the necessary characteristics are for a woman to be successful in a career, as a wife, and to be popular with men. Tan also asked the girls what characteristics they found desirable in a woman. The girls exposed to the beauty commercials rated the importance of beauty higher for them personally, as well as in terms of being popular with men. In his study on the impact of television on sex role attitudes and behaviors, Morgan (1987) writes, "Television is not likely to be the most powerful influence on adolescents, but it represents the most common, cumulative and broadly-shared potential source of values, images, and beliefs among otherwise heterogeneous groups of young people." In his longitudinal study of sixth through tenth graders, Morgan (1982) examined the effects of television viewing on sex role stereotypes. His findings are interesting. Morgan found a significant correlation between amount of television watched and sexism scores. The study provided no linkage between sex typing leading to greater viewing. For boys the results were just the opposite. He found no impact of television viewing on their sex role attitudes; however, heavier viewers tended to have more sexist attitudes. Controlling for demographics, Morgan found that both lower class males and females were more sexist, irrespective of how much television they watched. The implication here is that watching television may have its greatest effect upon those who are least likely to hold traditional sex role views. In another study conducted with eighth graders, Morgan (1987) found that those who watch more television are more likely to have traditional stereotypical sex role attitudes, but television is not related to their actual behaviors.

Mayes and Valentine (1979) studied whether children perceived sex role stereotyping in Saturday morning cartoons. Fifteen girls and fifteen boys aged eight to thirteen watched several episodes of different cartoon programs. Using the sex of the subjects and the sex of the characters as independent variables, Mayes and Valentine found significant differences in the evaluation of the characters by girls and boys. Both boys and girls in the study saw the characters they viewed as having sex-typed characteristics. These researchers suggest that entertainment media provide a fantasy setting in which young people can "try on" various roles different from what the child usually observes.

Fejes (1992) points out that, compared to studies on women and the media, only a few studies have explicitly studied the relationship between the media and social definitions of masculinity. While a number of studies have explored the relationship between the media and gender roles, Durkin (1985) notes that sex role research has "concentrated on the female role and the male sex role tends to be illustrated by default, and is often assumed to the converse of whatever characteristics are identified as associated with the female stereotype" (p. 110). Durkin suggests that one of the reasons that males have not received similar treatment in sex role research may arise from the fact that the women's movement has raised the level of consciousness and thus concern regarding women and, therefore, contributes to this emphasis on research on female sex roles. There has been no similar movement regarding the role of males in our society to stimulate such research.

In their study of heavy metal music and gender images, Denski and Sholle (1992) suggest that "the performative/bodily gestures of heavy metal are stereotyped and exaggerated reproductions of aggressive masculine behavior" (p. 50), for example, raising clenched fists, crotch grabbing, and pelvic thrusts. Heavy metal is not without its feminine and gender blurring features, however. Denski and Sholle point to clothing and heavy makeup, particularly lipstick and mascara. The music in concert or on recording is only part of a much more widespread heavy metal image. This message is found in the broader media as well. Denski and Sholle point to the comic book *Heavy Metal,* fanzines, clothing, electronic media such as video games, pinball machines, and the animated film *Heavy Metal.* Regarding the film, they write, "The vignettes that compose this film all rely on the young or weak taking up or conquering machines on their way to sexual initiation with large-breasted women" (p. 48). How these images affect the young adolescent male audience, the authors do not speculate. They suggest that the appeal of this kind of music and image to this age group reflects the particular development circumstance in which the young adolescent male finds himself. "These boys are confronted by girls who may be larger, stronger, and smarter than they are, while at the same time these boys are being socialized into the dominant masculine cultural position of pursuer of the female, thus generating a fear of the feminine." As a result, "Faced with intimidating females, the heavy metal fan finds fantasy escape in the aggressive, powerful figures of heavy metal, who sing about and seem to act out an extreme control of women" (pp. 53–54).

Studies have not only focused on music, but advertising as well. Both Postman et al. (1987) and Strate (1992) have explored the image of masculinity in beer commercials. Strate has referred to this commercial genre as a *manual on masculinity*. "The manifest function of beer advertising is to promote a particular brand," Strate writes, "but collectively the commercials provide a clear and consistent image of the masculine role; in a sense, they constitute a guide for becoming a man, a rulebook for appropriate male behavior, in short, a manual on masculinity" (p. 78). He argues that beer commercials speak to the masculine image in a number of ways. Beer is often associated with physical labor. The leisure time of men in these commercials is cast in terms of spending time out of doors or hanging out in bars. Beer is associated with initiation into membership (of which the group is all male). As an example of this, Strate points to the commercial in which the young Polish immigrant overcomes the pitfalls of the first day on the job. Walking into the bar after work, his foreman, who earlier stood corrected by the young man when he mispronounced his name, calls him and hands him a beer. Strate concludes: "Although targeted at an adult audience, beer commercials are highly accessible to children; between the ages of two and 18, American children see as many as 100,000 of these ads. They are also extremely attractive to children: humorous, exciting, and offering answers to questions about gender and adulthood" (p. 92).

In her study of comic books as a socializing agent, Pecora (1992) argues that, because comic books are so popular, particularly with young adolescent males, the characters that populate their pages are an important symbol of maleness in our culture. In addition, she points out that, for the most part, the males have dominated the ranks of comic book superheroes. Pecora presents the top ten comic book titles for 1990. Only one, *The X-Men,* includes women. For this reason she believes that comics have presented a particular idea of what masculinity is. Pecora points out that, with some exceptions, the world of the comic book superhero is one in which triumphant males make their way through action and violence. She believes that young adolescent comic book readers learn from these heroes rules about life in terms of what is acceptable, desirable, attractive, successful, and possible. "Young boys are still offered cultural representations that reinforce maleness as machismo. The superheroes are loners, fighting evil in their own way, a way that invokes violence. Technology," Pecora adds, "is used for power and control. Women are elderly and weak or voluptuous and unimportant. And it would appear, little has changed" (p. 77).

Depictions of male relationships on television have been around since its beginning. Some efforts have been made to transcend superficial "male bonding" friendships on television, as demonstrated in the drama series *thirtysomething*. More often than not, however, these efforts have been in comedies. Summarizing forty years of male friendships on prime-time TV, Spangler (1992) notes that "the majority of men on TV are seen doing together, not being together" (p. 110). A recent study by Berry (1992) examined the perceptions of low-income black adolescents to the images of black fathers and sons on television. These adolescents viewed an episode of *Good Times* and *The Cosby Show* in a media criticism class. Berry selected these two series because they represent differing images of the black male. The former represents the typical image of black manhood. Cliff Huxtable, conversely, presents a different portrait of the black male. He is more involved with his son Theo and more democratic in his decision making, while James Evans of *Good Times* is less involved and clearly in charge of the household. The economic circumstances are dissimilar as well. The Evans family lives in a housing project where the father is frequently unemployed. The Huxtable family lives very comfortably on the dual incomes of a doctor and lawyer. Berry notes that the sons in these two series are different. She describes Theo as "ambitious with average intelligence" and J. J. as "a buffoon, a modern day Stepin Fechit."

A majority of male respondents reported that they viewed James Evans as a stronger, more manly character. This was true of female participants as well. Contrary to her expectations, Berry did not find as strong a negative assessment of the J.J. character as she thought she would. Berry suggests that, while television is an important factor in gender awareness, there are clearly limitations when what appears on television is very different from the real world experience of its viewers.

As an electronic medium, it is not known how video games might affect gender socialization. Video games have been criticized for being sexist. Provenzo's (1991) analysis revealed that video games are "blatantly" gender stereotyped, and, therefore, they have the potential to amplify certain values, such as women as victims or women as dependent, as opposed to independent. He suggests that the combination of these stereotypes with those from other media leads males to assume that women are the "weaker sex." Research also demonstrates that video games are played more by boys and that boys enjoy playing these games more than girls (Kubey & Larson, 1990; Dominick, 1984). Kubey (1990/91) points out that most video games are designed by males for a young male audience. Whether this medium reinforces other media gender stereotypes is a question for future research. Nonetheless, Kubey argues that video games do promote gender inequality. "Since they represent many children's first exposure to technology, and since they're designed for boys, they contribute to boys getting a head start in becoming comfortable with technology." Therefore, "As our society becomes increasingly high tech, this may translate to career advantages later down the line" (p. 10).

If the media contribute to the development of sex role stereotypes, they can also be used to break down these stereotypes. The development of the television series *Freestyle* is a case in point. Originally conceived by the National Institute for Education, this series was created to reduce the influence of sex and ethnic group stereotyping on the career interests of nine-to-twelve-year-olds. The series contained three content themes. The first, childhood preoccupational activities, featured nine-to-twelve-year-olds in activities that might lead to specific career interests. Characters were portrayed in a number of activities, including mechanics, science, athletics for girls, and nurturant activities for boys. A second theme, behavioral skills, focused on skills that this age group could begin to develop that would be useful in later careers. Behavioral skills featured in *Freestyle* included leadership, independence, assertiveness, and reasonable risk-taking for girls, helping skills for boys, and cooperation for both sexes. The series also featured an additional theme of adult work and family roles (Johnston & Ettema, 1982).

The series aired on PBS stations and was evaluated in classroom settings where it was used by 268 teachers with over 6000 students in eighty-eight schools. To insure that the program would be a sound educational program, the developers sought to create a series that would be acceptable to teachers and entertaining and readily comprehensible to its audience. Students reported positive responses to all four characters.

Johnston and Ettema conducted an extensive study of the program's impact. Summarizing the results, they wrote:

> The world of *Freestyle* was created to be a coherent, compelling but different reality. It is now clear that exposure to this world changed some of what children believe to be true about their own world. The data show that one or both sexes reevaluated the competence of children in several nontraditional pre-occupational activities. Both sexes also reestimated the proportion of men and women in various jobs and family roles. Some of these changes made the worlds of boys and girls more alike; all of the changes made the worlds of the subjects more like the non-stereotyped world of *Freestyle*. Beliefs are, then, an aspect of children's lives which is open to the influence of the *Freestyle* experience. (p. 174)

Another promising outcome of the project was that 96% of the teachers recommended that their peers use *Freestyle*.

The data did reveal some limits to this television series, however. Neither sex changed its estimate of the proportion of family financial support contributed by both spouses. Changes were also not forthcoming in either the girls' or the boys' estimates of the competence of girls in three of the targeted behavioral skills, that is, independence, assertiveness, and risk-taking.

It should be noted that not everyone agrees on the effects of the media on gender socialization. Durkin (1985) has suggested that there are interpretive flaws in some of the studies. In addition, he notes a few studies that have found no effect. Walsh-Childers and Brown (1993), for example, examined the relationship between television viewing and sex role stereotypes among twelve-to-fifteen-year-olds. They found no significant positive relationship between television viewing and stereotype acceptance. In fact, they found a negative influence among one group, that is, white adolescent boys who watch female-oriented programming. Durkin does not, however, rule out media effect on sex role development but, rather, suggests different avenues for research.

CONCLUSION

This chapter opens with comments on the power of television to teach young people about who they are, as well as the world around them. Beyond television, other media perform this function as well, particularly for adolescents whose media habits typically involve a much broader range of experiences with other media. The lessons the media teach regarding life are many. The media contribute to children's and adolescents' understanding of what it means to be a girl or a boy. There is considerable evidence to suggest that virtually every medium—from Saturday morning cartoons and comic books to advertisements in computer magazines and video games—contains gender stereotypes. Powerful messages are provided on how to behave socially. This is particularly the case where other sources of information may be lacking. A shy adolescent may look to films or television to learn how to ask for a date. On the other hand, the media may provide lessons on how to get along well with others or how to behave aggressively. While children's educational programming frequently contains lessons about the former, messages about aggression and violence often emanate from the latter. As a source for socialization, the media exercise additional influences that are considered elsewhere. For example, the media rank with schools and parents as a source of information about other racial and ethnic groups and contribute to the development of stereotypes about other peoples.

CHAPTER 6

Growing Up on the Media:
Does It Affect Physical Development?

Some of our major sources of information about sex come from the media. Everything from the mildest innuendo on a network sitcom to the rawest pornography on X-rated video is contributing to our perceived reality of what sex is all about. We're continually learning about sex and modifying our constructed reality of its nature. How we act on that information may have serious consequences on our lives and the lives of others.

Richard J. Harris, *A Cognitive Psychology of Mass Communication,* 1989

The physical development of today's students is tied heavily to health issues. Health risks to young people have become a major concern. The recent attention that has been focused on adolescents, for example, speaks to this level of concern. The Carnegie Council on Adolescent Development's (1989) report *Turning Points* estimated that 7 million young people between the ages of ten and seventeen are vulnerable to high-risk behaviors, while another 7 million are at moderate risk. These risk behaviors may result in health concerns that include sexually transmitted diseases, drug usage, and pregnancy. Scales (1991) concluded that, if recent trends regarding young adolescents' health continue, these young people will have problems caused by early sexual activity, poor emotional health, and insufficient access to mental and physical health services. Most recently, Hechinger (1992) has argued that poor health among adolescents has reached crisis proportions. Presently, the United States has one of the highest teenage birth rates of any of the major industrialized nations. Also related to health is the number of adolescents who are victims of crime. Both *Turning*

117

Points and *Portraits of Young Adolescents in the 1990s* (Scales, 1991) indicate that adolescents are a major target population for crime and that a significant portion of these crimes occurs in school. Another issue linking the media to physical development is participation in sports. Students are encouraged to play sports as a means for developing and maintaining physical fitness. There is reason for concern over the messages young people receive from the media concerning sports that may impact indirectly on their physical development.

A number of health organizations have expressed concern over the relationship between children and teenagers and the mass media. The Surgeon General, the American Academy of Pediatricians, the American Psychological Association, and the National Institute of Mental Health have all issued reports, studies, or statements on this topic. In addition, medical journals such as the *New England Journal of Medicine* and the *Journal of the American Medical Association* have addressed concerns about media influence on health-related issues. Once again, because television has traditionally been the most persuasive medium, much of the concern has centered around this medium. It is also a major source of health information. *The General Mills Family Report* (Yankelovich, Skelly, and White, Inc., 1979) revealed that television ranked behind only doctors and dentists as a source of health information. Researchers have also looked extensively at advertisements in the various media. In recent years attention has also been focused on the movie and recording industries. A number of themes can be delineated in terms of the mass media and children's and adolescents' health and physical development based on the current research. Among those issues explored in this section are nutrition, sexuality, alcohol and tobacco use, and stress. In addition, the level of violence, which is considered in the next chapter, has reached epidemic proportions and is now considered a major health problem (Prothrow-Stith, 1990).

NUTRITION

Decisions regarding diet can have lifelong implications for one's health, such as obesity, inadequate nutrition, and female reproductive development. Clearly, children begin making these decisions at the checkout counter. McNeal (1992) estimates that children between the ages of two and twelve influenced $82.4 billion in food and beverage purchases in 1990. Advertising certainly contributes to these decisions.

Dwyer (1982) points out that advertised foods tend to be higher cost, brand name products that are high in calories and low in nutrients. Moreover, Atkin (1982) notes that food advertisements not only influence food preferences, but can also shape the basic nutritional beliefs and attitudes of children. Regarding the potential effects of food commercials, he writes:

> Since nutritional aspects of foods are not emphasized, youngsters may make good choices based on nonnutritional criteria that are promoted in the commercials. Specifically, nutrition may not become a salient dimension for evaluating products. In addition, young viewers may develop incorrect beliefs about presweetened products. By contrast, some positive learning may occur regarding the balanced breakfast concept that is mentioned in cereal ads. (p. 196)

Gerbner, Morgan and Signorielli (1982) found that 25% of all prime-time and weekend daytime commercials advertise food, and nearly half of them advertise for "junk" foods. Dietz and Gortmaker (1985) found a positive correlation between television viewing and obesity among children and adolescents. They suggest this correlation may be a combination of television viewing displacing other activities that require greater expenditures of energy, as well as consumption of the foods that are advertised on television. Tucker (1986) did not find the same correlation; however, he found a significant relationship between watching television and lower measures of physical fitness. Additionally, Dwyer notes that there is no balance between advertising and public service messages promoting good nutrition.

Davies (1993a) notes that early adolescents are particularly vulnerable regarding nutrition. Despite increased nutritional demands, a number of factors work against good nutritional habits of the young adolescent, resulting in poor diet. Few meals are consumed with the family, and more eating is done with peers. Because of physical growth, young adolescents become serious snackers, and the snacks they choose are often high in calories and low in nutritional value. Early adolescence is also a time of increased activities when young people argue that they don't have time to eat as they should.

Nutrition is also indirectly affected by the media-created image of the ideal body type in the media and advertisements. Silverstein et al. (1986) have studied the correlation between the mass media's image of a thin standard for bodily attractiveness for women with a similar standard in real life. They note that the last time there was an outbreak of eating disorders among women was in the 1920s when thinness was such a desirable image. Children as young as six years of age report dieting, and the number of children and adolescents who try dieting is increasing. Eating disorders among teenagers are now a serious health problem. Even preadolescents are showing symptoms of eating disorders (Scanlan, 1983). In the case of one very popular diet, the Beverly Hills Diet, Wooley and Wooley (1982) have argued that it represents the mass marketing of anorexia nervosa. While most of the attention has focused on females, males have not escaped the effects of the media's portrayal of the ideal body. Young adolescents, for example, may worry about being too thin and, as a result, attempt to "bulk up" through poor nutritional choices or steroids. And while steroids, in and of themselves, can be harmful, in some cases the chemicals that are used to cut them for sale on the black market are even worse that the steroids themselves. Recently, police in Canada seized anabolic steroids that had been cut with a popular car care product (Deacon, 1994).

Young people, as well as adults, may be adversely affected by the political and economic climate of the 1980s, which had ramifications for the advertising of foods. During the Reagan administration the Federal Trade Commission (FTC), the Food and Drug Administration (FDA), and the United States Department of Agriculture (USDA) tended to turn the regulation of food advertising and labeling over to the food industry, leaving the public vulnerable to misrepresentations and unsubstantiated claims. Moreover, takeover of two of the three major networks weakened self-regulation because of cost-cutting measures. Silvergladc (1990) points out the "new owners installed a bottom-line corporate mentality that is insensitive to public interest considerations that had been taken relatively seriously by network managers. The new coorporate officers," he continues, "argued that the networks need not spend large sums operating their own self-regulatory bureaus since the federal government itself was no longer placing a premium on regulating deceptive advertising" (pp. 91–92).

SEXUAL INFORMATION

Surveying the research on the role of television in sexual learning, Roberts (1982) observes: "Television is a sex educator of our children and a potentially powerful one. Contemporary television entertainment is saturated with sexual lessons, lessons which are likely to have an impact on young viewers' sexual development and behavior" (p. 222). Both formally and informally, young people learn about sexuality from the media. The media are important sources of sexual information for children and adolescents because of their nonthreatening and storytelling style (Signorielli, 1990b). Television is a source of sexual learning for several reasons. Roberts notes that children watch a considerable amount of programming for which they are not the intended audience. This adult programming contains aspects of life that, typically, would not be appropriate to a child. "Given the embarrassment, anxiety, or even anger that may characterize the response of an adult to a child's sexual inquisitiveness, television, " Roberts believes, "may seem to the child a relatively secure environment from which to glean insights into the meaning of sexuality in adult life" (p. 209). A second factor is that children have limited access to alternative sources of information. This situation is pertinent to other areas related to sexuality, such as erotic feelings and behaviors for which the child has even more limited access to information. Another characteristic that suggests that television serves as a source of sexual socialization is the "realism" in which subjects related to sexuality, such as relationships and lifestyles, are presented. Roberts notes Greenberg's study with British children, in which he found that the television realism of sexual roles, relationships, and lifestyles increases the likelihood of social and emotional identification on the part of the young viewer. Finally, television's potential to teach about sexuality is strengthened by the consistency with which the medium communicates sexual values and attitudes. Moreover, the potential for learning about sexuality extends beyond television. Jowett (1982), writing on "socialization by entertainment," argues that the movies played a role in shaping male/female relationships from 1920–1950. More importantly, the media influence values and norms, not just provide information.

Sex is clearly a topic that is common in the media. One study revealed that there are some 14,000 sexual references on television annually, and only 165 of these references deal with sex education, abortion, or sexually transmitted diseases (Strasburger, 1989). Louis Harris and Associates (1988) conducted a study commissioned by the Planned Parenthood Federation of America on sexual material on television. Researchers estimated that, on afternoon and evening television, 79,000 instances of sexual behavior occurred annually during the 1986–1987 television season during the afternoon and evening time slots. Using the Nielsen Company's estimates for the number of hours of watching television by the typical viewer, Harris concluded that the typical viewer would see about 16,000 instances of sexual behavior per year on television. Moreover, only 100 of those 16,000 would be "counterbalance references to sex education, STDs, birth control, or abortion." For teenagers these numbers translated into fifty-seven instances per week for afternoon viewing and 143 per week for evening viewing. Surveying the research, Liebert and Sprafkin (1988) concluded heavy viewing of sexual content on television by adolescents leads them to be less satisfied with their own sexual status, as well as to develop misconceptions about sex and sexuality.

Although television is the number one source of information on AIDS, this disease receives frequent treatment elsewhere in the other media. Wysocki and Harrison (1991) studied how information related to AIDS was reported in magazines for children and adolescents. They concluded that these periodicals failed to "provide a sufficient quantity and quality of information about this disease" (p. 23). In a Planned Parenthood poll (Louis Harris and Associates, 1986) teenagers indicated that television ranked fourth (out of eleven possible choices) as a source of information about how pregnancy is caused and about birth control. In addition, 20% of the teenagers polled listed books and magazines as a source of information about pregnancy, and 23% listed these media as an information source for birth control. Teenagers are willing to invest television with considerable credibility in the way that it deals with sexual topics. The Planned Parenthood poll revealed that 45% of the teenagers believed that television provides a realistic picture about information about sexually transmitted diseases, and 41% responded similarly to the topic of pregnancy and the consequences of sex. These percentages drop to 24% for people making love.

Few would disagree that the media have become much more sexually explicit in the last decade. Particularly disturbing to healthcare professionals have been rock music and music videos. The American Academy of Pediatricians' (AAP) Committee on Communications observed that:

> Rock music lyrics have become increasingly explicit over the last two decades—particularly with reference to sex and drugs. Some lyrics

communicate potentially harmful health messages. These lyrics are of special concern in today's environment, which poses unprecedented threats to the health and well-being of adolescents, including pregnancy, drug use, AIDS (and other sexually transmitted diseases), accidents, and suicides. (*American Academy of Pediatrics News*, 1988, p. 5)

Fedler, Hall, and Tanzi (1982) found the trend in popular music was to emphasize romance less and sex more. Music videos combine lyrics with the power of a visual image. A random content analysis of music video programs revealed that these programs contained heavy sexual content, including references to bondage and sadomasochism (Baxter et al., 1985). A similar content analysis by Sherman and Dominick (1986) concluded, "Music videos are violent, male-oriented, and laden with sexual content" (p. 92). What is unclear, however, is how music videos really affect viewers in terms of health concerns. Clearly, this is an area that warrants research in the future.

CIGARETTES AND ALCOHOL

With over $3 billion spent annually on advertising, cigarettes are the most heavily advertised product in this country, followed by alcoholic beverages. Despite protestations to the contrary, the evidence suggests that both of these industries market their products to attract young people. Since the introduction of the "Old Joe" advertising campaign for Camel cigarettes in 1988, the sales of Camel cigarettes to those under eighteen are estimated to have increased from $6 million to $476 million annually. DiFranza et al. (1991) based their conclusions upon advertisements from popular magazines. While this type of increase in sales seems unusually high, it accords with documents from tobacco companies, which demonstrate that they are trying to appeal to the adolescent market. These kinds of sales among adolescents also reflect a trend in tobacco consumption. Because smoking kills 418,000 persons a year and because more adults are quitting smoking, the tobacco industry must recruit new smokers to replace them. Pierce et al. (1991) concluded as well that cigarette advertising encouraged young people to smoke. Each day, 3000 teenagers, two-thirds of them female, begin smoking. Pollay (1991) notes that fifty years of advertising shows that the tobacco industry has tried to make cigarettes a symbol of health and good times. He notes that a good deal of research, including sophisticated psychological studies as well as marketing, are targeted at reaching adolescents beginning at age fifteen. Moreover, Pollay points out that tobacco companies knowingly capitalize on the adolescent's desire for independence and turn it into a motivation for smoking. In their analysis of cigarette advertising in popular magazines from 1960–1985, Altman et al. (1987) concluded that tobacco companies have tried to create the association of cigarette smoking with health and vitality. While smoking on television has declined considerably, movies reinforce advertising of tobacco. In his study of smoking in film over the last three decades, Glantz [quoted in Locke (1993)] writes: "Films portrayed the smoker in the same way that tobacco advertising does. The dominant themes of cigarette advertising were that smoking is associated with youthful vigor, good health, good looks, and personal and professional acceptance." Smoking also finds its way into movies through a new advertising trend called product placement, in which companies pay to have their product clearly featured in the film. Thus, Philip Morris paid $350,000 to have James Bond smoke Lark cigarettes in *License to Kill* (Miller, 1990). They also observed that women and young people are the target populations for these advertisements. The research of Aiken, Leathar, and O'Hagan (1985) suggests that cigarette advertising can be appealing to twelve-year-olds. Summarizing the research on the initiation of juvenile smoking, Covell (1992) points out that evidence suggests that young people who begin smoking frequently do so around age twelve. Finally, it is not likely that cigarette advertising will diminish in the near future. Cigarette advertising is very lucrative; consequently, the media are hesitant to refuse to run these kinds of advertisements. Moreover, because the tobacco industry provides so many advertising dollars to the media, cigarette companies are able to minimize negative coverage on the effects of smoking in the editorial content of the media (Weis & Burke, 1986). While lung cancer has become the number one cancer killer among women, adolescent females represent one of the few groups in which smoking is on the rise. Kessler (1989) surveyed six leading women's magazines with regular health columns or features. Only one refused tobacco advertising. Five of the magazines relied heavily upon tobacco advertising revenues. Despite the health risks, little coverage was devoted to smoking or related health hazards. The magazine that had a "no tobacco advertising" policy devoted more coverage than those without such a policy; however, this coverage was minimal. Kessler suggests that these magazines do not want to risk loss of advertising revenues by covering issues that are perceived as controversial. In addition, many of the products advertised are subsidiaries of tobacco companies.

As mentioned above, alcoholic beverages are heavily advertised. Wallack (1983) argues that, given the ubiquity and often misleading messages of alcohol advertising, coupled with the health issues arising from alcohol consumption, "the current permissive orientation towards advertising is out of touch with a broader social reality." By age eighteen, a young person will have seen 100,000 beer commercials (Postman et al., 1987). Results of a national survey on alcohol conducted with seventh through twelfth graders by the U.S. Department of Health and Human Services (1991) would seem to confirm Wallack's point. This 1991 report, *Youth and Alcohol: A National Survey,* revealed that 35% of all the wine coolers in this country are consumed by junior and senior high school students. They also drink 1.1 billion cans of beer. Half of the 20.7 million seventh through twelfth graders drink. When questioned, many students, particularly those fifteen and younger, could not distinguish between alcoholic and nonalcoholic beverages, leading some students to consume alcoholic beverages without even realizing it. Nine million young people get their information about alcohol from unreliable sources like their friends, or they "just pick it up." Clearly, alcohol consumption represents a significant health problem among young people today.

Like the tobacco industry, alcohol manufacturers have been criticized for using the media to make alcohol products appealing as a way of life for young people as they approach the legal drinking age (Jacobson, Atkins, & Hacker, 1983). Part of the appeal of alcohol among adolescents is linked to advertising (Atkin, Neuendorf, & McDermott, 1983; Atkin, Hocking, & Block, 1984; Aitken, 1989). Celebrity endorsements of alcohol products are also effective with adolescents (Atkin & Block, 1983). Strickland (1983) did not find a correlation between alcohol abuse and watching commercials for alcoholic beverages on television and only meager effects on consumption. In their study on adolescent reasoning about advertisements, Linn, de Benedictis, and Delucchi (1982) found that, while adolescents may be able to criticize the procedures used to generate results in product ads, when asked, they still often believe the results. Kilbourne (1991) points out that there are a number of myths that these advertisers want young people to believe. These myths include that drinking is a risk-free activity, that an individual cannot survive without drinking, that problem-drinking behaviors are normal, and that alcohol is a magic potion that can transform you. The transformative powers of alcohol are associated with happiness, wealth, prestige, sophistication, and sexual satisfaction, among others. Other misconceptions fostered by advertisers are that sports and alcohol go together and that, if alcoholic beverages were truly dangerous, the media would tell consumers. Finally, Kilbourne is critical of the alcoholic beverage companies for fostering the belief that they promote moderation in drinking. She notes that recent "moderation programs" like Budweiser's "Know When to Say When," as opposed to "Know When to Say No" actually suggest to young people that drinking beer is one way to demonstrate control. Kilbourne adds that these programs also perpetuate the myth that alcoholism is merely a question of irresponsible behavior, rather than a disease.

Children's and adolescents' exposure to alcohol in the mass media goes beyond advertising. While the incidents of smoking by characters on television, for example, have declined considerably (Breed & DeFoe, 1984), those of drinking have gone up (Signorielli, 1987; Wallack, Breed, & Cruz, 1987; Wallack et al., 1990). The most popular beverage of choice on television is alcohol (Signorielli, 1990). Moreover, when people on television drink, they most often do so because of a personal crisis (Breed & DeFoe, 1981). What effect these portrayals of alcohol consumption on television have on children and adolescents is difficult to determine because the research findings are mixed (Williams, 1993).

STRESS

The media may have an indirect effect upon the physical development of children and adolescents as contributors to stress. Cantor (1994), who has conducted considerable research on children's fright responses to media depictions, suggests that children often have strong negative emotional reactions to what they see in both network and cable programs. She and her colleagues conducted a study, for example, of children's reactions to coverage of the Gulf War. Parents of children at all three grade levels (grades one, four, and seven) used in the study reported that their children were frightened by aspects of the Gulf War coverage. The visual aspects of the coverage frightened the younger children, while the older children were disturbed by the coverage of the war in general. Cantor suspects that the media have the capacity to "overburden children with fears of horrendous disasters that are either unpreventable or highly unlikely to threaten them personally [which] may add undue stress to the process of growing up" (Cantor, 1994, p. 149).

Elkind (1986) and Hamburg (1974) have identified the middle school years as a particularly stressful time. Elkind observes that the stress comes at a time when this age group is least able to handle it. Postman (1982) argues that television is a "total disclosure medium" that exposes children to adult knowledge before they are ready. In doing so, this medium contributes to the breakdown between the social boundaries of childhood and adulthood. Chlubna (1991) observes that eleven year olds may believe that viewing cable movies and videos with sexual content may provide acceptable and sanctioned models for their own behavior. When they attempt to be more adult-like by mimicking the behaviors they see in these media, eleven year olds may experience confusion and dejection. Both of the situations described by Postman and Chlubna are stress-inducing situations.

Elkind (1981) has identified the media as a contributor to stress within his concept of "the hurried child." He maintains that a number of forces at work in our society are pushing young people to grow up too fast. Elkind explores television, popular music, and adolescent literature. He argues that they expose young people to adult issues and conflicts, thereby pushing them to grow up too quickly. The end result is unnecessary stress caused by the media through information overload and premature exposure to inappropriate information.

Another issue related to stress, for which there is a dearth of research, is the manner in which children and adolescents use the media to cope with stress. The evidence suggests that this is the case. Moreover, how do children and adolescents understand messages in the popular media about dealing with stress, for example, alcohol being depicted as a way to relieve stress?

SUICIDE

A somewhat controversial area of research regarding the media concerns the impact of media depictions of suicide on teenagers. Bollen and Phillips (1982) found that daily suicides increased significantly after highly publicized suicides appeared on television news programs. Gould and Shaffer (1986) examined the suicide rate of teenagers in New York State before and after three fictional films about suicide were televised. They concluded that the data suggested a significant increase in the suicide rate; however, Phillips and Paight (1987) replicated this study using data from two additional states based upon the same three television films. They found no evidence to suggest an increase in teenage suicides. Moreover, no significant increase was found when examining the data from New York. In their study of cluster suicides among teenagers, Phillips and Carstensen (1986) examined the impact of televised feature and news stories on suicide. After controlling for a number of factors, that is, days of the week, holidays, and yearly trends, Phillips and Carstensen found a significant increase in the number of suicides following the airing of these stories, whether they were about a particular suicide or a general information or feature story. Another finding of note in this study was that the clustering of suicides was considerably greater for females than males. The concept of media-induced suicide is not without its critics. Baron and Reiss (1985) have called into question the interpretations of the data supporting an imitative suicide hypothesis. Although they acknowledge that the data do not disprove imitative suicide, the analyses rendered in various studies are subject to other statistical interpretations; however, Phillips and Bollen (1985) have responded to this criticism and maintain that their interpretation of the data is accurate and that imitative suicide is in evidence.

MEDIA SPORTS AND THE STUDENT ATHLETE

Sports represent a major extracurricular activity in schools, as well as a source for physical development. Virtually every school, small or large, rural or urban, has some type of athletic program. The world of mediated sports presents conflicting messages to the ones that students should be receiving in these programs. As Goldstein and Bredemeier (1977) note, when winning, rather than playing, is emphasized as the primary goal of sports, the social and psychological experience of participating in sports is different. In their working paper on adolescent sports programs for the Carnegie Council on Adolescent Development, Seefeldt, Ewing, and Walk (n.d.) note some of the problems to which too much emphasis on competition have contributed. They highlight the trend to hire coaches whose professions are outside the field of education. One of the reasons is that fewer teachers want to coach because the pressure to win is too great. More distressing is the number of adolescent sports injuries, part of which can be attributed to too much emphasis on competition.

Goldberg [cited in Seefeldt, Ewing, & Walk (n.d.)] notes the increase in the number of "overuse injuries," that is, those caused by too much physical activity. Overly ambitious training programs also contribute to unnecessary injuries. One coach remarked that he had seen girls training by running sixty to eighty miles a week in the eighth grade! Another reason for the unusually high number of youth sports injuries is the overmatching of players. Again, too much emphasis on winning, combined with players involved in sports where other players are older and more physically developed, creates an environment for injuries. It would be unfair to hold the media responsible for the growing number of sports injuries among adolescents. There can be little doubt, however, that the emphasis placed upon winning in sports programming helps to create a competitive culture that impacts upon school sports.

Other health problems among today's atheletes have resulted from this "culture of competition." So much emphasis has been placed on winning that participation seems to matter little. It would not be an exaggeration to say that winning is "hyped" so much by the media that amateur athletes are under tremendous pressure to win. The potential to make substantial dollars in the future in product endorsements and media appearances adds to this pressure. The recent death of Christy Henrich, the gymnast, has focused attention, for example, on the problem of eating disorders among athletes, particularly females, who starve themselves to keep a competitive edge (Noden, 1994). Related to this culture of competition is the image of sports produced by media commentary. Again, increased risk of injuries may be the result. Tavris (1988) points out, "In recent years U.S. sports commentators have increased their attention to and praise of 'playing dirty,' inflicting pain, rules violations, and 'winning at any cost.' " She notes that research on sports coverage reveals that stressing conflict among players has increased significantly and that praise about exceptionally rough play occurs five times as often as negative comments.

CONCLUSION

The mass media form a nexus to which many issues regarding the physical development of students are connected. Several of these issues relate directly to the health of young people. 1) Through advertisements children exercise considerable influence over parents' nutritional purchases. Advertising continues to be a factor as they become older and make purchases themselves. 2) The media also serve as a sex educator in this country, particularly in the face of diminished alternative sources of information. Harris's (1989) observation is well taken. How students act on that information may have serious consequences for their lives, as well as the lives of others. 3) While the evidence suggests that the billions of dollars spent on advertising tobacco and alcohol products have some effect on the consumption of these products by adolescents, spokespersons for these industries deny that teenagers are the targeted market. In the face of these denials, health professionals continue to claim that the media are hazardous to young people's health. 4) The stress levels of students today are probably higher than they have been in decades. Homicides and suicides, for example, among adolescents have reached epidemic proportions. Again, the media play a role as a contributor to the increasing stress levels experienced by young people growing up in the 1990s. 5) Finally, sports play a major role in the life of young people and their physical development. More than 7 million teenagers play high school sports, and nearly three times that number of eight-to-sixteen-year-olds participate in community athletic programs (Mee, 1994). For many students being socialized into the world of sports in school will bring them directly into contact with a culture of competition encouraged by the media, which devalues participation and encourages an ethic of winning no matter what the cost. For some, the cost will be senseless and painful injuries; for others the price to participate will be much greater.

The physical development of today's students is impacted in numerous ways by the media. They provide students with a variety of health-related messages. In some cases those messages are very direct, such as in public service campaigns. More often than not, however, the messages children and adolescents take away from the media are less direct. By influencing purchase and lifestyle decisions the media have the potential to encourage unhealthy choices. Young people, for example, represent future tobacco sales. The high school student who chooses to participate in interscholastic sports does so in an environment in which overuse and other sports-related injury levels are unacceptably high, in part because winning has eclipsed participation in a culture where winning is everything. Media hype from the broadcast booth to advertising creates, as well as sustains, this elevated importance of winning. The media can also provide an adult window on the world before children and adolescents are prepared for it. This introduces unnecessary stress into young people's lives. Clearly, growing up on the media has important implications for the physical development of students from first to twelfth grade.

CHAPTER 7

Playing to Emotions:
The Media and Affective Development

Motion pictures are not understood by the present generation of adults. . . . Do the pictures really influence children in any direction? Are their conduct, ideals, and attitudes affected by the movies? Are the scenes which are objectionable to adults understood by children, or at least by very young children? Do children eventually become sophisticated and grow superior to pictures? Are the emotions of children harmfully excited? In short, just what effect do motion pictures have upon children of different ages?

W. W. Charter, Chairman of the Payne Fund Studies, 1933

Some of the pioneering research on media effects examined the emotional response of six-through-nineteen-year-olds to a variety of scenes in films. Zillman (1991) has noted that the invention of the motion picture represents a turning point because, previously, portrayals of emotions were limited to still pictures and print. With the advent of the film medium, "Uncounted characters exhibited a wealth of emotions to so-called mass audiences. The movies reached essentially all members of technological society. All members became more and more frequently exposed to emotions that were infrequent or nonexistent in the immediate environment" (p. 159). In their study *The Emotional Response of Children to the Motion Picture Situation,* Dysinger and Ruckmick (1933) conducted very sophisticated research for the time period, measuring the psychogalvanic response of subjects to a variety of movies. They found ample evidence that viewers respond emotionally to this medium, with variations depending on the age group and the subject matter. For example, they found that children under nine-

133

years-old did not respond "convincingly" to erotic scenes. Adolescents, on the other hand, did. "During the adolescent period, a definite response to amorous scenes seems to be characteristic." Dysinger and Ruckmick add, "The desirability or undesirability of such a degree of stimulation of the sexual emotions during adolescence is a point on which public opinion, mental hygiene, and ethics speak with authority" (p. 114). From a historical perspective this study is of interest because the same questions are being asked today although couched somewhat differently. For example, these researchers found that scenes of danger and conflict (translate action and adventure) incited strong emotions among children of all ages. Dysinger and Ruckmick ask if this kind of emotional arousal might be harmful.

> The question of the desirability of such emotional arousal is a difficult one. The necessity for quiet in the theater seems to be intimately related to the problem. These motion-inciting emotions must be suppressed to a considerable degree. At the extreme, this experience may be considered as questionable for the health of the children. It may be that this is an understatement; yet there is enough disagreement among authorities on the issues that are involved here to indicate that a more positive statement ought to come from the physiologist or the physician, rather than the psychologist. (p. 115)

Over sixty years later the question still is being debated. Despite decades of research since the Payne Studies, there still exist today major gaps in the research on media effects in terms of emotional development. Because popular music has a strong emotional appeal to adolescents, some of the research has been on emotions and the media; however, television has received most of the attention.

Zillman (1991) notes that both children and adults in today's society are "bombarded with portrayals of affects and emotions." Doubleday et al. [cited in Huston et al. (1992)] suggest that television can be a source of learning about emotions because the medium contains so much information about affect. This learning might include recognition of emotional displays and understanding how people experience emotions, as well as models for experiencing, expressing, and responding to emotions. Hoffner and Cantor (1991) point out that the emotions of media characters can be conveyed verbally or nonverbally through facial expressions, vocal tone, gestures, and overt behaviors. They may also be inferred based upon situational cues or, perhaps, knowledge of the character's goals and personality (Dorr, 1982). *Sesame Street* contains segments (affect bits) on recognizing basic emotions such as happiness and sadness. *Mister Rogers' Neighborhood* teaches viewers to identify and deal with certain emotions, for example, how one feels when a friend moves away (Graves, 1982). Summarizing the current research on emotions and television, Huston et al. (1992) note the following: very little research has been conducted on which emotions are portrayed on television or in the kinds of situations people express or experience emotions. There is a wide variety of documented affective responses to television, including happiness, interest, involvement, excitement, anger, disgust, sadness, and surprise. They also point out that empathy with characters in television and film can increase the emotional response of viewers. Cognitive development influences the affective response of children, as Feshbach (1988) observes:

> Children attend to cues that convey the emotions being experienced by characters. There are important age differences in the subtlety and range of cues to which children are sensitive. Preschoolers and young children are especially guided by the facial expression of the characters. Older children are more responsive to situation cues and are more able to understand the emotional implications that particular symbols and metaphors are intended to convey. (p. 262)

In addition, there is evidence to suggest that repeated exposure to arousing content on television can lead to desensitization.

In his study of children's perceptions of violence, van der Voort (1986) examined the emotional response of his subjects in three areas: excitement, empathy, and fear. Although van der Voort conducted his research with Dutch children, he used American programming. He found that, as children grow older, they are less inclined to respond emotionally to programs and less frightened of violent scenes. van der Voort reasoned that, with age, children become less absorbed by programs, resulting in greater detachment, and thus, less emotion. He also found a gender difference, with girls responding more emotionally. The realism of the program is an important variable as well. The more realistic the content, the stronger are the excitement and fear. A finding of particular note of van der Voort's was that emotionally responsive children watched fewer violent television programs.

Cantor (1994) and her colleagues have conducted numerous studies on children's fright responses to media. Two questions have guided their research: what type of mass media stimuli and events frighten children most, and what are the best methods for preventing or reducing media-inducing fears? Cable television has greatly expanded the potential for children to experience media with the potential to frighten them. This situation has bolstered the concern over children being frightened. Sparks [cited in Cantor (1994), pp. 139–140], for example, found that nearly half of the four-to-ten-year-olds in his study had seen *Poltergeist* and *Jaws,* and a substantial number had viewed *Halloween* and *Friday the Thirteenth* as well.

There is a dynamic at work, as Cantor has noted, regarding media and fright. She dismisses the contention that, as children grow older, they are less susceptible to emotional disturbances produced by the media. As children grow older, some things disturb them less, while others bother them more. Rooted in cognitive development, fright responses are, in part, determined by the child's understanding of the media presentation. Film, commercial programs, and the news are seen differently, depending upon the child's level of cognitive development. What follows is a summary of the findings from Cantor (1994) and her colleagues' research.

Because younger children are more concrete in their thinking, their perception of fear-inducing stimulus is an important factor. Thus, very young children are more likely to be frightened by something that looks scary that may, in fact, be harmless. Conversely, they are not likely to be frightened by something that appears less harmless but may, in fact, be quite dangerous. This point is illustrated by research, using the *Incredible Hulk* television series. Young children become fearful when the mild-mannered Banner is transformed into the Hulk. Older children do not report these levels of fear because they realize that the Hulk is really a benevolent character. Another finding from Cantor and her colleagues is that, as children grow older, they become more responsive to realistic rather than to fantasy-type dangers depicted in the media. Again, this relates to the cognitive development of the child. Over time children learn to tell the difference between fantasy and reality. When they see the media present events that can cause fear, they are able to translate the realism of the media into the potential for situations in real life that might pose a danger or threat to them. Summarizing findings in this area, Cantor writes: "In general, the tendency to mention fantasy offerings, depicting events that could not possibly occur in the real world, as sources of fear, decreased as the child's age increased, and the tendency to mention fictional offerings, depicting events that might possibly occur, increased with age" (p. 143).

Two additional generalizations that Cantor makes are also based upon children's ability to think in a more sophisticated fashion as they develop cognitively. First, as children mature, they are frightened by media situations that involve more abstract concepts. An example of this generalization is found in a study conducted by Cantor, Wilson, and Hoffner (1986) on a made-for-television movie. They conducted a survey on children's responses to *The Day After.* This movie presented a vivid portrayal of the aftermath of a nuclear attack in which a town is devastated. They found younger children (under twelve) the least frightened. Adolescents were much more frightened, and adults, proved the most frightened of all. While adolescents and adults could conceive of the idea of all mankind being annihilated by a nuclear war, younger children did not have the cognitive ability to entertain this notion, and, consequently, for them the movie did not have the same emotional impact. Cantor adds that most of the parents surveyed in this study could think of other shows in the previous year that had frightened their children more, while most of the parents of teenagers could not. A final generalization that Cantor presents is a corollary of sorts, based on the previous generalizations; that is, different strategies are needed for helping children of different ages cope with media-induced fear. Cognitive strategies work better with older children, while noncognitive strategies are more effective with smaller children. For example, visual desensitization can help allay the fears of small children much better than simply explaining to them why "there is nothing to be afraid of." In an experiment using the snake sequence from the film *Raiders of the Lost Ark,* Wilson and Cantor [cited in Cantor (1994), p. 144] experimented with various strategies to help children of a variety of different ages to deal with this scary scene from the movie. With the younger children an explanation proved ineffectual; however, when the researchers showed the children film footage that gradually introduced snakes until they were close up, these children were less frightened than those who did not see the footage.

Cantor points out that one of the implications of research on children's fright responses to media stimuli is that children respond in ways that are not always obvious from a parent's perspective. It is not easy to determine which shows a child will find scary or not scary. Age is clearly a factor. Another study (Hoffner & Cantor, 1990) involving children from kindergarten through third grade revealed that those who believed that a depicted threat existed in their local environment became more threatened than those who did not have the localized threat. Moreover, Cantor notes that, in surveys, parents report that their children have been frightened by shows such as *Little House on the Prarie,* which are typically available during afternoon programming slots. These shows often present themes such as accidental death, kidnapping, and others, which are upsetting to children.

There is evidence to suggest that frightening media depictions have a spillover effect. Cantor and Omdahl [cited in Cantor (1994), p. 145] showed children dramatic depictions of realistic life-threatening events involving fire and water. Other children saw scenes involving these two elements but not in a life-threatening way. Those children who were exposed to the former scenes were more frightened. The children who witnessed the threatening scenes reported less interest in canoeing, as well as building a fire in a fireplace.

The trend in more graphic news coverage has implications for children as well. In an effort to boost ratings, news coverage now includes more visually disturbing material. Two recent events covered extensively by the media provided researchers with an opportunity to see how children respond to this kind of coverage: the Gulf War and the space shuttle disaster. Not surprisingly, the studies conducted reveal that children responded to these coverages with fright. Wright et al. (1989) examined children's reactions to the *Challenger* disaster. He and his colleagues noted that, according to a national survey, 25% of five to eight year olds, 48% of nine to thirteen year olds, and 31% of fourteen to seventeen year olds watched the shuttle launch that day in school and saw the disaster as it actually happened. Wright et al. argued that the inclusion of a teacher-astronaut and the study keyed into McAuliffe's anticipated lessons in space made the launch even more significant and perhaps strengthened the effect. They interviewed fourth through sixth grade boys and girls to ascertain their emotional reactions and concluded that most of the children experienced "substantial emotional distress." Another study conducted regarding older students' (college age) response to the space shuttle tragedy indicated that over three-quarters of them reported strong or very strong emotional reaction upon first hearing about the disaster. Kubey and Peluso (1990) also found that many of the students in the study turned to both the media and interpersonal communication to help them cope with the unsettling news.

In their study of parents' and children's emotional reactions to television coverage of the Gulf War, Cantor, Mares, and Oliver (1993) surveyed the reactions of parents of first, fourth, and seventh graders. A substantial number of parents, 45%, reported that their children had been upset by the coverage of the war. In keeping with a developmental understanding of emotional reactions, the visual aspects of television coverage proved most disturbing for the younger children, while older children were bothered at an abstract level by the conceptual aspects of the coverage of the war in general. Similarly, Hoffner and Haefner (1993) found negative emotional reactions among children who reported feeling sad, angry, and fearful. Interestingly, studies conducted on the affective responses of children in other countries to the war did not yield similar results (van der Voort, van Lil, & Voojis, 1993; Morrison & MacGregor, 1993). Clearly, the nearly universal availability of television has created a situation where children, sometimes very young children, are exposed to events and situations that they would not normally have been exposed to. Moreover, some of this material provokes strong negative emotional reactions among the child and adolescent viewer.

Despite the need for more research in this area, some important observations have been made in terms of the media and the emotional life of young people. These observations center around two issues: identity formation and the emotional appeal of the media, particularly music. Violence and gender socialization, both of which relate to emotional development, have been explored previously. Over two decades ago Baranowski (1971) suggested that the adolescent may turn to television to answer the question, "Who am I?" by experimentally emulating television personalities. He also suggests that the message from television advertisements is that "you are what you own." Avery (1979) has suggested that the hero-worship of music and film personalities, common among adolescents, contributes to their search for identity and a new self-image. Research on early adolescents' secondary attachments to celebrities supports Avery's observation (Greene & Adams-Price, 1990; Adams-Price & Greene, 1990). Green and Adams-Price interpret these attachments as providing a safe avenue for experimentation for young adolescents dealing with identity issues.

The emotional appeal of music to teenagers can be found in the many associations they make between various emotions and this medium. Wells and Hakanen (1991), in their study of high school students, found that this appeal cut across social class, race, and ethnicity with females associating emotions with music more than males. Their research revealed that most of the respondents in their study used music for "mood management," that is, mood enhancing or tranquilizing. Similarly, Brown, Campbell, and Fischer's (1986) survey of adolescents revealed that over 36% of them indicated that they watched music videos "a lot" because they "get me in the mood I like to be in." Larson and Kubey (1983) suggest that one of the reasons music displaces television is because the sound and message of popular music is more relevant to adolescents and provides greater emotional involvement than watching television. Their research supports this hypothesis.

One of the most thorough explorations to date on the relationship between emotional development and the media is *Dancing in the Dark: Youth, Popular Culture and the Electronic Media*. In this study Schultze et al. (1991) reason that the electronic media, specifically film, music, and MTV, function as an "alternative high school on life" to which young people often turn to for guidance in identity formation and to satisfy intimacy needs. Because the media ultimately exist to deliver a market to advertisers, they contend that identity and intimacy turn into marketable commodities. The interaction of the media and identity formation occurs in a number of ways. Schultze and his colleagues maintain that the media perform a stabilizing function in the midst of a highly mobile society and a fluid culture. The media messages adolescents experience, however, tend to short-circuit the development of an adult identity. Young adolescents search out their identity in an electronic environment. "The crisis of identity is worsened by the electronic media's tendency to prolong adolescence by delaying the formation of stable mature identities." Later, they write: "Indeed, it is easy to argue that the electronic media effectively impede if not altogether reverse the development of maturity. A veritable 'cult of youth' encourages everyone, including adults and young children, to think and act like adolescents. As the media increasingly blur the many lines between youth and adults, adolescence and adulthood no longer seem nearly so distinct and identifiable" (p. 65).

The media represent a confluence of two different sets of needs, the one adult and economic, the other adolescent and psychological, that is, related to intimacy, identity, and meaning. The thesis of the authors of *Dancing in the Dark* is that youth and the electronic media have become interdependent. "The media need the youth market, as it is called, for their own economic survival. Youth, in turn, need the media for guidance and nurture in a society where other social institutions such as the family and the school, do not shape the youth culture as powerfully as they once did" (pp. 11–12). In order to hold the attention of this market, the media play to basic human needs that have a heightened relevance for adolescents, that is, identity, intimacy, and meaning. Aufderheide (1986) argues that music videos contribute to a feeling of instability among youth, which "fuels the search to buy and belong." This medium represents not only ways of seeing and hearing, but being as well. "Watching music videos may be diverting, but the process that music videos embody, echo, and encourage—the constant recreations of an unstable self—is a full-time job" (p. 77).

Since the advent of youth culture, a phenomenon that has really come into existence since the 1950s, both the content and appeal of the entertainment media have been emotional. Even the formal aspects of these media take into account the affective dimension of the adolescent. An MTV executive states, "What we've introduced with MTV is a non-narrative form. As opposed to conventional television, where you rely on plot and continuity, we rely on *mood* and *emotion*. We make you feel a certain way as opposed to you walking away with any particular knowledge" [quoted in Schultze et al. (1991), pp. 204–205]. Tannenbaum (1980) suggests that media entertainment provides vicarious emotional experiences. He also maintains that one of the reasons viewers watch the same program over and over again is to experience the emotional arousal that accompanies a favorite television series (Tannenbaum, 1985).

Evidence suggests that the media serve a therapeutic function for persons experiencing emotional difficulties. Klinke [cited in Potts and Sanchez (1994), p. 80] found that depressed persons used television viewing as a coping strategy. In their study *Television and the Quality of Life,* Kubey and Csikszentmihalyi (1990) found that television serves as an escape from adverse emotional states. Heavier viewers used television as a substitute for social interaction, that is, to escape feelings of loneliness. They also concluded, "Negative affect is more likely to cause viewing than the other way around" (p. 172). Much like the way music functions for adolescents, television may also serve as a form of mood management. The inability to deal comfortably with unstructured time and its attendant negative feelings contributes to more televiewing. Potts and Sanchez (1994) report similar findings in their study of television use, specifically watching the news, and depressive moods. They concluded that persons in a depressed state watched television to escape unpleasant feelings and stimuli that might exacerbate those feelings, While the viewers in this study watched news for information, they also found its content unsettling, a feeling that was more pronounced for depressed viewers, leading Potts and Sanchez to conclude that "regular exposure to TV news material in depressive moods is likely to maintain or even increase their initial negative mood state" (p. 88).

Zillman and Bryant (1985) have developed a theory regarding affective states and the use of media to modulate these states. Their theory of "affect-dependent stimulus arrangement" is based upon the premise that media selections are based upon the user's mood states and that the user selects certain media to minimize negative moods or to enhance positive moods. This theory emphasizes the active nature of the viewer inasmuch as the viewer selects certain media that consistently provide the desired effects. Bryant and Zillman have conducted experiments in which they measured the use of media's impact on boredom and stress, as well as mood states. Summarizing their research and that of others, Bryant and Zillman note that "the self-administered therapeutic scheduling of entertainment" indicates that media users can employ certain media genres to reduce aversion to particular states, for example, arousing material to alleviate boredom. Moreover, they maintain that, under certain conditions, individuals may deal with negative affective states by turning to the media for entertaining messages that they find comforting. A finding of note in their research is that there are gender differences, particularly in the way violent and hostile programming is used by males and females, with females generally showing a strong aversion to these kinds of media depictions and males seeking them out.

A number of theories exist regarding the function of empathy. Zillman (1991) has integrated several of these theories in an effort to understand the relationship between empathy and media use, particularly television. He argues that there are three basic components to empathy. The first is "reflexive" or "dispositional" and consists of an unconditioned motor response component to stimuli that might elicit empathy. The second he terms an "excitatory" component, which may be conditioned or unconditioned as is a nonmotor response. "Excitation is operationalized as heightened activity in the sympathetic nervous system, primarily, that prepares the organism for the temporary engagement in vigorous action such as needed for fight or flight" (p. 147).

The "experiential" component makes up the third component in Zillman's "three-factor theory of empathy." This aspect of empathy involves a conscious reaction on the part of the individual, in which a person monitors his or her emotional behavior continuing or discontinuing the behavior based upon its appropriateness. According to Zillman then, each empathetic reaction contains all three of these elements. An additional characteristic of his theory is what he terms "dispositional override," in which the individual may alter an initial response given a particular set of circumstances. This element explains "mixed affective reactions" that are not considered in other theories. Zillman gives the example of a student privately witnessing a much disliked professor having a bicycle accident. Her immediate response might be to cringe at the site of the fall, but then grin and chuckle. The dominant affective response is one of delight, despite the initial reaction. Taking the example a step further, Zillman notes that, if the student truly dislikes or hates her professor and had, in fact, hoped something misfortunate might befall him, then she might not cringe initially at all, but experience a feeling of euphoria. Thus, the student is dispositionally prepared for the accident. Moreover, if it became apparent that the professor might have injured himself, the initial joy that the student felt might be assessed as an inappropriate response, and this might be transformed into pity.

A final element identified by Zillman is what he calls "discordant affect." It provides a further dimension to the concept of dispositional override. As a person learns certain responses to situations, he or she may be disturbed when certain situations are encountered that do not seem ethical or moral. When an individual witnesses this kind of situation, he or she may react in an anti-empathetic manner. Thus, "discordant affect becomes associated with parties undeserving of good fortunes and deserving of misfortunes" (p. 153). Over time the individual may develop a conditioned response that is counterempathetic. As a result a person witnessing someone hurting another person may actually enjoy seeing the perpetrator be punished. The individual comes, then, to develop a disliking for certain types of individuals and the dislike "comes to signal that empathy is unnecessary and, in fact, inappropriate" (p. 153). Zillman and his colleagues have conducted research that supports the concept of discordant affect responses based upon "moral judgment mediation," which, in turn, is contingent upon the level of moral reasoning of the child viewer.

What are the implications of Zillman's theory for the relationship between media and emotions? The existence of the media makes possible exposure to both a larger number and a great variety of kinds of affective experiences. "A less obvious but potentially significant change lies in the portrayal of emotions itself. Whereas individuals in their own social environment tend to get only glimpses of someone else's affective responses, the media—nonfiction as well as fiction—present these reactions most graphically" (p. 159). Zillman notes that one of the key features that elicits empathy and discordant affect is facial expressions. The media user is treated to these facial expressions in a "supernormal" way; therefore, he argues that young children who witness these media presentations of facial expressions may learn "facial mimicry of great fidelity." Thus, they may learn what expressions are acceptable or unacceptable and portray them in novel situations—"situations for which their limited social environment may not have prepared them."

Another implication of mass-mediated emotional representations may be that these "iconic representations" make some of the imaginative activity needed in pre–mass media society unnecessary. Zillman makes a distinction between our technical society today and the pretechnical society of the past, which relied on print or verbal depictions of empathy. This absence of graphic visual depictions of empathy "made empathetic or counterempathetic reactions in all probability dependent on generating ideational representations that, in turn, depended on the experience by self with similar affect-inducing conditions. In short," Zillman continues, "to come from verbal reports of others' emotions, even when aided by some grimacing and gesticulating by the reporter, to intense concordant or discordant affect relied on considerable imaginative activity" (p. 160). The mass media have substantially altered this situation. He suggests that the combination of vivid affective images combined with their potential to induce emotional memories may have the effect of generating more powerful affective responses.

The concept of "construct accessibility" ties in directly with Zillman's suggestions that the media can stimulate recall of affective memories. Sanbonmatsu and Fazio (1991) have examined the implications of construct accessibility for media effects. It is necessary to grasp three basic concepts in order to understand construct accessibility. The first is construct. "A construct is simply a representation in memory consisting of coherent information about some entity" (p. 47). It is possible to develop a construct about a variety of things: persons, objects, events, rules, and attitudes. Accessibility, the second concept, is understood as the "readiness with which a construct in memory can by utliized in processing information" (p. 46). Finally, priming can be understood as a procedure that increases the accessibility of a construct. Priming, then, has the effect of serving as a stimulus for assisting the person to reach back into his or her memory to call forth a particular construct(s). Two of the key factors in accessing constructs are mood and emotions. Sanbonmatsu and Fazio offer the following generalizations based on studies in this area: 1) the person's mood state affects the accessibility to memory material, with the particular mood state increasing accessibility to memory representations of similar types of affective experiences, and 2) specific emotional states may serve to help retrieve associated constructs related to that particular emotion. Regarding emotional development and construct accessibility, the media can play two important roles. First, they provide information and experiences that contribute to the development of affective constructs. In some cases the construct may be nearly entirely media-generated; in other cases the media may simply contribute to construct development. Secondly, media use serves as a priming function to help recall affective memories. This ties in with Zillman's work on empathy, where a compelling media portrayal of an affective experience calls forth an emotional memory.

Given Zillman's (1991) three-factor theory of empathy, the activity of these components constitute a response that is a process. Returning to the difference between the portrayal of emotions in a media age versus one of an earlier time period devoid of the mass media, Zillman points out that the pacing of presentations of emotions in these two eras is different. Nonmediated perceptions of another's emotional experiences is allowed to follow its course, while those of the mass media are fast-paced, and sometimes the media user's affective reaction to an emotional experience is preempted. Whether it is an action program or the evening news, little time is allowed for the viewer to experience a full affective response, in part because the excitatory component requires time to occur. Moreover, this rapid pacing leads to a situation in which the excitation generated by one emotional depiction may carry over to a subsequent episode, heightening its intensity while depriving the initiating portrayal of its intensity. This dynamic can be used by advertisers to sell their products more effectively. Mattes and Cantor (1982) found that excitation may be transferred from a media depiction of a nonfictitious event to a subsequent television commercial, thus enhancing its appeal.

The realism and repetition of character portrayals in the media, particularly television with its serial programming, provide opportunities for emotional involvement with characters over an extended period of time. This long-term exposure provides an opportunity for getting to know a character and can lead to para-social interaction. In his studies with fourteen to fifteen year olds and college students in Germany, Strum found that they developed strong affective reactions to media characters [cited in Dorr (1982), p. 72]. Hoffner and Cantor (1991) provide evidence, both anecdotal and empirical, that persons become emotionally involved with media characters. The process of coming to distinguish a character from an actor occurs over time. Gradually, children come to make this distinction; however, even with adults, some seem to engage in a "suspension of disbelief" and treat television characters if they were real. Television villains are sometimes assaulted in public. Soap opera characters receive gifts after giving birth. Viewers become very upset when a popular chacter such as Henry Blake of *M*A*S*H* is written out of a series. Both children and adults report worrying and being concerned about problems of characters that they watch regularly on television. These reactions may be intensely negative towards some characters, as in the case of J. R. Ewing on *Dallas*.

The media may have a particular relevance to minorities in terms of psychological and emotional development. Brown (1993), a school counselor, writes: "Black girls learn early—from movies, television, magazines—that American popular culture extols the mainstream standards for beauty. Many black women suffer from low self-esteem because they have been made to feel that they are ugly" (p. 10). Brown points out that, because black women have been receiving these messages since childhood, the therapist faces a formidable task in getting these women to see themselves in a new light. In her essay on the impact of television on the self-concept development of minority children, Powell (1982) suggests that the consequences of watching television may have an added dimension for minority children. She notes the racial and ethnic stereotypes available on television. This concern for stereotypes can easily be expanded to include other media as well. "A growing person's conception of his or her selfness comes into being through the reflected appraisal of others. What are the reflections of the appraisals of our race-conscious society that television mirrors or projects to the minority group child viewer?" (p. 124). In some of the early research on the media and minorities, Gerson (1966) interpreted his findings to suggest that black adolescents used the media to learn how to behave as whites. Powell's concerns are not unfounded, as will be demonstrated in a later chapter that addresses the ethnic and racial stereotypes in the media.

Before leaving this chapter on the impact of the media on emotions, it is important to mention advertising. The use of emotional appeals in advertising is well documented (Fowles, 1986; Considine & Haley, 1992; Lloyd-Kolkin & Tyner, 1991). Harris (1989) points out that one of the best ways to begin influencing beliefs and behaviors is to influence emotions.

> For example, there are many ads that appeal to our love of friends, family, and good times and the good feelings that these bring us. We are asked to call people long distance to affirm our love, buy diamonds and flowers for them to show we care, and drink beer or soft drinks with friends as part of a good time. Such slogans as "Reach out and touch someone" or "The good times go better with _____" illustrate such appeals. Products are shown to be an integral part of showing our love and caring for others. The more closely the advertiser can link the product with those natural and positive emotions, the more successful the ad. (p. 76)

Therefore, because positive affective states are enjoyable, creating a linkage between them and a product constitutes a powerful method for selling a product. Clearly, this point has not been lost on the advertising industry.

CONCLUSION

In conclusion, despite the fact that the connection between emotional development and the media still warrants considerable research, the research that has been conducted has much to tell us. People of all ages resonate emotionally with every medium. In some cases the media may serve as a "school of affect," whereby the viewer/listener is cued to respond a certain way emotionally to a real or mediated experience. The formal features of the media may short-circuit emotional responses through fast-paced imagery, which precludes a full emotional response. Individuals may turn to the media to provide "video intimacy" or to alleviate adverse affective states such as loneliness, boredom, or depression. Finally, both entertainment and information media represent a potential source of fright for children and adults.

CHAPTER 8

Myths Created by the Media

A myth is a story through which the world is explained to us. When confronted with a myth, we should scrutinize its contents on two levels:
realism and ideology. A responsible attitude towards a myth demands
critical questioning of whether its contents stand up to reality, and of
whose interests it legitimizes. This is important, because stories about
the world never originate in a void; they always represent a pre-selected
point of view embedded in an existential position. In this way, the myth
transcends its descriptive brief and acquires a normative dimension.
The myth also tells us how the world ought to be, and provides us with
moral categories that indicate what kind of behavior is desirable and
what kinds of acts are objectionable.

Cees C. Hamelink, "Is There Life after
the Information Revolution?" 1986

A number of myths surround the media. In his essay Hamelink
(1986) explores what he terms "the myth of the information society."
His description of myth provides an excellent point of departure for
those seeking to understand the myths surrounding the mass media and
why it is so important that myth be understood as a function of media
literacy. In some cases the media have created these myths. Other cases
are based upon ignorance and misconceptions that the media have
helped sustain. It is critical for educators to understand these myths in
order for them to be able to explore them with students. All of these
myths relate directly to the components of media literacy as outlined in
Chapter 1. The nine myths presented here represent an effort to collect
in one place the various myths and misconceptions as identified by
various media scholars. And so it is revealing to explore how the world
of the mass media is explained to us.

MYTH #1: THE MEDIA TELL US HOW LIFE REALLY IS

There are really two dimensions to this particular myth. The first is the actual content of the media. The second is how the media shape a person's view of the world. It is difficult to distinguish between the media and the real world. Years ago, when *Marcus Welby, MD,* was a popular television show, tens of thousands of people wrote to Robert Young seeking medical advice, assuming that he was actually a doctor. In a similar vein, during the San Francisco earthquake in 1989, many people's first reaction was to turn on their television sets, validating their experiences by the media.

Improvements in communication technology have given the media, particularly television, the power to present an electronic world that appears so realistic that it is easily mistaken for the real world, which lies beyond the one created by the media. As media consumers, people use the media to fill in information gaps as they view drama unfolding on television. For example, while most of us have little actual direct experience with police work or the legal system, we learn, albeit often subconsciously, about how they work through the media, particularly television, such as reading someone their rights. Snow (1983) notes that television serves as a "legitimizing agent" in its capacity to create a media reality. Ironically, viewers come to expect the real world to conform to the world of television.

> The entire justice system from police detection and apprehension to the court system has and will continue to undergo change as a result of television's portrayal of the criminal justice system in fictional drama, sitcoms, and documentaries. What people see on television is what they have come to expect and demand in actual criminal justice procedures. Many viewers assume that police and court practice depicted in television fiction correspond to actual practices in real life. The so-called accuracy of Jack Webb's detective programs and the appearance of authenticity in attorney programs is at best atypical and in many cases a misrepresentation of real-life practice. However, the public's acceptance of TV reality is pressuring police and court professionals to change their ways despite the dubious value of these changes. (Snow, 1983, p. 152)

Related to audience perceptions of reality on television is the ongoing research with the Cultural Indicators Project at the Annenberg School of Communications. For nearly thirty years this project has been measuring the content of television, as well as the impact upon viewers in terms of how they come to conceive social reality. As noted previously, Gerbner and his colleagues argue that heavy viewing television has a "cultivating effect," that is, viewers come to see the world as it is portrayed on television. For example, heavy television viewers come to see the world as a dangerous place as it is portrayed in television drama (Gerbner & Gross, 1976).

A colleague once remarked, "You're more real once you've been on television." This comment relates to this issue of television as a legitimizing agent. It also underscores the fact that the media are used to draw attention, create interest, or change perceptions by slanting a story or even manufacturing what Boorstin calls a pseudo event. One recalls NBC's Frank Reuven's injunction to his new staff: "Every news story should, without any sacrifice of probity or responsibility, display the attributes of fiction and drama" [quoted in Levine (1977), p. 102].

In his work aptly entitled *Inventing Reality: The Politics of the Mass Media,* Parenti (1992) illustrates numerous cases where the media create reality. A couple of examples, each from a different part of the world, illustrate this reality-creating dynamic of the media. The Gulf War may be the most heavily covered conflict ever and one of the most widely discussed current events treated in social studies classes in years. It received ongoing coverage on a daily basis throughout its duration in a manner, thanks to improvements in comunication technology, far beyond that of the Vietnam War, the first conflict to be fought in living rooms on a daily basis. During Desert Storm the media dutifully reported events as they occurred. Viewers could not easily forget watching the nightly news when the U.S. attack on Iraq began. In his review of the media's role and coverage of the Gulf War, Parenti demonstrates the contradiction and omissions that took place on the part of the media. In particular, few seemed to look critically at the pronouncements of the president as the war unfolded. What emerges is a vastly different understanding of the war and its effects. Parenti notes that Iraq had been given assurances in 1990 that the United States had no interest in the dispute between Iraq and Kuwait. Shortly after the invasion, however, Bush called for sanctions by the United Nations against Iraq. Then the president sent troops to Saudi Arabia, announcing that Sadam Hussein intended to invade Saudi Arabia. Furthermore, Bush announced to the nation that the freedom of America and that of friendly countries would suffer if the world's great oil reserves fell into the hands of Hussein. Parenti points out that in neither case did the media question these presidential pronouncements. He correctly observes that no one person could possibly control the oil reserves of the Middle East and that the United States was getting most of its oil elsewhere.

When Bush announced that Hussein planned to destroy Israel, the media again accepted this pronouncement uncritically. Iraq did finally attact Israel in retaliation for U.S. air strikes. Thus, far from preventing an attack on Israel, the actions of the United States may have led to Scud missiles being launched against Israel. Parenti provides numerous other events during the Gulf War that gave the American public a vastly different understanding of what took place. Again, after opinion polls showed Americans' negative reactions to Iraqi nuclear capability, the White House announced that Iraq posed a nuclear threat. Parenti notes that the press "obligingly went along, never raising any question as to why a nuclear-armed Iraq was any more of a threat to the world than an already nuclear-armed China, Pakistan, Israel, or South Africa" (p. 164). In additional ways the media shaped Americans' image and subsequent support for the war. The media gave great attention to the technological aspects of the war. Here, Parenti cites a *Newsweek* cover headline: THE NEW SCENE OF WAR, HIGH-TECH HARDWARE: HOW MANY LIVES CAN IT SAVE? The Pentagon treated the American public to a very sanitized version of the war, with few civilian casualties. It is clear now that the Pentagon managed what the media reported from the beginning. What is instructive is that the war took place with very little critical questioning from the media. Norman Schwarzkopf became a household word, as well as a major media personality. His humor during Pentagon press briefings became nationally recognized. (He subsequently retired and signed a major contract with a media conglomerate for an undisclosed amount of money.) Predictably, Bush's special assistant, Richard Hass, noted that television was "our chief tool" in "selling our policy" to the country, as well as the rest of the world [Hass, quoted in Parenti (1986), p. 171]. On the eve of Desert Storm, public opinion polls showed that 50% of Americans supported military action. Just five days later, that support had risen to 80%, as the country was treated to carefully constructed images of success with minimal casualities and smart bombs. The Gulf War does not represent an exception to the rule in terms of international news coverage. Parenti provides other examples of where the media responded in a similar fashion, including the invasion of Grenada.

Snow (1983) argues that the media can envelop an event with believability, through its perspective, in order to create the impression that something is factual when it is not. He recounts the example of the Libyan inspired plot to assassinate President Reagan in 1981. The media reported a plot to kill the president and other high ranking government officials by an Islamic fundamentalist group of terrorists. This leak of information by a government official led to the calls for the return of American citizens from Libya. Daily news reports explored the dangers emanating from Libya. Again, a suspension of critical analysis by the news media contributed to the treatment of the story as a fact, instead of a rumor, despite the fact that no hard evidence was forthcoming. For example, no one seemed to question why Libya would jeopardize oil sales to the United States.

Lawrence (1989) is critical of the media for creating news in the business community when none exists. In their efforts to make headlines, the media issue stories and reports based on statistics or data that either lack reliability or need some sort of context in which to be properly understood. He notes that, every month, the media announce United States trade statistics, causing reverberations across Wall Street. Yet these statistics are among the lease reliable of the data the government issues. Similarly, stories carry statistics that mean little presented within the context of one isolated month. Much of the data on the economy and business makes sense if it is seen within the context of an extended period of time of at least several months. The impression created, however, is that a downturn or upturn in the economy is taking place based upon a few weeks' worth of data.

MYTH #2: THE MEDIA KEEP US WELL-INFORMED; THEY ARE OBJECTIVE AND BALANCED

Bill Moyers, a leading television journalist, has observed that objectivity is the greatest of all the myths of news journalism. People look to the news to keep them informed. In fact, decisions about what actually gets reported in the news depends upon what is considered "newsworthy." The research suggests that the concept of what is newsworthy can be a fairly subjective enterprise. Television is the most used source for international news. Yet Larson (1979) found that less coverage is given to underdeveloped than developed countries. Moreover, there is a higher proportion of crisis stories reported in Third World countries.

Levin (1977) found that networks have a tendency to bend stories, which may create a sense of learned helplessness among viewers.

MYTH #3: THE MEDIA AND OUR MASS-MEDIATED CULTURES ARE INEXPENSIVE, EVEN FREE

The popular media exist because of advertising. Over time there has been a switch in the roles of the mass media and advertising. Historically, advertisers helped pay the cost of media production by purchasing space. Still, the media had an existence in their own right. Today, most media, however, exist in order to deliver a market share to advertisers. This fact explains why one finds so much advertising in magazines, newspaper, television, even movies. For example, magazine industry general interest publications have given way to special interest magazines that deliver a special market to advertisers. Campaine (1980) notes that, for publishers and advertisers, special interest magazines represent little more than the delivery of a market. Readers pay for these advertisements every time they purchase a magazine. One observes a similar trend in radio programs that specialize in period music, for example, the sixties, or in musical genres, for example, jazz or hard rock. Likewise, Real (1977) writes that "a consumer may pay more to support TV and radio programs that he or she never follows and newspapers and periodicals that he or she never reads through the indirect support system of advertising than he or she pays in taxes for schools, highways, police, and other services" (p. 244). He notes that up to 50% of the price of a product that a consumer purchases may go towards advertising on television that is never even seen by the consumer.

Bagdikian (1992), in exploring this myth, traces the history of advertising in the mass media. In each case advertising has come to play a larger and larger role in the media in terms of space and programming. At the same time the media have told consumers that broadcasting is free and that newspapers and magazines are sold below cost because advertising dollars help subsidize the cost. In his example of newspapers, he explains that, in 1940, daily newspapers averaged thirty-one pages, of which twelve and a half pages (40%) constituted advertising. By 1980 papers contained an average of sixty-six pages, of which forty-three pages (65%) were advertising.

MYTH #4: THE MEDIA PROVIDE A FREE FLOW OF INFORMATION

Although the media industry would deny it, "information flow" largely exists only when the industry itself allows it. This dynamic is true locally as well as internationally. To appreciate the myth of free flow of information, it is important to understand the concept of the "gatekeeper." Gatekeeping occurs at each level of the media process, as decisions are made as to what and how an event, person, or concept actually appears in the media. Real (1989) provides the examples of reporters and editors as gatekeepers in the production of news. It begins when a newsperson summarizes an event in a story. The story is then further edited for local broadcast or publication. Some stories are picked up by the wire services where they are further abbreviated. Finally, only a portion of those stories are actually picked up by other news stations or publishers.

The criteria for the decisions as to what becomes news and what does not are made based upon a combination of factors, including editor and reporter subjectivity, what audiences consider newsworthy, and concerns of the media institutions themselves. For example, media conglomerates are reluctant to report or print information that reflects negatively upon them. All of these factors, in some way, inhibit the free flow of information. In some cases, decisions are made primarily for economic reasons.

Crane (1992) demonstrates how the gatekeeping process works in other mass media forms where there are separate gatekeeping systems. Popular music, for example, must find support from a record producer. Recording, however, is no guarantee that one's music will be heard. Each year, many more recordings are produced than can realistically receive air time on the radio, Thus, the DJs form a second and separate gatekeeping system by deciding which recordings they will play.

In some cases advertisers themselves perform a gatekeeping function and control the free flow of information. Cigarette advertising is a multi-million dollar business. The tobacco industry provides millions of dollars of advertising to the media. Moreover, the clout of tobacco industry advertising dollars allows cigarette manufacturers to minimize coverage in the editorial content of the media on the effects of smoking (Weis & Burke, 1986). For example, there is evidence to suggest that women's magazines are reluctant to print stories on the risks of smoking-related illnesses, because publishers do not want to forgo lucrative advertising dollars from the tobacco industry. Meanwhile, lung cancer has become the leading cause of cancer-releated deaths among women.

Beyond advertising there has been an ongoing debate in recent decades over who will control the flow of information worldwide. While the final vestiges of political and economic colonialism are fading away, the communications industry is creating an "electronic colonialism" in developing countries. The New World Information and Communication Order (NWICO) came into existence in order to help third world countries establish some sense of control over their information systems in terms of their flow and content, as well as domestic communications policies (McPhail, 1987).

Presently, the issue over the flow of information is centered around two opposing groups. The communications industry of the developed, that is, Western world, maintains that there is a free flow of information between the developed and underdeveloped worlds. The lesser developed nations, often represented by NWICO, approach the concept of information flow differently. Their governments often want greater input and control over information systems. The vast majority of the news comes from a handful of wire services. Large multinational corporations exert influence in terms of tariffs, communications regulations, rates, and so on. In many cases electronic colonialism is in these companies' best interests. Information has become a powerful commodity that is controlled by transnational companies. "Clearly, the information revolution is nowhere in sight, except in the offices of stockbrokers, bankers, spy masters, meteorologists and the headquarters of transnational companies" (Traber, 1986, p. 2).

MYTH #5: INFORMATION OVERLOAD IS INEVITABLE

In identifying this myth, Fore (1990) writes: "The media also carry the myth that the tremendous avalanch of words, sounds, and visual images that invades our lives through the media is part of the price we must pay for living in modern society. If we expect," he continues, "to benefit from the wide variety of audiovisual experiences now available, the media tell us that we have to expect demands, sales pitches, commercials, and sheer volume that issue from them" (p. 52).

An area in which the media claim that information overload is the most inevitable is in advertising. Bagdikian notes that the media support this myth by arguing that the broadcasting media are free, another media myth explored previously. Thus, they come to use one myth to prove another!

> To growing complaints about proliferation of commercials, television replied that radio and television broadcasting is free, that advertisers give the public something for nothing. The public has never heard the something-for-nothing assumption debated over commercial radio and television or in newspaper and popular magazines. As a result, it has become an article of faith that mass advertising is essential to the preservation of a free press and free broadcasting. (p. 141)

This use of the myth that the mass media are free to bolster the myth of the inevitability of information overload reflects the mass media's confidence in these myths to operate effectively in our culture. This further underscores the need to address these media myths within the framework of media literacy.

MYTH 6: OUR MASS-MEDIATED CULTURE IS DEMOCRATIC AND EGALITARIAN

As media consumers students are led to believe that they have a wide variety of choices. Witness the expansion of cable, the plethora of stations one can pick up with a satellite dish. In reality, however, despite the sense of having all kinds of media choices, the media are concerned with money and profit, not democracy and egalitarianism. Over ten years ago, Bagdikian (1992) observed it was quite possible that, by the 1990s, a half dozen large corporations would dominate the media industry. At that time fifty national and multinational corporations controlled most of the major media. A look at the mega-media conglomerates today validates Bagdikian's prediction. Today, that number is down to twenty. Consider the merger of Time, Inc. and Warner Communications a few years ago. One conglomerate now owns two of the most popular entertainment cable systems, a major textbook company, many of the top popular magazines including *Time,* a leading book publishing company, a recording company, and a motion picture studio. Even as I write, two other communication companies are negotiating a merger.

Masterman (1985) highlights the trend towards the privatization of information. He notes Schiller's observation that, when information becomes a commodity, its role and character change. "When this occurs, not only do those with the ability to pay gain advantaged access, but eventually – and, ultimately most importantly – they become the arbiters of what kind of information will be produced and what is made available. The market unsentimentally yet inexorably confers this on those with the fatter bank account" (Schiller, quoted in Masterman, pp. 15–16).

The melding of the media into large corporations has an impact on not only who own the media, but what is said as well. McPhail's (1987) comments on the media in Canada clearly parallel what has taken place in this country. Corporate culture understandably means profits, but when the bottom line becomes the standard, not only accessibility to the media, but what the media tell us are greatly affected. Addressing the situation of the press in Canada, McPhail points out that the most obvious goal is profit, but an underlying "latent goal" is to convey an ideology that will continue to create a climate for profitability. In his study of the corporate elite in Canada, Clement argues that the media perform an ideological function and that a media elite sets the agenda for the attitudes and values that this elite wishes to see reflected in society (cited in McPhail, p. 26). At first glance this might seem almost conspiratorial or propagandistic until one examines, for example, advertising; however, few would deny that one of the goals of this segment of the media industry is to try to shape attitudes and values about consumption. Fore (1990) notes that this value is part of the cultural world view encouraged by the media and will be examined below.

MYTH #7: THE ISSUES OF LIFE ARE SIMPLE

The tendency of the media industry to reduce even the most complex of life's issues to a simplistic level is one of the most strident criticisms of the media. MacNeil (1983) argues that this simplicity derives from the fact that the media, in this case television, must appeal to the broadest audience possible. He notes with irony that, as our society becomes increasingly more complex, television, with "its dominating communication instrument, its principal form of national linkage, is an instru-

ment that sells simplicity and tidiness; neat solutions of human problems that usually have *no* neat solutions" (p. 5).

Fore (1990) believes that this myth, that the issues of life are simple,
has its roots in another media myth explored previously, that is, that information overload is inevitable. "Since we live in a world full of information overload, it is necessary and possible to reduce everything
really worth knowing into simply good and bad. The media help us
identify who and what is 'good' and 'bad,' whether we should respond
'yes' or 'no' to a particular issue or situation" (p. 52).

In a similar vein McPhail (1987) notes one of the trends in international journalism is what he terms "parachute journalism in which
masses of foreign correspondents, assorted paparazzi, and belligerent
camera crews descend by the plane-load to international scenes of conflict." This kind of journalism "tends to trivialize or sensationalize
events that are far more complex than a 30-second clip" (pp. 14–15).
He predicts this trend will continue until the public demands more
in-depth news coverage of events abroad.

In his exploration of media culture, Phelan (1977) examines two
media cliches emanating from this desire for simplicity: stereotypes
and issues. Obviously, the media are not the inventors of stereotypes,
but they rely heavily on them. In *Mediaworld* Phelan writes: "Stereotypes are useful necessities to help people deal with the complexity of
the world by selecting and simplifying the overwhelming amount and
variety of material that assaults them indirectly and through the media"
(1977, p. 17). The use of stereotypes by the media is now well
documented. From sex roles to occupational images, the media rely on
stereotypes. Phelan believes that issues are employed much like stereotypes. He describes them as "simplified and selective statements of
stereotypes." Echoing Fore's description, he notes that issues simplify
complex situations to the point that any middle ground is eliminated,
and we are presented with an either/or set of answers. "Public debate
selects views in order to reach decisions; the multiplicity of public
policy alternatives is simplified and sharpened by debate to clear-cut
dichotomies: war and peace, save or spend, hire or fire" (p. 17).

Booth (1982) observed this tendency to stereotype in the visual
media. He points out that television "reinforces a general trend in *all*
media toward simplification and polarization of the unlimited complexities of our lives. A citizen of the country presented to me by TV,
whether that country is literally the United States or some imagined

world, I learn quickly that all problems could be solved simply, if only other people would think about them the way I am being taught to do *now*" (p. 44).

Booth approaches the media from a unique perspective. He believes that the use of different media represents different ways of being in the world. With its appeal to stereotypes and simplicity, television represents a "passivity of imaginative engagement, with a resulting simplified emotional engagement." He wonders aloud philosophically what the long-term effect of this kind of media experience will be.

> No doubt there will be great consequences for our future selves from all of these controls over our characters as we enter and leave the video worlds. But we do not know, we cannot prove, what those consequences will be. What we do know, what we need no experimental proof for, is that our lives are lived in *these* ways, sitting, now before the screen, and not in possible other ways. The selves, souls, persons, characters that we are likely to become as a result of living in print or a video culture for decades will matter greatly, but they are unavailable as evidence in our debates. (p. 44)

MYTH #8: CONSUMPTION IS INHERENTLY GOOD

This myth, possibly more than any other, drives the media industry although it is in no way confined to the media. At first glance advertising comes to mind, and that needs to be explored. But even before advertising is considered, the media industry is concerned with consumption of the media itself. Consider that there are well over 12,000 magazines in circulation. Viewers have access to hundreds of cable channels. Thousands of movie titles are now available on video. The discriminating listener can find a radio station that specializes in virtually any type of music that he or she wishes to listen to. Recordings are now available on tape, vinyl, or compact disc. The media possibilities seem endless.

Much of the function of today's mass media is to entertain. As a measure, however, media success is not based upon how well they entertain, as much as how well they are consumed. A film cannot simply be a good entertainment film. It must be a blockbuster! It is interesting to note that many good family entertainment films remain obscure because they do not become mega-hits. Nielsen ratings for television have little to do with quality programs. It is largely an economic question of how many people are watching a particular program on a given night. Many people watch television with little selectivity. The explosion in media technology has only fueled this penchant for media consumption. Look at the VCR phenomenon. The VCR is the fastest growing technology in the history of communication technology. In its wake it has spun off a whole new industry, for example, video rental stores. This technology has greatly expanded the boundaries of media consumption. Because the media industry is driven primarily by economics, not the communication of information, consumption is encouraged at every turn. This encouragement of consumption is a fact of media life even before advertising is dialed into the equation.

As noted above, advertising is largely what now makes the media possible. It is a multi-billion dollar business. More money is spent on advertising as an art form than any other. Despite disclaimers from the industry, advertising deals with creating "wants and needs" in people. That is why there is such an abundance of advertising. Creating habits of consumption starts when children are young and continues throughout life and explains why companies begin to try to establish brand loyalties beginning with two year olds. Little wonder then that Ronald McDonald ranks only behind Santa Claus as the most recognizable character among the nation's school children. It also explains why Joe Camel is one of the most recognizable consumer icons, even among six year olds.

The primary function of the media today is to deliver a market to an advertiser. This is why there has been a tremendous increase in advertising over the years in the media. Every time the Super Bowl rolls around, viewers are reminded in the pre-game hype how companies pay hundreds of thousands of dollars for thirty seconds of air time. Clearly, the sponsoring network is not creating an entertainment extravaganza simply for the benefit of the home viewers. Invariably, there is a linkage between the acquisition of material goods and happiness. The good life is merely an extension of having a lot of material possessions. And by all accounts the media are very successful at perpetuating this myth, starting with very young children. Children influence their parents to spend about $200 billion a year (McNeal, 1992).

One of the supreme ironies is that many of the products and the good life portrayed in advertising are beyond the means of most Americans. This myth reaches its most logical, if not bizarre, extreme in *Lifestyles of the Rich and Famous*. One notes an occasional wealthy person doing some good with his or her money; however, mostly, the show is an object lesson in consumption carried to the extreme. The lives of the rich and famous are always happy, thus reinforcing the myth that consumption is inherently good.

MYTH #9: THE MEDIA HAVE NO IMPACT

Volumes have been written exploring the question of whether the media have any impact and, if so, what the effects of the media are. Beyond issues of violence, learning, and gender socialization are questions about how society has rearranged itself around the media. American culture is a media culture in the biggest sense of the word. Virtually no facet of American culture has been left unchanged by the media. Even the spiritual dimension has been vastly reshaped for millions of Americans through the electronic church. It is now no longer possible to imagine life without the media. On those rare occasions when people are cut off from the media, it often proves to be an unsettling experience, as noted in Winick's (1988) research with those who have lost their television sets.

Chapter 1 notes that the four primary functions of mass communication are to entertain, inform, transmit, or reflect culture and to persuade. In analyzing the myth that the media have no impact, it is possible to locate numerous examples where mass communication has impacted upon society as they function in each of these four areas.

The Entertainment Function of Mass Communication

Mediated sports provide an excellent example of the entertainment function of mass communication. The impact of the media upon sports is well documented. From the living room to the press box or to the negotiating table, the media have transformed the way we understand and use sports for entertainment. Beyond the huge salaries and tremendous accessibility of sports on television, most sports enthusiasts are unaware of the many changes (in some cases the rules of the games themselves) that have taken place to accommodate the media, particularly television. Crabb and Goldstein (1991) and Harris (1989) provide numerous examples of these kinds of changes in sports. Beginning in the 1970s rules for football, baseball, and basketball were changed to create more spectator appeal and to make these sports fit better into programming requirements. In some cases these changes came about directly to accommodate television; in others the changes were more indirect. Among the changes these authors note are, in baseball, lowering the pitcher's mound from fifteen to ten inches to make curve and slider pitches more effective; in basketball, changes in rules to facilitate scoring such as the twenty-four–second clock; in football, moving the goalposts back to the endline and reducing the penalty for offensive holding from fifteen to ten yards; in golf, changing from match to medal or stroke play to insure big-name golfers in the final stages of PGA tournaments; and in tennis, introduction of sudden-death tie-breakers to eliminate nontelegenic deuce games. In some cases changes have been superficial, such as adding more color to sports uniforms, changing the color of tennis balls from white to "optic yellow," or changing the center line in hockey from the solid to a broken line to show up better on television. The sudden-death overtime is another media-induced change. Crabb and Goldstein point out that a number of changes have taken place in scheduling to make sports more "media friendly." More games are played at night, and team schedules are arranged to have the better teams play more often to boost market appeal. The recognition that sports are one of the most entertaining and, thus, watched program genres on television, particulary by males, has led to the creation of "synthetic sports" or "trashsports." Harris observes that, on ABC's *Wide World of Sports,* synthetic sport "runs the gamut from cliff diving at Acapulco or national logrolling championships to a rattlesnake hunt in Keane, Oklahoma or national wrist-wrestling championships in Petaluma, California . . . the 'World Buffalo Chip-Tossing Contest' and the 'Joe Garagiola/Bazooka Big League Gum Blowing Championships' " (pp. 119–120).

The Information Function of Mass Communication

Throughout this book numerous examples of the way the media provide information have been explored. An additional example of the effects of the information function can be found in American foreign policy. O'Heffernan (1993) has observed that the crisis of the Gulf War firmly established television as a player in world politics. Larson (1986) has identified a number of ways that the media, in their efforts to provide the public with information, can have substantial effects on foreign policy and foreign relations. The information that is provided on these two areas often comes from overseas wire services and television footage from other sources. Transmitting news from overseas locales often involves local censorship.

A second feature Larson describes is the presence of the media making private or secret negotiations between governments more difficult, a point also made by O'Heffernan. The end effect Larson argues is that public opinion becomes a third party in negotiations because the visual component of news is now so important that what becomes available for reporting is often contingent upon the video choices that a network has access to. Visual demands then lead to overcoverage of photogenic issues and undercoverage of other issues for which video footage is unavailable. News coverage is often episodic with intense saturation coverage, which may lead to an ahistorical account.

Larson also notes the coverage of the Islamic Revolution and hostage crisis in Iran in 1979. Based upon news reporting, many people believed that this crisis in the Middle East came out of nowhere. In fact, the signs had been there for a long time but were ignored or unnoticed by the media. The media can affect public perceptions about foreign affairs. Visual information can have a strong impact, especially when it is presented over an extended period of time. The change in public opinion over the Vietnam War is a good example. Similarly, daily coverage of the Iran hostage crisis certainly created frustration with the president. Carter became the scapegoat for the failure to obtain their release and this, most certainly, contributed to his loss to Reagan in 1980. In some cases the media actually participate in foreign policy by serving as a direct communication channel. Larson notes Walter Cronkite's role in bringing Begin and Sadat together for their historical meeting. In other cases the media may have more information than the government, reversing the usual government-to-media flow. These observations, as well as others by Larson, demonstrate that the media, in performing their information function, can have very serious effects on foreign policy.

The Transmission of Culture

As noted previously, an understanding of mass communication as transmitter of culture carries two dimensions. The first dimension is that of relaying culture as it is. The second is mass communication as a creator and shaper of culture. An example of this function at work is the mass media's role in the creation of the "cult of celebrity." Celebrities are not a new cultural phenomenon. Henderson (1992) observes that the rise of a celebrity-based culture can, in part, be traced to America's shift from a producing to a consuming society. The growth of the entertainment industry, made possible by the media, fueled this shift from what Henderson calls a "hero-oriented stance to an embrace of celebrity." A more novel development, however, is the numbers and interest and influence that they command. Cultural observers point out that society's preoccupation with celebrities has a much deeper meaning that transcends the glitz and glamour. In *The Culture of Narcissism,* Lasch (1979) observes: "The mass media, with their cult of celebrity and their attempt to surround it with glamour and excitement, have made Americans a nation of fans and moviegoers. The media give substance to thus intensify," Lasch continues, "narcissistic dreams of fame and glory, encourage the common man to identify himself with the stars and to hate the 'herd,' and make it more and more difficult for him to accept the banality of everyday existence" (p. 21). Borrowing from a previous theme, Harris (1989) maintains that, in trashsports' creation of celebrity contests, viewers are not attracted by the sport but, rather, the celebrities. "Because of the para-social interaction we have with our TV 'friends,' we will watch them participate in events we would find totally uninteresting in most other circumstances. It is not unlike watching one's own child in a ball game," Harris observes. "We are there because of our relationship with one of the participants, not necessarily because of intrinsic interest in the sport itself" (p. 120). As cultural icons, celebrities then perform a variety of functions that are media-related. To that end the media have a "monopoly," as it were. They are instrumental in helping create a social market for celebrities, and they supply those market demands by creating a stable of movie stars, rock stars, and literary and television personalities. Even the production of news, what one would generally consider an information function, is now dependent upon celebrities for its delivery.

Still another example of the impact of the media on culture is the way in which communication itself is being transformed. Beniger (1987) observes a profound impact of the mass media on society in terms of its replacement of interpersonal communications. Technology both within the communications industry and elsewhere has created a situation in which the mass media ape personal communication. Thus, the mass media are capable of "personalizing" their messages so that the distinction between interpersonal communication and mass communication are now blurred. The end result is that the traditional community has now been transformed into an impersonal association, resulting in what Beniger calls the *pseudo-community.* An example of this personalizing of mass communication is the use of prerecorded messages. In 1986 the Republican party telephoned hundreds of thousands of voters each day with a recorded message from President Reagan, in which he urged them to vote in the November election. Hang-up rates ranged from an unprecedented low of 5% to 17%. One political consultant noted that using a politician's voice created a psychological bond. "You'd be amazed at the number of people who say the next day that 'the President called me on the phone last night'" [Eichenwald, cited in Beniger (1987), p. 355].

A theme that Beniger presents, which is related to the concept of pseudo-community, is the way that the media manipulate sincerity. He explores in detail Merton's 1946 study *Mass Persuasion,* which examined how Kate Smith helped sell $39 million in war bonds; the key to her success—sincerity. In the face of decline of interpersonal communication, the media have seized upon creating an image of sincerity very similar to that of Kate Smith's over fifty years ago. Moreover, technology makes it possible for the media to feign sincerity to huge audiences simultaneously. Beniger provides numerous examples of how effective manipulating sincerity can be. He cites a *USA Today* poll on the most believable sports figures selling products. Heading the list were John Madden and Bob Uecker, both unglamorous, simple, unpretentious, almost self-effacing. Both are persons to be believed because they come across with sincerity, not unlike Kate Smith who, in describing herself, said, "I haven't any stories or fancy phrases to fling at you . . . no sound effects to capture your attention. I'm a plain simple woman" (as quoted in Beniger, p. 359).

Mass Communication and Persuasion

As Black and Whitney (1988) observe, the lines between the information and persuasive functions of mass communication are sometimes blurred. The concept of persuasion can operate at a number of levels. In some cases the persuasive intent is blatant or obvious. At other levels it may be much more subtle.

Lasch (1979) points to the distinction between truth and credibility and how the latter is often passed off as the former in an effort to persuade. He writes:

> The role of the mass media in the manipulation of public opinion has received a great deal of anguished but misguided attention. Much of this commentary assumes that the problem is to prevent the circulation of obvious untruths; whereas it is evident, as the more penetrating critics of mass culture have pointed out, that the rise of mass media makes the categories of truth and falsehood irrelevant to the evaluation of their influence. Truth has given way to credibility, facts to statements that sound authoritative with conveying any authoritative information. (p. 74)

Borrowing a situation from the Nixon presidency, Lasch relates how the president's press secretary Ron Ziegler announced that his previous statements on Watergate had become "inoperative." While many commentators interpreted this description as a euphemism for lying, Lasch maintains that what Ziegler was saying was that his previous statements were no longer believable. "Not their falsity but their inability to command assent rendered them 'inoperative.' The question of whether they were true or not was beside the point" (p. 75).

In some cases truth is pressed into the service of deception in an effort to persuade. Advertising provides a ready example. "The type of advertising claim which is potentially most damaging is the statement which is literally true, but miscomprehended, thus deceiving consumers by inducing them to construct a meaning of the ad that is inconsistent with reality" (Harris, 1989, p. 74). Relying on an understanding of information processing, advertising draws upon a number of linguistic techniques to persuade the consumers to purchase products by inviting them to make inferences beyond the information presented in the advertisement. Harris and others have conducted extensive research, demonstrating that the strategic use of the truth to induce deception works, so much so that he notes it is difficult for subjects not to make such inferences.

CONCLUSION

Media literacy draws its meaning from the proposition that those who live in a media culture must think critically about the media that shape culture. Hamelink (1986) observed that myths demand critical questioning to see if they stand up to reality and whose interests they legitimize. The kind of critical reflection he calls for is clearly relevant for the nine media myths analyzed in this chapter. As educators, we must address these myths at some juncture. Bird and Dardenne (1988) remind us that, to have power, myths must constantly be retold. The media retell these myths on a daily basis. Exploring them within the context of media literacy takes the power away from the media industry and allows us to tell our own story. To do any less leaves it up to the mass media to create our reality for us.

CHAPTER 9

In Search of the Hidden Curriculum:
The Case for Media Literacy in Schools Today

The growing influence of the mass media—particularly television and popular music—raises troubling moral questions. Through simplistic coverage of issues, many television programs project a "quick fix" mentality that discourages thoughtfulness and encourages violence and questionable social mores. Television programs and commercials encourage such values as materialism, overconsumption, superficiality, and casual sexual behavior, and reinforce racial, ethnic, and sex-role stereotypes. How can school encourage more responsible attention to the values content of the mass media or, failing that, counteract this influence?

Moral Education in the Life of the School: A Report from the Association of Supervision and Curriculum Development Panel on Moral Education, 1988

There are three compelling reasons for making media literacy a part of the curriculum. The first speaks to the influence that the media exercise on young people. In a number of cases, these influences are not positive, for example, health concerns, the link between media violence and aggressive behavior; however, as noted in the Introduction, concern over the negative impact of the media is scarcely new and has not provided sufficient momentum over the last two decades to make media literacy a universal curriculum component. A second reason for teaching media literacy touches on the pervasiveness of the media in our culture. One of the axioms of effective pedagogy is to provide learning experiences that are relevant to students. As the chapter on media use indicates, the media are a major part of the life experience of today's students. Virtually any subject taught offers numerous possibilities for pulling the media experience into instruction, thereby providing a point of reference with which students can relate. Here, then, the media should be seen as providing abundant opportunities for teachers to create meaningful learning by appealing to an experience that is relevant to virtually every student, regardless of ability, gender, ethnic, or economic background. Consequently, media literacy contains within it the seeds for making teachers better teachers. Another important reason for teaching media literacy is that it is virtually impossible to fully teach many of the traditional subjects in the curriculum without including the media. This fact is sadly overlooked in most instructional materials. Similarly, other issues uppermost on the educational agenda can neither be fully understood nor addressed without including the media and teaching students how the media shape their understanding of themselves and their world, such as multicultural education, government, health, and gender equity. For all of these reasons, then, media literacy should become an issue worthy of serious curricular consideration.

The media constitute a significant part of the environment of students of all ages. Starting with preschool and *Sesame Street, Barney,* and *Mister Rogers' Neighborhood,* television is a focus for preschool children's learning. At children's entry into an academic program, media literacy should be infused in the curriculum. Media literacy becomes a serious topic of study for children who begin to depend on knowledge and influences outside the family and school. Previously, Davies (1991a, 1993a) has noted that, at the middle level, there are a number of characteristics of early adolescence, as well as educational, needs of the middle school student, which makes this a particularly valuable and necessary time to address media literacy. Nearly all of these characteristics and educational needs can be expanded to include elementary and high school students as well. Those areas to be examined in this chapter include critical thinking, consumer education, the developmental tasks of children and adolescents, character education, citizenship, global and multicultural education, gender equity, health education, and the emergence of a new kind of learning.

CRITICAL THINKING

As noted in the Introduction, the ultimate goal of education, as well as media literacy, is to create independent thinkers. Crucial to independent thinking is teaching students to become critical in their thinking.

Beyer (1988) notes that critical thinking "consists essentially of judging the authenticity, worth, or accuracy of something." It is primarily evaluative in nature. Schwartz and Perkins (1990) describe this type of thinking as concerned with "the critical examination and evaluation—actual and potential—of beliefs and courses of action." These understandings of critical thinking reach to the heart of Considine's (1992) definition of media literacy as "the ability to analyze and evaluate information carried and conveyed through the media." Beginning three decades ago with the critical viewing skills of television, the foundation of what was to become media literacy, critical thinking was identified as one of the goals of this literacy.

Today, the idea of teaching critical thinking has found a permanent place in teaching media literacy. For example, Dorman (1994) identifies two dimensions of "media logic." The first is "a way of thinking implicit in a given medium's format that is supported by certain professional assumptions, beliefs, and values" (p. 35). He uses the example of television news, which relies on visuals, particularly dramatic ones. Given this understanding of media logic, the emphasis is on quick-breaking, high-profile stories, instead of "process stories" such as the societal violence against children. Dorman suggests that there is another dimension of media logic that addresses the relationship between media studies and critical thinking. He poses the question: "What might a teacher of critical thinking conclude about 'media logic' of this second sort?"

Dorman argues that there are three areas of inquiry here. The first speaks to one of the media myths identified earlier. He writes:

> In the logic of television news, the world is a certain and simple place in which to live. Unpleasant to be sure, but nonetheless filled with certainties. There are good guys and bad, either this alternative or that one, a right way to do things and a wrong way. Put another way, television encourages us to think deductively in a largely *inductive* world by its systematic reliance on stereotyping and its deference to established austerity, conventional wisdon, and the existing social, political, and economic arrangements. (p. 35)

A second characteristic of the logic of television news is that all things are pretty much equal. Dorman believes that this "fallacy of lack of proportion" in the network news is the most widespread. Because of the demands of news, events are given a similar amount of attention as if they were all of the same significance. For example, a feature on a prominent personality's athletic achievements receives the same attention as a massacre in Rwanda. Still a third principle that drives media logic is that more is less. "Put another way, if it can't be said in under thirty seconds, it's probably not worth saying." Dorman provides an example from the last presidential race. CBS established a guideline in which the network's evening news would use a presidential sound bite no shorter than thirty seconds. This requirement was then reduced to twenty seconds.

The most disturbing dynamic of media logic regarding the news is that emotion and imagery predominate over reason.

> Whether it be the treacle that passes for conversation among news anchors or the sentimentalized presentation of community charity as a solution to hopelessness, what matters is the feeling an image produces. Whether it be commentators who said of newly-elected President Bill Clinton's economic summit that it was a success because he *looked* presidential, or the Gulf War, which was presented on American televsion as a mini-series, a kind of "Lonesome Dove with Smart Bombs," television news sets viewers adrift in a sea of images and an ocean of sensation. What is not important is a line of argument that can be analyzed, thought about, tested, accepted or rejected. (Dorman, 1994, p. 35)

As Dorman has suggested, exploring the world of media logic provides fertile ground for encouraging critical thinking about a medium that has become the major source of information about worldwide activity today.

O'Reilly and Splaine (1987) provide another perspective for thinking critically about the news. They have developed various models for critically thinking about television. One of these models (BASE) employs four perspectives for analyzing news reports on television. Students are encouraged to look at what came *before* the news report. O'Reilly and Splaine note that this is important because what comes before a news report affects the tone of the report. The second stage of the model requires students to look at what came *after* the news report. Again, what comes after it affects how a news report is perceived. Students need to analyze what they really *see* in a news report. Among those elements of critical analysis needed to determine what one sees, O'Reilly and Splaine suggest determining the report's point of view, what inferences are being made, and use of persuasive techniques. Finally, the student must weigh the evidence presented in the news report. Here, quality and quantity are important. What sources are being used? Who or where are they from?

Numerous other examples demonstrate how the media can be used as a point of departure for teaching critical thinking. At a time when teaching for thinking has become a major issue on the educational agenda of the nation, media literacy provides an excellent opportunity for helping students become better thinkers.

CONSUMER EDUCATION

Advertising is a multi-billion dollar business. Kellner [cited in Smillie & Bowen (1993)] estimates that fully 2% of the United States' gross national product, a total of $110 billion, is spent on advertising. A young person is estimated to have seen 1,000,000 television commercials by high school's end (Postman et al., 1987). At the same time the combination of children and adolescents represent a multi-billion dollar market for advertisers and businesses. Graham and Hamdan (1987) speculate that the teenage market is between $50 and $55 billion. And while the number of teenagers has declined, their purchasing power has doubled. Whittle Communications earns $100 million a year selling commercial spots to advertisers who want to tap into the lucrative teenage market in the classroom. McNeal's (1992) research illustrates that, in 1990, young people between the ages of four and twelve spent $7.29 million and influenced another $132 million in purchases. This combination of volume of advertisements to which they are exposed and the growing influence of children and adolescents as consumers has contributed to the growing concern about advertising on consumer socialization. "Consumer socialization is the developmental process by which young people acquire the knowledge, attitudes, and skills relevant to their functioning in the marketplace" (Atkin, 1982, p. 191). Brecher writes that "advertisers and marketers face an eternal challenge; find new ways to sell us products we already have, don't need or may not even want. They must innovate constantly, since we become immune to both the medium and the message in much the same way cockroaches develop resistance to pesticides" (Brecher, 1993). The infomercial, infozine, home shopping networks are some of the kinds of "innovations" that need to be considered as young people experience consumer socialization.

ADVERTISING AND CHILDREN

A growing concern over the impact of commericals on children led the National Science Foundation (NSF) to issue a report in 1977, identifying important research issues, as well as summarizing the research to date. The authors of that report identified ten areas of concern. The first revolves around children's ability to distinguish television commericals from program material. The report noted that a number of studies had documented the difficulty that children under the age of eight had in comprehending the difference in purpose between commericals and programs. A second area of concern was the influence of format and audiovisual techniques on children's perceptions of commercial messages. The research up until that time suggested that disclaimers proved insufficient for nonreading children. Subsequent research suggests that a third of children's advertisements contain some sort of disclaimer, usually appearing at the end of the commercial and containing adult language [Stern and Harmon, cited in Harris (1989), p. 80]. The concern of source effects and self-concept appeals revolved around advertisers' usage of characters to sell products. The research suggested that the mere appearance of a character could significantly alter children's evaluation of a product positively or negatively. Research at the time of the report was inconclusive regarding the use of overt premium offers to improve product appeal, particularly of cereals, among children. A fifth issue identified in the NSF report focused on the use of violence or unsafe acts in television commercials. Despite variations in the research, the report suggested "that usage act portrayals may be hazardous, even in context, and should probably be avoided, whenever possible" (p. v).

Most of the research on the impact of advertisement for proprietary medicines had been conducted with teenagers. The NSF report noted some influence in terms of affecting children's attitudes towards illness and medications. Heavier viewers reported a greater frequency of illness, believed more in the efficacy of medicines, and were more receptive to their use. A major area of research summarized in the report addressed the effects of television food advertisements on children. The authors noted two findings of interest: the empirical evidence supports the general effectiveness of food advertisements regarding children, and the children can learn nutritional information when it is included in commercials. According to the authors, children see 20,000 commercials per year; therefore, they noted the effects of the volume and repetition of commercials as an issue. Again, summarizing the research, they noted that, as the understanding of commercials increases with age, so do negative attitudes towards them. However, this negative attitude is accompanied by only a slight decline in children's requests for advertised products. The authors also noted that heavy television viewing does not seem to have any effect on the understanding of commercials. It does, however, seem to contribute towards a more favorable attitude towards both advertisements and advertised products. Considering the impact on consumer socialization, the report states quite clearly that commercials play a role in initiating consumer behavior in children of all ages. Research also indicates that children rate commercials as a source of information on products behind information actually gathered in stores, but ahead of interpersonal sources. The last concern mentioned in the report is the issue of television advertising and parent-child relations. Among the findings reported is that parents tend to overstate the degree of control they exercise over their children's viewing and overestimate their children's understanding of commercials.

It would not be an exaggeration to say that the makers of advertised products view children primarily as a lucrative market. One popular children's cable station, for example, conducts 150 research studies a year, with focus groups of nine-to-twelve-year-olds (Laybourne, 1993). As Atkin has noted, rules proposed to restrict advertising to children have largely been thwarted. Research since the National Science Foundation study suggests that there is continued cause for concern. Ross et al. have noted that children have processing limitations when it comes to commercials

> Children are limited in: (1) their ability to apply conceptual knowledge to override perceptual impressions; (2) their ability to search systematically for relevant information, rather than responding to immediate stimulus salience; and (3) their ability to consider multiple properties of stimuli (e.g., visual and verbal) simultaneously. [quoted in Goldberg & Gorn (1983), p. 141]

Moreover, as Graves (1982) notes, black children may be more vulnerable to the influence of advertisers because they are more likely to fail to recognize the intent of advertising and accept it as truthful. As a consequence she maintains that this may leave them more open to advertising's messages about social roles.

Hundreds of studies have been conducted since 1977 and are beyond the scope of this chapter. One area of concern, however, warrants further mention because it has become increasingly more popular in advertising, and children are particularly vulnerable to it, that is, the use of celebrities and characters from children's programming to sell products. Atkin (1982) points out that advertisers achieve a high level of trustworthiness using professional characters, including celebrities. Congress passed the Children's Television Act to protect children from excessive advertising. Still, advertisers are allowed twelve minutes per hour for weekday children's programming.

Two techniques that advertisers use to increase the effectiveness of their ads beyond time limits are host-selling and what has come to be referred to as the "program-length commercial." Host-selling is the use of the same primary characters in a commercial who also appear in the program slot of which the commercial is a part. Kunkel (1988) studied the effectiveness of this technique with four- and five-year-olds and seven- and eight-year-olds. He showed both groups the same commercials in both a host-selling context and in a nonhost-selling context. He found both groups were significantly less likely to discriminate commercial from program content when viewed in the former context. Moreover, the older children were more favorably influenced by the same commercial content viewed in the host-selling context. Kunkel also notes that, despite the prohibition against this form of advertising by the FTC since 1974, there are more characters showing up in commercials. He believes that this signals that host-selling is no longer being effectively restricted. The effectiveness of the advertising techniques is evidenced by the fact that toy companies use their marketing budgets to subsidize the production of Saturday morning children's television shows. Thus, Hasbro, Inc. used its marketing budget to help defray the costs of *G.I. Joe, Jem,* and *The Transformers* (Harris, 1989).

The "program-length commercial" (a term coined by the FCC) or product-based program also trades on the connection between characters popular with children and their advertising potential (Kunkel, 1988). Greenfield et al. (1993) note that, previously, companies created commercial products as a spin-off from programs such as *Sesame Street.* Today, that process works in reverse. The trend now is for the product to come first. Nor is this trend limited to television programs. Some films directed at children achieve the same effect while also generating tremendous profits for the companies that make them. Witness the tremendous popularity of the Teenage Mutant Ninja Turtles movies. Even young gifted children, who are better able to discern the selling intent of commercials than other children, may have difficulty identifying the selling strategies behind the program-length commercial (Abelman, 1992).

A relatively new advertising ploy related to the program-length commercial is interactive television. Diamond [cited in Harris (1989), p. 81] reports the tie-in of interactive toys with television. Using high-frequency tones or infrared light keys, viewers turn on their interactive toys. Diamond gives the example of *Captain Power and the Soldiers of the Future*, in which children can turn on their $30 Mattel Power Jet and fire at the television screen while an electronic signal keeps track of their "hits" and records the players' scores. Harris points out that not only does the program-length commercial encourage the purchase of the toy, but makes it *necessary* to fully enjoy the program.

ADOLESCENT CONSUMERS

Davies (1990) has observed that the emerging adolescent is an emerging consumer. Advertising and the media are inseparable. The overwhelming objective of the media is neither to entertain nor to inform but, rather, to deliver audiences to advertisers. Schultze et al. (1991) point out that corporations realize that they can vastly increase profits by promoting "distinct generational groups." While adolescents make up a significant part of a huge youth market, little is done to help them become wise consumers. Stevenson (1981), Schultze et al. (1991), and Arnold (1993) have addressed the vulnerability of the early adolescents to advertisers and their potential to be exploited by them. Nowhere is the media's efforts to influence early adolescent consumer socialization more apparent than with Music Television (MTV). As one MTV creator observed, "We don't shoot for the 14-year-old—we own them." In *Dancing in the Dark: Youth, Popular Culture and the Electronic Media,* Schultze and his colleagues (1991) examined how MTV represents a very creative and powerful tool for consumer socialization of the youth market. They argue that there exists a symbiotic relationship between the youth culture and the electronic media. This relationship is one of mutual dependence. To survive economically, the electronic media need a consumer youth market. On the other hand, young people derive guidance and nurturance from the media because other social institutions do not shape youth culture as powerfully as they once did.

A significant part of the media is made up of the entertainment industry. Schultze et al. echo Stevenson's thoughts on the media, consumerism, and youth.

> The entertainment industry sees youth as a prime market—a distinct, ever-renewing demographic group possessed of ample leisure and money to make sales soar. Further, adolescents have shown themselves, because of their particular state of life, to be especially susceptible to the marketing wiles of the entertainment industry. This industry is adept at perpetually recycling timeless adolescent anxieties and hopes into easily adaptable formulaic fads and fashions. (p. 77)

One of the principles of Arnold's (1993) empowering curriculum is to help young adolescents understand the forces at work that exploit them and to develop strategies that counteract this exploitation. He notes that "advertisers prey on the insecurities of young people, convincing them that they should look a certain way, dress a certain way, and act a certain way to be acceptable—all of which purchase of the advertiser's product will help bring about." He concedes that the advertising industry uses a similar approach with other age groups, but that "the practice seems especially insidious and exploitative given the vulnerability of youth" (p. 6).

Upon closer examination one finds that much of the world of MTV is about selling. Music videos are really advertisements for the recording industry. In fact, most of the music videos produced are made by the same people who create advertisements. Not surprisingly, then, the commercials on music television are very similar in style to the music videos themselves! MTV, as well as other media, encourage consumption on a less direct level as well. Adolescents are expected to buy the latest fashions, electronic gadgets, and so on that are identified with a media-generated youth culture. Aufderheide (1986) maintains that music videos, because they are commercials, have erased the distinction between commercials and programs. "Music videos have also set themselves free from the television set, inserting themselves into movie theaters, popping up in shopping malls and department store windows, becoming actors in both live performances and the club scene. As omnivorous as they are pervasive," Aufderheide maintains that music videos "draw on and influence the traditional image-shaping fields of fashion and advertising—even political campaigning" (p. 57). Gow's (1993) research underscores another technique that music videos employ for commercial purposes. He notes that music videos persuade by promoting both recordings and performers. Among advertisers this is called "positioning," that is, a product is not sold directly, but "rather involves creating, maintaining or changing consumer perceptions of a product." As Ries and Trout (quoted in Gow, p. 319) explain: "Positioning is not what you do to a product. Positioning is what you do to the mind of the prospect." Gow has demonstrated how music videos employ the production strategy of "pseudo-reflexivity." He describes this strategy as "employing imagery that demystifies some, but not all, of the aspects of the video making process in order to draw both audience attention away from the promotional motives underlying video production and enhance the anti-commercial stance typically adopted by hard rock musicians" (p. 318). This kind of subtle "impression management" represents a very subtle, but effective, way in which the recording industry sells.

The introduction of Channel One into the classroom increases education's responsibilities, as well as opportunities for teaching adolescents to become critical consumers. As Greenberg and Brand (1993, 1994) have noted: "The care that goes into crafting the advertising is at least as extensive as that which goes into designing the news portion of Channel One" (p. 57). It is worth noting that the major study cited earlier (funded by Whittle Communications) by the Institute for Social Research on the effects of Channel One, was not permitted to look at the effects of advertising! In their study Greenberg and Brand examined the impact of commercials on Channel One on students' purchasing intentions and their desire to "want" things, that is, materialism. They found student viewers thought more highly of advertised products than nonviewers, and viewers reported that they were more likely to purchase products appearing in Channel One commercials than nonviewers. Greenberg and Brand found no difference, however, between students who watched the program and those that did not, in terms of recent purchases of products advertised on Channel One. Their study also provided evidence that Channel One advertisements reinforce materialistic attitudes among viewers.

Finally, Gitlin (1982) argues that the plethora of commercials that both children and adults encounter on a day-in and day-out basis have an "*indirect* consequence on the contours of consciousness over all:

they get us accustomed to thinking of ourselves and behaving as a *market* rather than a *public,* as consumers rather than citizens" (p. 434). Later, he notes that this process need not even require commercials, but simply commercial forms. "Even public broadcasting children's shows take over the commercial forms to their own educational ends. . . . The producers of *Sesame Street,* in likening knowledge to commercial products ('and now a message from the letter B'), may well be legitimizing the commercial form in its discontinuity and in its invasiveness" (p. 434). Clearly, then, some critical analysis of advertising is warranted in schools to serve as an antidote to the consumer socialization forces at work in our society.

CHARACTER EDUCATION IN A MEDIA CULTURE

In recent years a new emphasis has emerged on moral and character education in American schools. Recently, the Association for Supervision and Curriculum Development (ASCD) devoted an entire issue of *Educational Leadership* (November 1993) to this topic. *Why Johnny Can't Tell Right from Wrong* (Kilpatrick, 1992), *Moral, Character, and Civic Education in the Elementary School* (Benninga, 1991), *Reclaiming Our Schools: A Handbook on Teaching Character, Academics, and Discipline* (Wynne & Ryan, 1992), as well as *Educating for Character: How Our Schools Can Teach Respect and Responsibility* (Lickona, 1991), call for the need to return character education to the classroom. Indeed, values are one of the cornerstones of the Edison Project (Schmidt, 1994). By now, the disturbing statistics on the country's youth are all too familiar. More specifically, *Turning Points* (Carnegie Council on Adolescent Development, 1989), *A Portrait of Young Adolescents in the 1990s* (Scales, 1991), *A Matter of Time* (Carnegie Council on Adolescent Development, 1992), and *Fateful Choices* (Hechinger, 1992) underscore the at-risk nature of today's early adolescent. Many of these at-risk behaviors relate to character and values issues. A report from the Association for Supervision and Curriculum Development Panel on Moral Education (1988) identifies the disturbing trends in increased homicides, suicides, and out-of-wedlock births as contributing to the increasing concern about moral education in schools.

It would be easy to blame the mass media for the values crisis that confronts society today; however, this would not only be unfair, but counterproductive. On the other hand, it would be shortsighted to pretend that the media not only help shape our culture, but our values as well. The ASCD Panel on Moral Education names the mass media as one of those factors that has heightened concerns about the moral life of students today. Glasser (1990/91) believes that television, the most pervasive of the mass media, is a powerful moral teacher and that every show, whether it wants to or not, supplies an answer to the question, "What is ethical behavior?" Media today help fill a void created by other social institutions (e.g., family, church, and school) that do not exercise the influence they once did.

Another point regarding values and the media is raised by Arnstine (1977) in "Learning, Aesthetics, and Schooling: The Popular Arts as Textbook on America." Concerned with popular media, particularly television and film, Arnstine believes that the media may simply reflect and reinforce pervasive values. As a result, the media may create a sort of cultural inertia as they reinforce mainstream values but fail to suggest any action that might deal effectively with the forces at work that are transforming culture. An example can be found in consumerism and its attendant materialism, which is so prevalent in our culture today. Instead of questioning this value, the media reinforce it.

Loundsbury (1987) perhaps summarized best the need for moral education for early adolescents, stating that: "Education is a moral enterprise and middle school teaching is inherently a matter of morality. It cannot be otherwise, for all human behavior involves valuing. It is not a matter of whether we should teach values or not, but rather a matter of what values are we teaching" (p. 2). His comment has application for children and older adolescents as well.

A mandate to pursue character education needs to include a critical analysis of those socializing influences that help shape the values of the young. This chapter opens with a passage from the ASCD Panel on Moral Education, which poses the question: "How can schools encourage more responsible attention to the values content of the mass media or, failing that, counteract this influence?" (p. 45). Finding a home for more media literacy in the curriculum provides a suitable response. Students need to know how to decode and respond to the messages that they receive on a daily basis from the media. Fore (1990) has identified five such values that the media communicate: 1) happiness consists of material acquisitions; 2) consumption is inherently good; 3) violence is a legitimate way to solve conflict; 4) love and sex are synonymous; and 5) sexuality consists of satisfying one's own gratifications. In a field test for a program designed to help teenagers resist social and peer pressures to engage in early sexual involvement, these teenagers acknowledged pressure from the media. When asked about such pressures, more teenagers cited television than any other single source. Music followed television. Eighty-one percent of the teenagers indicated that they had recently heard songs that emphasized sex. Movies followed, with 70% of the respondents identifying this source of pressure. Advertisements from magazines and television constituted the final pressure, with 64% of the teenagers indicating they felt pressured to be sexually involved (Howard, 1985). Responding to a survey on what influences teen values regarding sex, one girl best summarized a frequent media message: "It's better on TV than in real life."

In his study of values on prime-time television, Selnow (1990) considered examples of portrayals of values incidents, and these incidents generally played an integral, if not principal, role in these programs. Moreover, these values are often portrayed positively. He did note that values are frequently identified with characters. Because law enforcement characters are overrepresented as characters with personal values, "Displays of positive values are linked strongly and disproportionately with authority and power figures. Such displays help perpetuate the cultural norm that associates goodness and positive values with the state, power, and recognized authority" (p. 72).

Research exploring the possibility of a link between moral development and character education and the media is difficult to conduct. Moreover, as Bryant and Rockwell (1994) have observed, this subject is considered taboo because it tends to overlap with things "religious." They conducted a series of experiments on the effects of massive exposure to sexually oriented prime-time television programming on adolescents' moral judgements. The results of these experiments are significant. They concluded: "For teenagers, who are one of the most vulnerable groups of family members, heavy exposure to prime-time television programming featuring sexual intimacy between unmarried persons can clearly result in altered *moral judgment*" (p. 195). Bryant and Rockwell added that, given the amount of this type of sexual behavior on television, some teenagers' moral values might be affected. They also noted that some factors clearly mitigate, if not eliminate, this kind of effect altogether: a well-defined family value system, free and open discussion of television programming, and *active and critical viewing.*

Rock music has been widely regarded as a negative influence on adolescents' values. As noted previously, some heavy metal and rap songs contain lyrics that have been identified as sexist and violent. Clearly, the lyrics of some of these songs are cause for concern. As Leming (1987) has observed in his study of rock music and the socialization of moral values, to have some impact on values, students must first be able to "attend to the music with sufficient sensitivity to be aware of any moral message and must define those messages the same way adults do" (p. 369). How much of rock music lyrics adolescents actually understand is not clear. Researchers have reached different conclusions. Greenfield et al. (1987) found that lyric comprehension develops with age and that the intended lyrics are often misunderstood. Rosenbaum and Prinsky (1987) surveyed junior and senior high school students about their favorite songs. Respondents could explain only 37% of their favorite songs. Miedzian (1991) notes that there is reason to believe that fans of HSS (homicide, satanism, suicide) rock music, which contains some of the most objectionable lyrics, spend more time listening to this music and know the lyrics of their songs better than those of other rock genres. While Leming found some agreement in interpretations between adults and early adolescents, in some cases the adolescents found socially desirable values overlooked by the adults. While Leming concludes that popular music does influence values, the evidence suggests that their interpretations are also based upon the adolescents' existing value systems. Seventy-one percent of the adolescents in his study rejected one song's message because it advocated casual sex. Leming's findings suggest that adolescents are not simply passive listeners soaking up negative messages, as has been intimated by authors such as Gore and Miedzian. This does not mean that some rock music should not be overlooked as a source of values, only that the messages that young listeners hear may be very different from what adults hear.

An issue strongly related to moral values, as well as other aspects of life, is decision making. Children, and perhaps adolescents, are called upon constantly to make decisions, many of them moral or ethical. Recall that Havighurst (1972) listed constructing an ethical system as a key developmental task. Pertinent to the relationship between character education and decision making is the role the media might play in how decisions are made. Janis (1980) addresses this question, and while he looks at major questions such as choices concerning career, marriage, lifestyle, health, and the welfare of one's family and not values choices per se, his essay is relevant because values ultimately require action, which means making choices and decisions.

> Perhaps much of the power of television to influence the decisions of large numbers of people, whether for good or for ill, resides in its capacity to increase the availability of images of specific outcomes, desirable ones as well as undesirable. The greater availability of that particular image of any positive or negative outcome increases the probability of that particular image becoming dominant over images of other outcomes when people are trying to decide what to do. (p. 165)

Janis suggests that television contributes to individuals' personal scripts, that is, a "coherent sequence of events expected by the individual, involving him either as a participant or as an observer" (Abelson, quoted in Janis, p. 165). The key question is whether vicarious experiences based on television can be incorporated into individuals' personal scripts. Janis's observations can be generalized to include other mass media as well. There would seem to be enough evidence to date to validate Janis's suggestion. Both children and adults routinely avail themselves of countless mediated images, and some of those images are translated into behaviors.

Finally, depending upon how one frames the argument, the use of Channel One in classrooms presents an interesting dilemma for educators. In exchange for televisions and ten minutes of current events, schools allow Whittle Communications to show two minutes of commercials. This author has maintained since its inception that allowing commercials in the classroom sends students the wrong message. Rank (1993/94) argues that this is really an ethical issue. "The main issue is the presence of television advertising—of commercial persuasion—aimed at the audience of children within the classroom and sanctioned by the schools" (p. 52). In his mind this is exploiting children, and exploiting children is unethical. Rank is critical of Channel One advocates who avoid this question, as well as those who justify its use as a "reasonable trade-off." He notes that some teachers like the program because it entertains students. No doubt, some consider that Rank is overstating the case. But consider what has been written about advertising and youth culture thus far.

The tremendous commercial success of MTV has resulted because it has successfully delivered the youth market to advertisers. Recall the MTV executive's comment: "We own the fourteen year olds." Regardless of how one looks at providing class time for commercials, this means that advertisers have a captive audience of 12,000,000 students for two minutes a day. The rationale may be different, but the dynamic is the same. While Channel One is informing, the more important issue is the underlying message about the values of schools, Rank's choice of word, "exploitation," may be too strong, but his point is well made. Materialism is an important value to advertisers; inviting it into the classroom is difficult to justify under any circumstances, let alone for ten minutes of news and a television set. This point has not been lost on some school systems. The state boards of education of New York, North Carolina, and California have all argued against the adoption of Channel One for ethical reasons. As Muffoletto (1994) points out, historically, the curriculum and the institutional structures of schools have served a gatekeeper function "for keeping out selected world views and values and letting in others." As a result, "Requiring children, as a captured audience, to view promotional, noninstructional, and value laden programs (meaning advertisements) is a breach of trust" (p. 201).

PREPARING FUTURE CITIZENS

Fontana (1988) notes that television is a major determinant of what citizens know about history, economics, political systems, social issues, and interpersonal relationships. Preparing students to become good citizens has traditionally been one of the goals of American education. Similarly, media literacy has been concerned with issues of citizenship as well. Society faces a situation today where the numbers of voters, particularly young voters, has declined for the last two decades. Why? It is not enough to say that the American public is apathetic. A Kettering Foundation study [cited by Thoman (1992)] offers three reasons: that people lack knowledge of how the political system works; that people do not believe that they can make a difference; and that Americans do not feel like they have access, that is, there is no process for engaging policymakers to discuss their concerns and seek solutions. Thoman notes that the media bear directly on all three of these explanations. For example, Bowen (1992) argues that the communications industry has become so commercialized that the average citizen does not have the opportunity to have any input. He writes: "In this era of corporate journalism, citizen speech is either confined to letters to the editor or carefully packaged and labeled in public opinion polls. Responses which do not fit into polling categories are simply discarded or placed into the never-never land of 'other' " (p. 15).

The present situation is unlikely to change unless the education system can begin to school a generation of media-literate young people who understand the role of the media in the political process and are willing to change it. In *Charting a Course: Social Studies for the 21st Century* (Brody, 1989), a curriculum task force noted that one purpose of political science education in elementary and secondary schools is to teach students about the "realities" of political life. The report notes that another purpose for political science education should be to "develop an understanding of the capabilities and skills needed to participate effectively and democratically in the life of society" (p. 62). In a similar vein Atkin (1981) suggests that mass mediated political socialization can have important consequences to voting behaviors for two reasons. First, patterns of news exposure, political interests, and values in the prevoting years may carry over into adulthood. Secondly, the participation of prevoters in campaign activities and discussion with voters may have peripheral influence on those who are old enough to vote. Media literacy, as it relates to the political process then, is clearly needed if students are to understand these realities and develop the skills to participate meaningfully in this process.

A related issue is the mass media's impact on political socialization. The research in this area is not extensive. Political socialization as a specific area of study is relatively new. Political socialization is "the process by which a junior member of a group or institution is taught its values, attitudes and other behaviors" [Hess & Torney, quoted in Renshon (1977), p. 5]. As a process this socialization begins with emotional attachments to political figures and institutions in the elementary school years. During these years political concepts are quite global (Atkin & Gantz, 1978; Hawkins, Pingree, & Roberts, 1975; Conway, Stevens, & Smith, 1975). Chaffee et al. (1977) note that the mass media constitute the major source of political information for young people, with television and newspapers as the dominant sources. Moreover, they note that young people attribute to the mass media considerable influence in terms of their political opinions, as well as the power to inform. As a source of knowledge, the programming need not be strictly informational. Atkin and Gantz (1978) argue that entertainment programming can have important consequences for the child's development of cognitive and affective orientations towards political actors, issues, and institutions. For example, Dominick (1974) found that watching police shows was positively correlated with knowledge of one's civil rights when being arrested.

Hawkins, Pingree, and Roberts (1975) conducted a study using fourth, sixth, eighth, tenth, and twelfth graders during the Watergate hearings. Students received a list of sixteen problems from which they were to pick the three most important. They conducted three surveys over several months, with the final one following John Dean's revelations. Previously, no fourth grader had selected "honesty in government" as a problem. In the final survey 21% indicated it was. For eighth graders the percentage rose from 3 to 31% and for twelfth graders from 24 to 60%. Conway, Stevens, and Smith (1975) found a positive association between media use and fourth through sixth graders' perceptions of party differences. In their study of the CBS National Citizenship Test (which aired in November 1965), Alper and Leidy (1969/70) showed how resilient the effects of a single program could be. The study involved high school students. The program affected some of these students who expressed attitudes towards the constitutional laws discussed on the program. Some effects dissipated, while others could be found six months later.

Studies involving adolescent populations have shown that the media, particularly television, are a source of political information (Hirsh, 1971; Conway, Stevens, & Smith, 1975; Tolley, 1977; Rubin, 1978). In their survey of sixth and tenth graders' media uses, Greenberg, Ku, and Li (1989) found that these students relied heavily upon television for their news. Neither their findings nor those of Cobb (1986) indicated newspaper readership is a major source of news. Of the sixth graders surveyed Greenberg and his colleagues found that 68% depended upon television the most for news and 17% indicated they relied heaviest upon newspaper. By tenth grade these percentages changed somewhat—64% for television and 21% for the newspaper. Radio is used roughly 10% of the time when one averages the responses of these two grades.

Dominick (1972) examined the role of television as a teacher of political facts and attitudes among sixth and seventh graders. He concluded that the mass media are the primary source of information about government. In his sample roughly 80% name the media as their source of information about the president, 60% Congress, and 50% the Supreme Court. Of the media, students ranked television as the major source of information about the Supreme Court and the second most important teacher regarding Congress. In addition, he found that students who showed high usage of television for political information were more likely to believe that television commercials for candidates would help them make up their minds. Jackson-Beeck's (1979) study with middle school students revealed that newspaper exposure was a positive predictor for political information and interest, while television exposure worked in the reverse.

Tolley's (1973) comprehensive study on socialization to war found that parents were the dominant influence on attitudes related to the Vietnam War, while the media affected information levels the most. He also noted that children know more about war today than in any other generation in the past because of the media. Similarly, Hollander's (1971) study found that, among high school seniors, the mass media was the dominant source of information about the Vietnam War and war in general. Students cited television most often among the media, followed by newspapers and magazines. The mass media surpassed school as an information source by a considerable margin. There is ample evidence since the Gulf War to prove this point (Greenberg & Gantz, 1993). Rubin (1978) found that adolescents who viewed more television were less cynical politically. He concluded, however, that heavy viewing may have a negative impact on the acquisition of political knowledge and an understanding of how government works. Conversely, Berman and Stookey (1980) found a positive correlation between the extent of viewing and negative feelings towards various levels of government. Conway, Stevens, and Smith (1975) noted that media use contributed to civic awareness on a very concrete level for fourth through sixth graders. Contrary to their hypothesis, however, they did not find that heavier media exposure raised students' understanding of government at a more abstract level, for example, importance of political parties. Chaffee, Ward, and Tipton (1970) studied media use and effects among adolescents during the 1968 presidential campaign. They found media use produced gains in knowledge about the campaign. Moreover, the junior and senior high school students who participated in this study rated the media as more influential than parents, teachers, or peers in terms of developing political opinions. In their study of adolescents and the 1976 presidential debates, Hawkins et al. (1979) found that a majority of the students in their study watched some part of the debates. Moreover, these researchers concluded that viewing the televised debates did impact on political socialization.

Two factors regarding the media and political socialization should cause concern, given what has been written thus far. As noted above, adolescents rely on television news more heavily than any other source for information about the country, as well as for international news. Secondly, adolescents invest television news with a higher degree of believability than newspapers. Greenberg, Ku, and Li (1989) found that belief in news from television dominated the other media. Using a Likert Scale (1 equals very little and 4 equals very much), sixth and tenth graders rated their belief in TV news 3.1 and 3.3, respectively. Both grades gave newspapers ratings of 2.8. These findings have implications both quantitatively and qualitatively for learning about what is going on in the world. After commercials and infotainment are subtracted from the regular evening network news, there is some question as to how much of substance actually remains. Because of time constraints and ratings considerations (not that newspapers don't have similar constraints), television news cannot begin to approach the number of stories nor the depth of treatment that newspapers can. Given these data and Cobb's (1986) conclusion that the prospects of developing newspaper readership among half of the students she studied are not good, today's adolescent runs considerable risk of being both underinformed and poorly informed. Whether these habits can be reversed remains to be seen. Clearly, however, exploration of this topic would constitute part of a media literacy curriculum.

Comparative studies of Soviet and American adolescents regarding the news media and nuclear issues also point to the role of the media in providing information and shaping attitudes as well. Generally, students from Moscow knew more about nuclear issues than their American counterparts. While Soviet students also watched more television news and read more newspapers than American students, media use, combined with other factors such as age and school performance, served as a predictor of knowledge about nuclear issues in both countries. An interesting finding in this study was that, while students from both countries indicated television news was their major source of information, American students seemed to learn as much from newspapers (Andreyenkov, Robinson, & Popov, 1989). In their study of news media use and adolescents' attitudes about nuclear issues, Robinson, Chivian, and Tudge (1989) found a number of differences between Soviet and American adolescents, including greater use of the news media among Soviet youth. Adolescents in both countries demonstrated a relationship between media exposure and perceptions of greater nuclear risk and destruction. Moreover, in both the Soviet and American samples in the study, those adolescents who watched more television news and read more newspapers were more optimistic about the future, with this relationship being stronger among the Soviet youth. This is a significant finding, as the authors of this study note: "It is hard to see how the news media can be said to foster greater alienation (or 'videomalaise') given the solid positive correlations that prevail between media use and optimism about the future" (p. 113).

Adolescence is a period of political skepticism (Mereleman, 1972). Simultaneously, the evidence suggests that schools are neither the source of political information or civic values that we would like to believe (Merelman, 1972; Jackson-Beeck, 1979; Langston, 1969). At the same time Austin and Nelson (1993) maintain that television can serve as a "major bridge" for adolescents' (as well as immigrants') learning about the political world. Their research, as well as that of Adoni (1979), reveals that political learning from the media takes place within a complex relationship connecting the media, family, peers, and cultural background. Austin and Nelson (1993) found that the family establishes styles of communication that carry over into other contexts, including the media, which then become socializing influences in their own right. Adoni's work with fifteen- and seventeen-year-old Israeli students found that mass media use helps structure social contexts in which the adolescent can exercise newly acquired political orientations. He found a positive relationship between the strength of social relations with parents and peers and the perceived utility of the media in developing political attitudes. He concluded that "those adolescents who are well integrated in the primary groups can better 'use' the media for the development of their social identity" (p. 10). A somewhat disconcerting implication arising from the research of Austin and Nelson is that political knowledge predicted political efficacy, which is the belief that an individual's political participation will somehow make a difference in the political systems. They note that, if the source of this information comes from shallow coverage of politics via advertising and news bites, this may "have long-reaching consequences for political participation" (p. 431). This concern provides still another reason for helping students become media-literate, particularly regarding the world of politics as presented in the mass media.

GLOBAL AND MULTICULTURAL EDUCATION IN A MEDIA CULTURE

In the last five years multicultural and global education have received a great deal of attention in education circles. What is often forgotten in these studies is that a cultural understanding of others and the world is shaped by the media. Sometimes this learning is formal, at other times informal. Long before the explosion in electronic media, Lambert and Klineberg (1967) found that much of what American children learned about other nationalities came from the media. From a multicultural perspective media literacy addresses two issues. How do the media shape the images of one cultural group or another, and how do the media contribute to a particular ethnic or minority group's understanding of itself? On the influence of television on the ethnic identity of minority children, Takanishi (1982) writes: "Television serves as a socializing agent not only by the frequency of its presentation of blacks and other minorities, but even more potently through the multiple images it transmits about the values and appropriate roles for individuals of different ethnic groups" (p. 87).

Dorr (1982) points out as well that television can have three possible socialization effects. She notes that children are not simply passive receptors. They bring their own life experiences to viewing, and this can dramatically affect the way they view minority groups on television. Comstock and Cobbey (1982) provide examples of how racial and ethnic groups process television differently. Secondly, entertainment television provides an image of white power and prestige, which provides minority viewers with a picture of their place in society. Thirdly, for reasons mentioned previously, minority children looking to television for role models will find few to choose from. A summary of some of the research findings on the media and Afro-Americans can serve as an example. Poindexter and Stroman, in their review of the literature, found blacks were underrepresented on television, and when they did appear, their roles were minor, and they were depicted in low-status occupations. Television portrayed this minority group negatively and stereotypically. They also found blacks relied heavily on television figures for information, including information about themselves and their community. The work of Northcott, Seggar, and Hinton (1975) suggests that the civil rights movement may have contributed to a more favorable image of blacks on television for a time. Similarly, Berry (1980) refers to the improvement in the representation of blacks as "The New Awareness," arising out of the national attention given to the discontent of blacks following the Watts riots. Asante (1976) credits television with elevating black consciousness through its coverage of the treatment of blacks in the 1960s. If improvements have been made in the portrayals of blacks on television in the wake of the civil rights movement, Guerrero (1993) questions whether this has occurred in other media. In his study of the image of blacks in film, he argues that, in the interest of profits, movie companies (often part of huge mega-media conglomerates) do not want to make movies with any elements that might impinge upon their commercial success. Guerrero writes: "The commercial cinema system has continued to stock its productions with themes and formulas dealing with black issues and characters that are reassuring to the sensibilities and expectations of an uneasy white audience. These filmic images," he continues, "tend to mediate the dysfunctions and delusions of a society unable to deal honestly with its inequalities and racial conflicts, a society that operates in a profound state of racial denial on a daily basis" (pp. 162–163).

Allen (1993) summarizes these issues when he writes:

> The print and the electronic media, and especially cinema and television, have shown African people and other people of color in comedic stances and in degrading ways. The depictions have suggested that African peoples are not interested in and do not care about serious matters, are frivolous and irresponsible, and are unable to participate in the mainstream of U.S. society. Television has been notably powerful in implying, suggesting, and maintaining this myth. (p. 156)

Nor is this concern a new one. Cripps [cited in Kindem & Teddlie (1982), p. 195] observes that concern about Hollywood portrayals of ethnic minorities spans at least eighty years, when a group of blacks rioted in Boston in protest of D. W. Griffith's film *Birth of a Nation*.

Research conducted several years later for the Payne Studies validated these concerns. When Peterson and Thurstone conducted research on films and the social attitudes of children, they showed this film to children as part of their study. They found dramatic increases in negative racial attitudes, which lasted for months (Greenfield, 1984). As Greenfield points out, this study, although conducted over sixty years ago, underscores how a single exposure to a powerful film can impact a young person's view of the world. Using a medical model, Pierce (1980) argues that television contains "social trace contaminants." In medicine these contaminants are subtle but, over time, can destroy an organism. He believes that television contains just such elements of racism. Pierce finds these elements in sports, the news, television series, and advertising. Similar observations can be made about Arabs, Hispanics, Asians, and Native Americans (Shaheen, 1984; Hamamoto, 1993; Woll, 1980; Arias, 1982; Iiyama & Kitano, 1982; Morris, 1982; Geiogamah & Pavel, 1993; Greenberg & Brand, 1993).

In his exploration of the role of mass communication on racial consciousness, Winston (1982) offers an intriguing explanation of why television has perpetuated false and stereotypical images of minorities. He draws upon the formal features of television for his explanation:

> Television's basic communications technique — the transmission of information by a rapid succession of coded images — is neither discursive nor reflective. Although television can, of course, project ideas, it may be incapable of matching the capacity of print to present complex ideas and arguments. Free of the restraints of syntax and linear discussion, television conveys a "sense of authenticity" through the intrinsic superiority of the visual image, giving the viewer the impression that he or she has grasped a matter intellectually, when in fact only the absorption of definite visual images that *suggest* ideas and conclusions has occurred. It is simply easier for television to give the viewer the feeling that the images are accurately reflective of a complex reality than it is to achieve the same effect with print. (p. 173)

There is evidence to suggest young people construct their understandings of other ethnic and minority groups based upon media images. Dorr (1982) notes that, since most of us have relatively limited contact with other ethnic groups, television "could be especially potent in filling our experiential gaps with these groups — to the extent that television includes them in its world" (p. 29). Berry (1980) argues that the portrayal of blacks on television reflects and reinforces the images whites have of blacks, as well as their culture and social status. When Greenberg (1972) asked white elementary school children their source of information regarding appearance, talk, and dress of blacks, he got varying responses. Of those that had few direct experiences of blacks, for example, rural children who seldom lived near blacks or attended school with them, two-thirds cited television as their principal source of information. A third of surburban youth cited television. Conversely, urban youth, with their frequent contact with blacks, were the least likely to rely on television.

In *The TV Arab* Shaheen (1984) provides anecdotal evidence of young people developing stereotypical images of Arabs based upon media portrayals. In one case a group of students became angry when the teacher challenged television's stereotypical image of the Arab as the "bad guy." In her research using six- to eight-year-old white children, Graves (1975) found that, when minorities were positively portrayed in a cartoon, children's attitudes were more positive. Conversely, a negative portrayal resulted in more negative attitudes. Leifer, Graves, and Phelps [cited in Christenson & Roberts (1983), p. 87] found a similar reaction among viewers using prime-time television. Even commercials may impact and reflect how a particular group sees itself. Donahue, Meyer, and Henke [cited in Goldberg & Gorn (1983), pp. 137–138] highlighted the difference between how two groups viewed the same commercial. Compared to their white counterparts, black children saw the food in a McDonald's commercial as better than the food they received at home, and they viewed the family portrayed in the commercial as happier.

Lichter and Lichter (1988), in their study of adolescents, ethnic images, and television, produced some interesting findings. They found from high school students surveyed that 24% said that people on television are real life, and 26% said that television influences their racial and ethnic attitudes. This also supported the findings of Poindexter and Stroman [cited in Greenberg (1986)] noted previously, which suggested that black children tend to believe in the reality of television and to learn behaviors from television characters. The Lichters also reported that blacks use television more than any other group to learn about life, in that 51% reported they learned a lot from television, and 23% identified often with ethnic television characters. In her cultivation analysis of fictional blacks on television characters, Metabane (1988) found that blacks who were heavier viewers perceived racial integration as more prevalent, that blacks and whites were more similar, and that more blacks were middle-class. Dates (1980) found that black adolescents evaluated black television characters more positively than nonblacks and identified more strongly with black characters than whites.

Other studies indicate that young people can develop attitudes and understandings of other ethnic groups based upon the media, particularly television. Roberts et al. [cited in Christenson & Roberts (1983)] conducted a study using the television series *The Big Blue Marble,* a program specifically designed to help children in America develop more favorable attitudes towards children of other cultures. Nine to eleven year olds made up the study population. Summarizing the results of the study, Christenson and Roberts note that children experienced significant increases in their estimations of the well-being of children in other parts of the world and decreases in measures of ethnocentrism. The series had a greater impact upon younger children. In another study three to five year olds viewed two Canadian-produced *Sesame Street* inserts with Oriental and Indian children. The children who viewed these inserts showed a strong preference for playing with nonwhites, rather than whites, compared to the control group (Gorn, Goldberg, & Kanungo, 1976). Atkin, Greenberg, and McDermott (1983), contrary to their hypothesis, found only a limited effect of blacks on commercial television among fourth, sixth, and eighth graders. According to the authors of the former study, these seemingly contradictory results may be explained by two factors: one study involved younger children, and the latter study did not use programs intended to change multiracial attitudes. Kindem and Teddlie (1982), in their study of film effects and ethnicity, found that serious drama was effective in reducing ethnic prejudices, although the effects were strongest for those who were not "highly prejudiced."

The media are the major global educator in our society. (Consider that more people use the national television news than any other source for information about the world.) At the same time the media and other advances in telecommunications have linked the various countries of the world together. Africa provides an excellent example of the linkage between global education and media literacy. Home to over 500 million people and nearly a third of the United Nation membership, this continent represents a significant part of our global village. Africa is *terra incognita,* however, in the minds of too many citizens, teachers, and high school students (Lampton et al., 1990). What is known is frequently learned from the media, and that should be cause for some concern.

News coverage serves as an example. In a study of representations of race in network news coverage of South Africa, Kozol (1989) focused on the impact of visual imagery. She concluded: "In the news coverage of South Africa, visual images construct complex messages that primarily reinforce, although at times they challenge racist stereotypes" (p. 179). As evidence of this conclusion, Kozol noted black South Africans depicted as perpertrators of violence, their leaders elevated to celebrity status, and the failure to interview black South Africans in the same number as whites. This is the South Africa portrayed on the nightly news.

Of equal concern is the geographical bias in the media's coverage of the world. A study of the *New York Times* coverage of Equatorial and Lower Africa revealed that coverage was based upon economic interests of the United States and that violence got most of the front page attention (Charles, Shore, & Todd, 1979). Here, the failure to be included in news coverage creates not only a lack of information, but a sense of unimportance or what Tuchman has called "symbolic annihilation." Again, an example from Africa will make this clear. During the 1984 famine in Ethiopia, when 1 million deaths occurred, the international community responded with aid. Even the entertainment industry responded with a recording to raise money for relief efforts. In 1991 a more serious situation threatened the lives of nearly thirty times the number of people in the Horn of Africa. While CNN elected to do a weeklong series on famine, the other networks limited their coverage because of costs, difficult working conditions, and lack of interest. Explaining the lack of coverage, one reporter expressed the networks' reluctance because "they don't get much bang for their buck." She also noted that Americans have never paid much attention to news from Africa. The fact that this country pays little attention to the news about Africa may relate to the fact that the news media do not pay much attention to Africa. In a study aptly entitled *Television's Window on the World,* Larson's (1984) work mirrors earlier research on Africa. He examined how the U.S. networks covered international affairs. With the exception of three nations, the rest of Africa received very little coverage. When U.S. Network coverage did occur, it tended to involve crises, countries, and issues that reflected U.S. interests.

In those situations where information is presented, critical analysis is warranted. Medhurst (1989) demonstrates how what is presented as an objective documentary on television borrows from filmic propaganda techniques. Even television journalists question the way the world is presented on network television. Dan Rather (1990) notes that the networks rely on focus groups to find out which stories are more popular, instead of which stories are more important. Confirming research, he acknowledges that "we have, by and large, accepted the proposition that people don't care about foreign news, don't really care much about hard news at all" (p. 6). Forrest Sawyer (1988) speaks to the impact of commercialism on television news. He notes that, early on, television news lost money, but networks provided it as a public service. Today, television news is a tremendously profitable business (up to 40% of the profit for local stations). He observes that the business constraints of the news business make fair and accurate reporting difficult.

Textbooks contribute to the problem. Though not a mass medium, they do represent an important one because of their role in driving curriculum. When a committee of the Middle East Studies Association conducted a study of the image of the Middle East in secondary social studies texts (Griswold, 1975), they found numerous examples of error and bias. "This often occurs in regard to Islam and the Arab World when authors display latent prejudice abetted by careless research, poor writing and inadequate editing" (p. 25). The committee also pointed out that, comparatively, the Middle East received far less coverage in world history books, leading to cursory coverage in the classroom.

When the African-American Institute (Hall, 1977) surveyed educational materials in the United States, it identified thirty problems with the way Africa was treated, many of them textbook related. Among some of the problems the institute identified are the depiction of traditional societies as static, the treatment of physical geography in a vacuum, and the "dark continent syndrome." Nearly twenty years later, the American Federation of Teachers Education for Democracy Project has issued a series of papers on how school materials teach and mismatch world affairs. The papers on the Middle East and Africa note improvements; however, a number of problems are still in evidence (Rubin, 1994; Herbst, 1994).

In their examination of Australia in elementary social studies textbooks, Birchall and Faichney (1985) concluded the information was accurate but generalized. They concluded that, having been exposed to this information, "one might be excused for conceiving of Australians as far off, remote groups of desert dwellers, some of whom are aboriginal people who work on sheep stations, regulary attend the opera in Sydney, go surfing and own exotic pets such as kangaroos, koalas, and wombats" (p. 122). The problem is that, while this information is valid, it only represents about 14% of the population, thus having the effect of creating a stereotype, the authors contend. They note this picture is the equivalent of a picture of Americans as "Indian cowboys who visit Disneyland, go skiing, and have racoons and beavers as pets" (p. 122).

As noted previously, there is a tendency for the media to be more influential in the absence of direct experience or other information sources. Motion pictures, though not intended to be "educational," do provide a "multicultural and global educational window on the world." Kindem and Teddlie's (1982) research suggests that films can positively or negatively affect ethnic stereotypes and prejudices. Ukadike (1990) notes that much of our image of Africa has come from the movies. Nor are we inclined to challenge these images. "It is amazing how, when films with exotic images reach Western screens, their hollow content does nothing to diminish their anthropological value or rating. Nor is the audience inclined to seek detailed and accurate information for a true anthropological rendition of the culture" (p. 42). Guerrero (1993) has identified a number of stereotypes of blacks in commercial movies. Woll (1980) noted that, after considerable progreess in the movie portrayal of Latins, American films in the post–World War II decade heralded the "return of the greaser" image.

The recognition of the appeal and influence of comic books has generated debate as well. Mainstream comic producers such as the Marvel and DC Comic groups are producing comics with black super heroes. Nearly a quarter of the $700 million comic book industry is black (Waters, 1993). Dissatisfied with the dearth of black heroes and their stereotypical portrayals, four blacks formed their own company, Milestone Media, in 1991 and created their own series of comics to provide a black audience with their own heroes. Milestone later signed a distribution agreement with DC Comics. Not satisfied with a black hero whose alter ego is a successful conservative lawyer, another group of blacks formed another black comic book publishing company called ANIA, a Swahili term meaning protect and defend. Waters notes that there is an ongoing battle between these two companies over which is the best image to portray to black youngsters. As one of the ANIA partners noted: "When your superhero is a black Republican, that just doesn't work for inner city kids. Our stories are straight from the streets." The debate is significant because the issue is not comic book sales; it is over which black heroes best represent the black image—a concern that is based upon the assumption that these images affect impressionable young minorities.

In his call for media literacy and multicultural education, Considine (1994) summarizes this need:

> Given what we know about media content and the proclivity for stereotyping, we must begin to explore the way in which these media messages cumulatively construct a world view. We must also consider the way in which these messages can contribute to social attitudes. While a single media message seldom causes anyone to do anything, the repetitive nature of these messages can be influential particularly on impressionable young people whose identities and attitudes are still forming. (p. 12)

DEVELOPMENTAL TASKS AND THE MEDIA

In *Developmental Tasks and Education* Havighurst (1972) identifies three sources for the tasks he outlines in his book. Some tasks arise from physical maturation; others arise from the cultural pressures of society. The third source of these developmental tasks is personal values and aspirations. The media have some bearing on all three of the sources. Havighurst acknowledges the media as agents involved in these tasks, but only conservatively. The research cited in this book, however, demonstrates that the media have some connection to most, if not all, of the tasks that Havighurst identifies for middle childhood and adolescence.

It is beyond the scope of this book to examine the relationship between the media and all of these tasks; however, it is instructive to briefly mention the eight developmental tasks Havighurst outlines for the adolescent in order that the reader can see from the research that has been presented how relevant the media are in terms of contributing to the development, or perhaps the lack of development in some cases, of these adolescent tasks. The eight tasks he identifies are 1) achieving a new and more mature relation with age-mates of both sexes, 2) achieving a masculine or feminine social role, 3) acceptance of one's body and using the body effectively, 4) achieving emotional independence of parents and other adults, 5) preparing for marriage and family life, 6) preparing for an economic career, 7) developing a set of values and an ethical system as a guide to behavior, and 8) desiring and achieving socially responsible behavior.

Some of these tasks are clearly impacted by the media. For others the influence may be more subtle. Acceptance of one's physique would be a costly enterprise to the cosmetics advertising industry, which trades on women's fears that they never look good enough (Barthel, 1988). Preparing for an economic career is a case in point. The media may operate on two different levels. First, one's choice of an occupation is often guided by material expectations that are partially shaped by the media's version of "the good life." It is not at all uncommon to hear a high school senior announcing his or her chosen major "because that's where the money is." Secondly, the media are a source of information about various professions. Atkin, Greenberg, and McDermott (1983) found that, in self-reports among elementary children, almost half said that what they learned about occupations came from television. After the movie version of Woodward and Bernstein's *All the President's Men,* schools of journalism reported an upsurge in the number of applicants.

GENDER EQUITY AND MEDIA IMAGES

As noted in an earlier chapter, the media image of women has improved somewhat. Nevertheless, stereotypes still abound in virtually every arena, for example, sports and business. Recent studies on gender bias in the classroom indicate that students and teachers still have much to learn. It will be difficult to change behaviors without affecting some change in attitudes. This can only be accomplished by critically examining cultural images and understandings of gender. Not surprisingly, then, books on gender or women consistently note the mass media's role in the reconstruction of the female image. An additional concern is the portrayal of gender in textbooks. Sleeter and Grant (1991), in their content analysis of forty-seven textbooks written for first through eighth graders, from the core content concluded that these textbooks "have successfully addressed the gender issues mainly by eliminating most sexist language. Males predominate in most books; but even in books in which females have a major presence, females of color are shown fairly little. One gains little sense of the history or culture of women," Sleeter and Grant continue, "and learns very little about sexism or current issues involving gender. . . . The books convey the image that there are not real issues involving sexism today, that any battles for equality have been won" (p. 98). A particularly disturbing feature of the books analyzed is that minority women are rarely shown as change agents in the political, social, and economic struggle for equality. Despite images of gender in the media, these sources of images can be overlooked when working towards gender equity in the classroom. Grossman and Grossman (1994), for example, devote an entire chapter in their book *Gender Issues in Education* to excellent strategies for reducing gender-stereotypical behavior in the classroom. Examining gender images emanating from the media, however, is not mentioned at all.

There are numerous opportunities within the curriculum to address the image of women in our society, and to do so in any meaningful way necessitates an examination of the way females are portrayed in the media.

MEDIA MESSAGES AND HEALTH ISSUES

One avenue for addressing concerns about the state of health of students today is through health education. New advances are taking place in research, such as participatory research, and developing models for understanding how children and adolescents construct what it means to be healthy. As Frith and Frith (1993) and Davies (1993a) have pointed out, however, if the health education of young people is going to be useful, some critical examination of the media's health-related messages will be required. The media affect the health of students on a number of levels. Therefore, opportunities for introducing a media literacy component into health education curriculum are readily available. First, the media provide a source of health-related information, as in the case of sexual information. Secondly, the media, particularly advertising, provide a vast array of products and behaviors that have implications for the health of students. Smoking and alcohol consumption are the most obvious. Nutrition is another. Considerable research still needs to be conducted on the impact of mediated health messages on children and adolescents. At present, there is enough documentation to warrant teaching young people to bring critical analysis to bear on the health messages they are receiving on a daily basis.

THE NEW LEARNING

Development in communication technology has provided some profound questions regarding the nature of education, learning, and thinking. Recall Salomon's research. Davies (1993b) argues that the mass media are ushering in a new period of learning, which he refers to as "the new learning." The advent of this new learning literally turns the world into one big classroom. Based on the media as the dominant educator in this country, learning depends heavily upon visual imagery. While 8 million students watch Channel One daily, England (1983), in his study of teacher attitudes about television, found that only 49% of the respondents believed that it is the school's responsibility to teach students to become more critical viewers. There is little evidence that this percentage has changed much.

Masterman (1985) notes the contrast between education in the classroom, which is heavily print-based, and that outside of school:

> Schools continue to be dominated by print. To have difficulties in decoding print is, in school terms, to be a failure. Outside of school the most influential and widely disseminated modes of communication are visual. As we have seen, television is probably the most important source of political information in our society and is regarded by most people as the most reliable source of news, perhaps because of its ability to present a visual record of events. Even print itself is coming to be regarded as a visual medium. Layout, design and typography are widely understood to be a significant part of the total communication process, whilst even the term "print media" is frequently a misnomer, since in most texts print is rarely unaccompanied by visual images. (p. 13)

Masterman goes on to argue that it is only a matter of time before schools realize that they must teach students to analyze visual images critically. The increased use of video and other visual materials will require students to "assess visual evidence" and "will be a cross-curricula skill which will need to inform teaching and learning in all subjects" (p. 14).

Olson (1988) reasons that media literacy is a skill that one learns just as one learns to read the written word. "For all new media, new categories for interpretation and criticism must be developed and taught to children so that they will have interpretive skills that are as powerful as those exploited in the literate tradition" (p. 34). Boorstin's (1981) observation that things that appear on television are now considered more real than what actually occurs in real life holds true for the other media as well. Again, Olson points out that television is considered as authoritative as the *Encyclopaedia Britannica.*

Related to the issue of learning is a much deeper question of whether the media alter our concepts of thinking and intelligence. Papert (1993) notes that becoming literate involves thinking in a different way. Thus, becoming proficient at understanding the media, particularly the visual media, requires educators to examine how they expect students to think and, ultimately, how they learn. Here, a brief historical overview underscores this situation. Civilization began with the spoken word. The development of the alphabet led to the written word. The invention of the printing press eventually gave birth to what Postman (1985) has termed the *typographic mind.* He writes:

> In the eighteenth and nineteenth centuries, print put forward a definition of intelligence that gave priority to the objective, rational use of the mind and at the same time encouraged forms of public discourse with serious, logically ordered content. It is no accident that the Age of Reason was coexistent with the growth of print culture, first in Europe and then in America. . . . Almost all of the characteristics we associate with mature discourse were amplified by typography, which has the strongest possible bias toward exposition: a sophisticated ability to think conceptually, deductively and sequentially; a high valuation of reason and order; an abhorrence of contradiction; a large capacity for detachment and objectivity; and a tolerance for delayed response. (pp. 51, 63)

Culture was almost totally dependent upon the printed word until the advent of photography. However, the proliferation of visual images from advances in photography and commercial lithography, coupled with the development of advertising to sell the flood of products resulting from mass production in the latter part of the nineteenth century, changed all of that.

Some years ago, McLuhan (1978) addressed this question in an essay on the hemispheres of the brain and the media. Echoing Postman, McLuhan argued that the Western world is primarily left-brained. Ours tends to be a culture that thinks in a linear sequential fashion. He attributes the dominance of the left brain in the West to the invention of the phonetic alphabet, which, in turn, shaped our experience of the world. Conversely, the media today, particularly the visual media, appeal to the right brain. "Today, the paradox is that the most recent Western technologies are electronic and simultaneous, and are thus structurally right hemisphere and 'Oriental' in their nature and effects" (p. 58). As a result, the media are creating a "right-hemispheric environment" in a culture that thinks in a left-brained fashion. One may take issue with McLuhan's assumption that this situation creates a "formula for complete chaos." His observations, however, do point to the need for helping young people think in a fashion that helps them understand the media.

CONCLUSION

There is every indication that the current level of influence the media play in the lives of children and adults will continue to grow. This media presence is a fact of life—one that cannot be ignored. Even so, there is still controversy over the need for media literacy in our schools. Once students exit the four walls of the school, they enter a much larger classroom in which the media function as a "parallel school system." It would be a mistake to underestimate the tremendous amount of learning that is taking place in this extended classroom. This level of learning is so great that the mass media can legitimately be described as affecting a "reschooling of society," beginning in the preschool years. For all of these reasons, it is incumbent on educators to help students become critical users of the media if they are going to be the best students and the most informed citizens that education wants them to be. The hidden curriculum need not be hidden any longer.

CHAPTER 10

Dimensions of a Media Literacy Curriculum

Television and the newer electronic media, if used wisely, have great positive potential or learning and development. They give children different mental skills from those developed by reading and writing.

Patricia M. Greenfield, *Mind and Media: The Effects of Television, Video Games, and Computers,* 1984

Someone once remarked, "Curriculum is like a suitcase. Every time you put something in, you have to take something out." Given the additions to the curriculum in recent years, the first response of teachers is understandably one of reluctance to add something else. Nevertheless, a careful evaluation of existing curricular objectives will yield opportunities for those "teachable moments" where introducing media literacy into a lesson can be done in such a way that teaching other curricular objectives can be accomplished more creatively. At the middle and high school levels media literacy can even be taught as an elective or an exploratory as well.

It is not the purpose of this chapter to present a detailed media literacy curriculum; rather, I identify the basic components of a media literacy program at the elementary, middle, and high school level. Reading through this chapter will provide teachers with some idea of the scope of a media literacy program. In order to move from theory into practice, the chapter draws on some of the best teaching materials available. As teachers, we not only want to know why, but how as well. And so this chapter includes a variety of activities from these resources and provides educators with a fuller picture of how the teaching of media literacy might be accomplished. In order to make these activities more accessible, the appropriate grade level—i.e., elementary, middle, high school—for each activity is provided. In some cases, however, the activity will require some modifications to make it more responsive to the needs of students of different grade levels. If an activity has been taken directly from a resource, I have noted its source. All of the resources from which I have borrowed activities are listed at the conclusion of the chapter and are easily obtained. Many are very reasonable in cost as well.

Virtually all of the activities presented in this chapter can be translated into instruction in such a way that objectives in the core curriculum are not compromised. On the contrary, they can be enhanced as one draws upon the daily media experiences of students to make those objectives more relevant.

One of the joys of being an educator is learning new things. Because both teachers and students live in a media environment, teaching students about the media can be both a learning experience, as well as fun. One of the most rewarding things for me in studying and researching what it means for students to grow up in a media-saturated culture is how much one can learn about their world.

INTRODUCING THE MEDIA

Those media that should be explored within the context of media literacy are television, film, radio, popular music, music videos, advertising, newspapers, the news media, and magazines. Some of these media clearly overlap. Advertising is common to all of these media, for example. Similarly, the news media are part of the world of both print and the electronic media. The point of departure for any media literacy program will be acquainting students with a basic model of communication, as well as the terms *media* and *mass media*. Given this understanding, as Considine and Masterman have pointed out, students need to develop some idea of how the media industry is structured. Research suggests that, as children grow older, they begin to develop some understanding of the economic structure of the media industry. Nevertheless, among older students, this understanding is often very rudimentary. This is not surprising when one considers that many adults do not understand the economic realities of the media either. Developing an appreciation for what Considine refers to as the "sources and structure" of the media is critical because it has both short- and long-term

Media Activity and Grade Level

Activity	Elementary	Middle	High School
Media log	X	X	X
Adventure in mass media		X	X
Media dependency check-up		X	X
Advertising inventory (TV)		X	X
Defining communication	X	X	X
Understanding media audiences	X	X	
Media scavenger hunt	X	X	
Media survey		X	X
Basic TV camera features	X	X	
Day without media	X	X	X
Programming strategies		X	X
Visual and aural codes	X	X	X
The pace of TV	X	X	X
Creating a storyboard	X	X	X
Making a flip book	X	X	
Exploring film shots	X	X	X
Analyzing film clips	X	X	X
Identifying film genres	X	X	X
Writing a movie review		X	X
Teaching films		X	X
Classic radio programs		X	X
Comparing TV and radio scenes		X	X
Radio survey		X	X
Looking at sound effects		X	X
"Radio days" interviews		X	X
Radio formats and advertising		X	X
Discussing pop music		X	X
Audience participation in pop music		X	X
Exploring music technology		X	X
Music and social issues		X	X
Audio and visual recall of music videos		X	X
Music video gender check		X	X
Music video jolt check		X	X
Values analysis of music videos		X	X
Product survey	X	X	X
Defining advertising/product evaluation	X		
Targeting audiences	X	X	X
Product placement	X	X	X
Ad "rip up"	X	X	X

(continued)

Activity	Elementary	Middle	High School
Advertising claims/appeals	X	X	X
Using vivid language		X	X
"The power of packaging"		X	X
"Ad up" exercise	X	X	X
Comparing new and old ads		X	X
The "human billboard"	X	X	X
Creating an ad	X	X	X
Elements of a newspaper	X	X	X
Survey of student readership		X	X
Writing press releases and letters to the editor		X	X
Tour a local newspaper	X	X	X
The inverted pyramid	X	X	X
Creating a front page	X	X	X
Researching newspaper statistics		X	X
Creating a Revolutionary War newspaper		X	
The media as information source	X		
Visual analysis of the news		X	X
Hard and soft news		X	X
News station tour	X	X	X
Ranking the newsworthiness of events	X	X	X
Creating a student magazine	X	X	X
Collecting magazine samples	X	X	X
Content analysis of magazine advertisements		X	X
Comparing print and film versions of literature		X	X
Censorship and parent advisory labels		X	X
Analyzing the "pseudo event"		X	X
Discussing political advertising		X	X
The rise of advertising and the second Industrial Revolution		X	X
Content analysis of science information in the popular media		X	X
Analyzing health related ads	X	X	X
Commercials on TV sports		X	X

consequences. Consider, for example, the trend towards the concentration of the media in the hands of fewer and fewer corporations. This pull towards the "privatization of information" needs to be understood by students because it can have profound implications for society, particularly this country's political and economic life.

In their media literacy curriculum for elementary grades, Lloyd-Kolkin and Tyner (1991) identify several objectives related to helping students develop a basic understanding of the media. While developed for elementary grades, these objectives have application for middle and high school students and can be explored at a deeper level. These objectives include the ability to define mass media and to list several examples, as well as to identify the various functions of the mass media. They also suggest that students describe their personal viewing habits and identify different rules about media use. Finally, Lloyd-Kolkin and Tyner's curriculum includes objectives on teaching students to consciously select and use media, as well as to consider the impact of television on their lives. These seven objectives represent an excellent beginning for helping students to begin to reflect on the media. Two additional elements that can be added to Lloyd-Kolkin and Tyner's list are teaching students a basic communication model and the economic features of media ownership. These additional features can be introduced at the elementary level; however, respecting the cognitive level of elementary grade students means that younger students will be able to have only a very basic understanding. The teacher can show younger students a rudimentary communication model, that is, sender-message-medium-receiver, whereas more sophisticated models can be employed with older students. For example, middle and high school students can more readily discuss the difference between the intended message and the message that is actually received.

Classroom Applications

Elementary, Middle, and High School

A number of media literacy resources include keeping a media log. *Media & You* (Lloyd-Kolkin & Tyner, 1991) even includes a worksheet (Figure 10.1) to assist younger students with their logs. Having students keep this kind of log helps them to identify the various kinds of media, as well as the amount of personal time that they actually spend in media consumption. For some students this activity can be quite revealing!

Your Media Log

Each symbol below equals one hour. Color in one symbol each time you use an hour's worth of media. Color in half a symbol for one-half hour. Follow the example below.

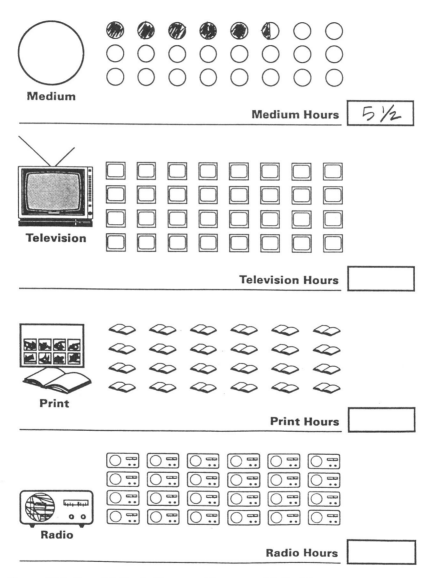

Medium

Medium Hours $\boxed{5 \frac{1}{2}}$

Television

Television Hours

Print

Print Hours

Radio

Radio Hours

Figure 10.1 From Media & You: An Elementary Media Literacy Curriculum *by Donna Lloyd-Kolkin and Kathleen Tyner (1991). Used with permission.*

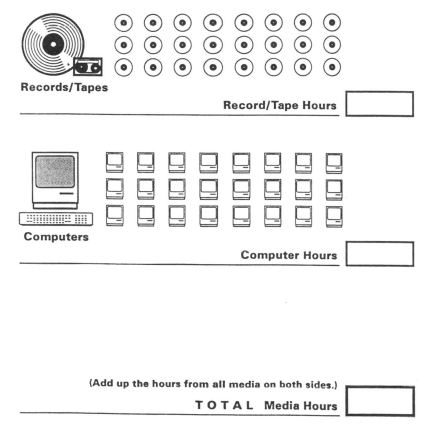

Records/Tapes

Record/Tape Hours

Computers

Computer Hours

(Add up the hours from all media on both sides.)

T O T A L Media Hours

Figure 10.1 (continued) From Media & You: An Elementary Media Literacy Curriculum *by Donna Lloyd-Kolkin and Kathleen Tyner (1991). Used with permission.*

The teacher can request that younger students keep a log for one evening and bring it to class the next day. A math class can provide an excellent setting for processing the logs along the lines of Lloyd-Kolkin and Tyner's suggestions. They recommend that the teacher have individual students report their media use, particularly television, and then total the number of hours for each medium on the board. A class average can be determined for each medium, and students can compare themselves to the class averages. Lloyd-Kolkin and Tyner also suggest that the teacher ask students to develop a list of activities that they might have done instead of using the media the night before. In addition, they suggest that students make lists of alternative activities and take them home to place by the television set to be looked at when they become bored with watching.

A manual for parents and teachers, *Television and the Lives of Our Children,* by DeGaetano (1993) has a television and video survey as well. DeGaetano's survey includes how many televisions and VCRs there are in the home and where they are located. Students also survey which are their favorite programs, who makes the program recommendations in the home, and whether they are asked not to watch certain programs. In addition, Considine and Haley (1992) recommend that media logs also include those persons present, that is, parent, siblings, or friends, when media are consumed.

Shrank (1991) suggests that students keep a media log for a week. Each day, they record how much time they spend with each medium. The students then take the three media they spend the most time with and multiply the time by fifty-two weeks per year. Using these times, the students translate how many years in their lifetimes that they will spend with each medium. Shrank also provides some interesting data from a survey on how much time people spend on other activities with which the students can compare. For example, the average American in a lifetime will spend six months sitting at stoplights, one year looking for "lost" objects, four years doing housework, five years waiting in line, and six years eating [from Lloyd-Kolkin & Tyner (1991), pp. 29–32; DeGaetano (1993), pp. 14–15; Shrank (1991), p. 9].

Middle and High School

In the introductory lesson from the *Mass Media Workbook* (Hollister, 1993), students are given a definition for medium, that is, "a channel or system of communication." This definition is then expanded to include communication with large numbers of people over time and space. One of the activities Hollister suggests is to have students experience an "adventure" in mass media. The teacher presents students with a list of ten famous people from the past before the advent of the electronic mass media. Students are asked to select four of these "celebrities" and bring them into the present and expose them to each of the major media. Students select an example of each of the media, which best typifies values held by today's audience. Then, they imagine their selected celebrities' responses and record their reactions. In another activity Hollister encourages students to participate in a media dependency checkup. Students rank their dependence on ten different media, including television, radio, advertising, and recordings. Then they graph the results and compare them with their classmates. Students give the survey to parents and grandparents, and the results are compared. Finally, students can learn a very quick lesson in the economics of the media industry by conducting an "advertising inventory" of one or several media. A class might even be divided into groups, with each group taking one medium. The teacher instructs students to record one hour of prime-time television. Using a stop watch, they can determine how much of that viewing hour is actually taken up with commercials. Likewise, any printed media can be examined quantitatively to see how much space is taken up with advertisements [from Hollister (1993), pp. 2–4, 7–10].

Elementary, Middle, and High School

Any definition of mass media is predicated on an understanding of communication. For elementary students Lloyd-Kolkin and Tyner (1991) distinguish between "face-to-face" and mass communication. Middle and high school students can explore this distinction in terms of interpersonal and mass communication. Regardless of the age level, all students need to understand the basic differences between these two forms of communication. Personal communication typically relies on more direct forms of communication, for example, talking, letters, and allowing for a response from the other party. Moreover, the message is intended for an individual or a limited number of persons. The mass media, conversely, are generally not interactive inasmuch as there is no allowance for clarification of the message and the message is one that is intended for a very large audience.

Elementary teachers can bring in a variety of different media or pictures or illustrations of media and have the students discuss them. Lloyd-Kolkin and Tyner also suggest that students search through their homes for examples of face-to-face and mass media. Older students can participate in a brainstorming session and see how many different kinds of communication they can come up with. The teacher should be prepared to include additional examples that students might not come up with, such as early forms of writing, sign language, and pictographs (Shrank identifies over two dozen). The teacher might want to make up two columns, listing personal communication on one side and mass communication on the other.

Previously, the four main functions of mass communication have been elaborated. These functions include to inform, to entertain, to persuade, and to transmit culture. At the elementary level students have the capacity to understand the first three at a basic level. Lloyd-Kolkin and Tyner suggest that the persuasion function for younger children largely be limited to the selling of products. Middle and high school students can develop a more sophisticated understanding through activities such as the analysis of political advertisements. Likewise, by relating the media to youth culture or gender images, teachers can help both the young and older adolescent to see the role that the media play in helping transmit and shape culture. Moreover, older students are able to sound the meaning of advertisements in terms of creating a spirit of commercialism and materialism. Students at all three levels should be able to make distinctions between the various media in terms of their functions. Generally, print media tend to be more informational, while broadcasts of the electronic media are heavily given over to an entertainment function. In the beginning each of the functions is introduced to students with an initial experience related to each function provided. Because the concept of function is so important, however, each of the four functions should be explored at greater length as they relate to each individual medium, for example, music videos both entertain as well as persuade and transmit culture.

Because the media have become so explicit in recent years, media literacy activities, which include using media, particularly with elementary age children should be chosen carefully and with parental cooperation. As noted previously, watching certain programming can be a frightful experience for children. Younger children might be asked to watch the weather and to discuss how that information might impact on them. The teacher might select suitable articles from the newspaper and bring them into class for discussion. Making the connection with entertainment is a rather straightforward task. Students can discuss their favorite programs and/or magazines and why they use them.

Once students understand a basic concept of communication and what the mass media are, then they can begin to explore other elements of media literacy, such as media influence and the audience. The dimensions of media influence and audience, like the functions of mass communication, need to be explored within the context of each individual medium. It is helpful, however, for students to have a basic understanding of who uses the media and what impact the media may have on the user, both individually and collectively. The teacher may want to give middle and high school students a brief explanation of media effects theories, based on the overview provided in a previous chapter. To make this more relevant to students, a "gratifications and uses" perspective should prove fruitful. Again, this makes the media experience immediately and directly relevant to them. As Davies (1993b) has noted, lecturing students about the "bad effects" of the media is counterproductive for two reasons. First, it communicates to students that media influences are rather straightforward and simple (the hypodermic needle theory), when they are not. Secondly, it turns students off. In examining rock videos, for example, it is important to get the students to explore the messages not only from an objective, but also a personal and more subjective, point of view. If media research has demonstrated anything, it is that young people often take away different messages from their media experiences than adults.

Elementary School

Lloyd-Kolkin and Tyner (1991) suggest an activity that helps younger children develop an appreciation for the various media audiences.

> Tell the students you'd like to talk about television with them. Which shows are their favorites? Let each student tell you his or her favorite show. Write the answers on the board in two columns, one for boys and one for girls (do not mark the columns "Boy" and "Girl" yet). Looking at the lists on the board, which are the favorite shows? Why do people like them? Students may respond in generalities, like "It's funny" or "It's scary." Ask for more specific reasons about why they like the show: Do you like the characters? Which character is your favorite? Why? Is this character like people you know in real life or is this character someone out of the world? What about the plots, the stories in the show? Are they things that could happen in real life? What do you learn from watching this show? Would you like to be like the characters? Why or why not? (pp. 25–26)

The teacher then pares down the lists, eliminating the duplicate programs. Boys are asked what programs they think girls like and vice versa. If the students don't see that boys and girls have different preferences, then the teacher tells the students that their responses were recorded by gender. The columns are then labeled "Boy" and "Girl." A third column is added, which contains programs that are favorites of both the boys and girls. Lloyd-Kolkin and Tyner note that the purpose of this activity is not to reinforce gender stereotyping but, rather, to show that different groups use the media in different ways, both as individuals and as groups. This sets the stage for later lessons on advertising where students learn that media are created to appeal to specific groups based on their mass media usage.

Having identified their favorite programs, the students can then discuss if their favorites are the same as those of their parents and other adults. Why or why not? This idea can be further expanded, and the students can discuss media preferences. Are some types of media used more by other groups? For example, parents might be newspaper readers, while teenage siblings probably spend more time listening to the radio [from Lloyd-Kolkin & Tyner (1991), pp. 25–27].

Elementary and Middle School

The teacher can plan a media scavenger hunt. A list of several examples of different media can be put together. Students can be divided into groups of four or five and given a short time period, such as a weekend or holiday, to work together [from Lloyd-Kolkin & Tyner (1991), p. 43].

Middle and High School

Children and adolescents, as well as adults, use a variety of media for a number of different reasons, that is, gratifications. Students can conduct a survey of their own reasons for media use. After they have brainstormed what some of those uses might be, they can develop a survey for themselves to fill out individually. Research cited previously can provide additional categories of gratifications that are relevant. For example, Greenberg, Ku, and Li (1989) developed the following categories of gratifications: relaxation, company, excitement, today's news, passing time, learning about life, forgetting problems, entertainment, learning about oneself, something to do, some thrills, getting away from what one is doing, fun, easing loneliness, calming down, and learning how to handle problems. The teacher might want to check the list from the brainstorming session against this list developed by Greenberg and his colleagues. For each category several different mass media are included. Students can tabulate the results and see if any patterns develop. Are there differences between males and females, for example? If the class is culturally diverse, do other differences emerge? Students might want to speculate on how answers might compare with adults, or they might want to even conduct the survey with adults and see if there are differences.

Against this background of understanding what the media are and how they are used, students can begin to explore the particulars for being media-literate in each respective medium. What follows is a presentation of those basic elements that should be included in a media literacy curriculum. It is by no means inclusive, but represents the key components.

TELEVISION

A number of elements make up a basic literacy for television. A brief overview of television history is helpful and can be found in any number of media texts. Students, with some assistance, will be able to identify the numerous television genres. This makes for a good introductory brainstorming project. Helping students distinguish between the form and content of television provides a good framework for how to approach the other media as well. Students should begin to analyze the different media in terms of these two categories as a matter of habit. Moreover, within the context of form and content, the teacher directs students to appreciate that each medium has its own strengths and limitations.

Understanding television's formal features is critical in order for students to be able to decode this medium. The formal elements of television can further be broken down into visual and auditory features. Among those that students need to analyze are the different kinds of camera shots and angles, sound effects, background music, other dubbed-in sounds such as laugh tracks on sitcoms, special effects, and story features such as narrative and plot. Another concept that is relevant here is called a "jolt." This is a term used in the media industry "to refer to moments of excitement generated by a laugh, a violent act, movement by people or objects within the frame, high decibels in the soundtrack, or rapid cutting" (Ministry of Education, 1989, p. 45).

It is helpful for students to understand how programming decisions are made on commercial television. The general rule of television programming is to try to hold the largest viewing audience for the longest amount of time possible. In its resource guide *Media Literacy,* the Ministry of Education of Ontario, Canada, has identified a number of programming terms with which students at the middle and high school level should be familiar.

Both young and adult viewers develop their own versions of social reality, based upon what they see on television; therefore, it is very important to get students to critically examine the way in which the television industry constructs social reality. A number of different themes are appropriate, depending on the age level of the students: the family, relationships (soap operas are very popular with adolescents), minority and ethnic groups, gender portrayals, social problems, sexuality, and various professions, for example, teaching, law enforcement, medicine, and politics. Students also need to explore which groups are rarely seen on television, for example, handicapped and the elderly, and discuss why this is so. The Pacific Mountain Network has produced an excellent video, *Creating Critical TV Viewers* (1992), which explores stereotypes on television, as well as several other themes such as the economics of this industry and how a television newscast is created.

Finally, television violence should be included as a media literacy component. Because it has become a fairly common staple in both children's and adults' programming, students are most certainly being exposed to it. Recently, the Center for Media Literacy has developed a workshop kit for helping students explore media violence, which can be obtained by writing the Center at the address listed in the Appendix. Considine and Haley (1992) note, however, that, before any discussion of television violence can take place, a definition of violence must be forthcoming. Because exposure to media violence is a sensitive issue, teachers need to be careful about how they deal with this issue. One discussion that is likely to generate considerable debate is whether viewing violence on television makes viewers more aggressive. Middle and high school students may even be able to explore some of the theories regarding the effects of media violence.

Classroom Applications

Elementary and Middle School

Students can develop an understanding of some of the basic features of a television camera with paper towel rolls cut into three different lengths. The shorter length reveals a larger field of vision, while the longer ones frame a smaller area. Students can learn about the different kinds of shots by trying each "lens" at different distances. Thus, they can see firsthand how a close-up shot is done. It is possible to simulate shots such as a pan or zoom by moving the lens slowly in a horizontal sweeping motion or moving forward or backward. Likewise, students can learn the different angles by positioning themselves, taking various positions and looking through the rolls.

Elementary, Middle, and High School

An activity suggested in many media resources is a day without the media. For younger children this activity would focus primarily on television since that is the most prevalent medium among this age group. Lloyd-Kolkin and Tyner (1991) suggest informing parents in advance to secure their cooperation. For middle and high school students a number of media should be included. This exercise performs a number of functions. It helps students identify their personal media habits in terms of both how much and why they use the media. Students can discuss how they felt about not having a particular media in their lives for a day. Another topic of discussion can center around what students did with the time that they ordinarily spent watching and listening. With older students the teacher should be prepared for discussion about the emotional reactions of students, given what the research shows in terms of media use for "mood management."

Middle and High School

This activity begins with the teacher sharing with the class the following terms as they are defined in *Media Literacy:*

- Audience flow is the carryover of an audience from one program to another on the same channel.
- Block programming is the running of similar shows to hold the same audience as long as possible.
- Blunting is a scheduling ruse designed to prevent a large audience from tuning into a competing network program by offering a similar program.
- Bridge is a form of blunting whereby, for example, a network will schedule a big miniseries at 8:00 P.M. to offset a big movie due to start at 9:00 P.M. on another network.
- Counterprogramming tackles a highly rated program on another network by scheduling a completely different program to deliver a different kind of audience.
- Hammock is the time period between two successful programs, where a new show can be introduced and guaranteed a sizable audience.

- Prime time is the time when there are more people watching television than at any other time of the day, that is from 8:00 P.M. to 11:00 P.M. on Mondays to Saturdays and from 7:00 P.M. to 11:00 P.M. on Sundays.
- Rating is the percentage of all homes with televisions that are tuned to a given program. Each rating point represents approximately 763,000 homes or almost 2 million people. Each rating point also represents about 10 million dollars in advertising revenue each year.
- Share is the percentage of all television sets in use that are tuned to a given program (Ministry of Education, 1989, p. 69).

Once students understand the terms, the teacher has them go through a copy of the local television listings and find examples of each of these programming strategies. While they will not be able to find examples of ratings or shares per se, they should be able to find an article in the entertainment section of their newspaper or an entertainment magazine that gives the ratings of commercial programs [from Ministry of Education (1989), pp. 69–70].

Elementary, Middle and High School

The following activity from *Meet the Media* is excellent for helping students explore the formal aspects of television:

Watch 10 minutes of any television program. (The content does not really matter). Read the questions below before you watch, but do not try to answer them yet.

Visual codes
(a) What did you learn from the performer's faces?
(b) What did you learn from the performer's movements and gestures?
(c) What did you learn from the way the characters were dressed?
(d) What did you learn from the background? Did the place of the action tell you anything about the characters?
(e) Which character(s) did the camera concentrate on? Which character(s) did we see in close-up most often?
(f) Did the camera change focus? Did the changes in focus shift your attention?

Aural (sound) codes
(a) What did you learn about the characters and the situation from what was said?

(b) What did you learn about the place and situation from the sound effects?

(c) What did you learn from the music? [from Livesley et al. (1990), p. 158]

After students understand that the economics of commercial television consists of attracting the largest number of viewers, the teacher has them brainstorm a number of different genres of programs that appear on the major networks. The teacher should make sure that Saturday mornings are included. Students then discuss each of these kinds of programs and what kind of audiences they are designed to attract.

One of the simplest and most effective ways to acquaint students with the fast pace of television is to have them track the length and number of cuts in a television program. This activity works better in pairs and can be done in the classroom or at home. One student should count (it won't be highly accurate because some scenes last only a few seconds) aloud to get a general idea of how long a scene lasts. The other student should record this information, as well as the number of cuts. The count need only last a couple of minutes. This activity is repeated for at least four or five different program genres, using the same amount of viewing time with each program. Students should be sure to include an educational program such as *Sesame Street* or *Mister Rogers' Neighborhood*. The teacher then has the students discuss the results. Are there variations in counts from genre to genre? If so, why? Which programs have the least? the most?

Creating storyboards is an activity that can be done at all levels, with older students generating a more sophisticated product. By making their own storyboards, students learn a very basic production technique used in most visual media. As a production technique storyboards serve as the outline or format that a program or advertisement will take. The teacher can create a series of boxes on a master that can be numbered and labeled by students (see Figure 10.2). At the elementary level a scene number and a very brief description of what is occurring in the scene will work. Middle and high school students might include the types of shots and duration of the scene, in addition to a description of what is occurring. Likewise, elementary students will want to create a storyboard that is brief and simple. Older students can develop longer sequences with greater complexity. Moreover, if a video camera is available, they might even be able to film based on the storyboard.

Your Name: _____

Tell Your Own Story

Plan your own TV program or ad the way TV professionals do. Use the storyboard frames below to plan your show by drawing each scene in order and numbering them.

Figure 10.2 *From Media & You: An Elementary Media Literacy Curriculum by Donna Lloyd-Kolkin and Kathleen Tyner (1991). Used with permission.*

MOVIES

Motion pictures are popular with students of all age levels. Again, it is helpful to begin by acquainting students with a short history of film. Shrank provides a very brief, but good, overview of the beginnings of the motion picture industry. Another good resource for a short history of film, as well as television, advertising, and radio is Inge's (1982) *Concise Histories of American Popular Culture.* Students need to be able to identify the four major types of camera shots: long shot, medium shot, close-up, and extreme close-up. They also need to be familiar with camera angles and movement and how they affect what is being filmed, for example, pan, zoom, track shot, dolly shot, and tilt. In addition, the teacher should familiarize students with elementary editing terminology/techniques: cut, dissolve, fade-in, fade-out, jump cut, and superimposition. Limpus's (1994) *Lights, Camera, Action: A Guide to Using Video Production and Instruction in the Classroom* is an excellent resource for helping students learn basic film terminology/techniques. Because it focuses on video, it can be used for other video-based media as well, such as television, music videos, and the news.

Because special effects have become such an important aspect of movie making today, students should spend some time learning what special effects are: fast and slow motion, freeze frame, animation, masking, changing colors, pop ons and pop offs, use of models or miniatures, and sound effects. Other aspects of film making appropriate for middle and high school students that the teacher might want to expose students to are costuming, props, lighting, background music/sound, and set designs.

Classroom Applications

Elementary and Middle School

Students begin by developing an understanding of how films are made, by exploring the concept of "persistence of vision," that is, an image stays in the mind until the next one appears. This explains why a series of individual images shown quickly appear as a fluid motion. They need to learn that the actual film of a movie consists of a series of still pictures moving through a projector at twenty-four frames per second. The teacher might want to share that, in the early history of movies, cameras were hand-cranked. "Over-cranking" (the term used at the time) thus exposed more film to produce slow motion sequences. Conversely, slowing the film down reduced the number of individual images and created a faster pace.

An excellent and inexpensive activity for helping students understand the idea of persistence of vision and how motion picture film works is to make a flip book. To be effective, students need three or four dozen cards of the same size. In *Media & You* Lloyd-Kolkin and Tyner (1991) include a ready-made flip book that students need only cut out and staple. Students decide on a simple sequence involving motion and draw a series of figures. Each successive card records a slight change in motion. (Students need to be reminded to position the figure in the same place each time.) The cards are numbered and stapled. When students flip through the book, the illusion of motion is achieved. If a large number of cards are used, students can experiment with what happens when cards are added or subtracted.

Elementary, Middle and High School

Familiarizing students with formal features of film making can be done in a number of different ways. Considine and Haley (1992) suggest giving students brief plot descriptions and then having them indicate what type of shot would be used. For example, they provide the following scene

- A platoon of soldiers marches across the desert.
- Some of the soldiers worry about the mission they are on.
- The enemy opens fire.
- One of the platoon is hit.
- His friend is shocked.

The teacher might even tell the students to make up their own scenes in which they must use so many types of shots and editing techniques [from Considine & Haley (1992), p. 206].

Another way to help students become more familiar with these formal features is to show film clips with examples of various shots and editing techniques. Have the students discuss them and why the film maker chose to use a particular technique.

Students of all ages should be able to identify the major film genres, including westerns, romance, comedy, sci-fi, fantasy, adventure-action, and documentary. With younger elementary age students the number of genres will be limited. For elementary and middle school students the teacher will need to help students develop an understanding of what the term *genre* means. Considine and Haley suggest providing a simple definition of genre as a type of story, for example, fairy tale, folktale, or fantasy. The teacher then brings the entertainment section of the newspaper to class and has the students look through the advertisements for movies to see how many different genres there are.

Middle and High School

In *Media Literacy* the Ontario Ministry of Education (1989) encourages middle and high school students to review films. This is an excellent way to combine language arts skills with critical film analysis. Because film reviews require a journalistic writing style, it also provides students with another type of writing experience. Students might want to read a couple of reviews from the entertainment section of the daily paper. Written by teachers, *Media Literacy* provides an outline for writing a movie review that can be adapted to the individual audience. The entire class can be shown a film appropriate to the grade level and can share or compare the reviews they have written.

Because of their wide variety and versatility, films can be used to enhance the curriculum in any number of ways. Recently, the National Council of the Teachers of English published *Reading the Movies: Twelve Great Films on Video and How to Teach Them* (1992) by Bill Costanzo, which provides an excellent list of films to teach, as well as ways to approach them. Films work very well in language arts. Because many novels are made into films, students can read the book and then watch the film. The number of ways to approach literature as film is virtually limitless. Comparing and contrasting sharpens thinking skills. Students can apply plot, mood, point of view, and other literary components to the film. Movies can easily be integrated into history and social studies. Students can study an important historical figure and determine what elements of his/her life should be included if the person's life was going to be made into a film. This helps them learn history, as well as experience the decisions that need to be made in trying to condense a person's entire life into a ninety-minute film. Considine and Haley (1992) provide an extensive list of historical persons who have been memorialized in film. Similarly, significant historical happenings have been powerfully captured on film. *All Quiet on the Western Front* provides a compelling portrait of trench warfare during World War I. *The Grapes of Wrath*, with its documentary-like character, gives students a powerful visual image of the poverty brought about by the Depression and Dust Bowls of the 1930s. With the necessary background students can also analyze the formal aspects of these films.

Examples of stereotypes in film abound. Any number of movies can be used to teach lessons in this regard. *Birth of a Nation*, for example, is an excellent film for teaching some of the early film techniques developed by D. W. Griffith, as well as the blatant stereotypes of blacks that persisted fifty years after the Civil War. Students might want to compare how images of groups have changed over the years, as in the case of the depiction of Native Americans in westerns.

A good way to demonstrate films as transmitters of culture can be accomplished by showing students movies with similar themes from different time periods. Teachers should keep in mind film content, however. An important rule for teachers is never to show students films that have not been previewed by the teacher first. *The Green Berets*, made early in American involvement in the Vietnam War, gives a much different picture than the films made in the 1980s after the nation had time to reflect on its experience.

Finally, film is an excellent medium for exploring moral issues. In his essay "The Power of Film," Mallery (1994) demonstrates how films can be used to explore moral issues. He notes that teachers should not assume that students will pay attention only to "schlock" or that movies have to be "old" or "classic" to be used. Mallery provides very practical suggestions for leading discussions about film in this manner. Rather than beginning with a formal question on symbolism or the message of the film, Mallery encourages teachers to begin a film discussion by asking a question like, "Can you point to a single moment in the movie when you found yourself moved?" Everyone should have an opportunity to respond so that the "serious discussers" don't take over early on. He also notes that it is important to get students to connect the characters in the film to real life. This moves viewers beyond generalizations such a "I hated it," or "Why did we have to watch *that*?"

RADIO

Radio represents the first of the electronic mass media. Studying radio will not require the time commitment that other media does.

Snow (1983) points out that there are more radios in this country than televisions and telephones combined, yet it is the most taken for granted of all the mass media. As noted previously, middle and high school students spend a lot of time listening to the radio. Because it is entirely aural, it represents an interesting medium.

As with television and film, students should read a brief history of radio. They will be particularly interested in the 1950s and the role the transistor radio played in the birth of rock 'n roll and youth culture. Students also need to understand the basic economic realities surrounding the radio industry. They will be most interested in the importance of radio to the success of their favorite music groups. Additional elements that students need to explore are the various uses of radio, other than listening to music, the variety of radio stations/formats, various uses of sound, and voice-overs.

Classroom Applications

Middle and High School

An excellent way to introduce students to the study of the radio is using Orson Welles' Mercury Theater dramatization of H. G. Wells' novel *War of the Worlds*. The recording of this historical broadcast is readily available and provides a number of tie-ins with various themes. It is a very good introduction to understanding the power of radio (the absence of visual images). This broadcast also is a significant event in the history of radio, as hundreds of thousands of listeners believed that it was real. As a very popular medium during the Depression, students can explore the idea of the use of entertainment as a form of escape during periods of severe economic crisis. Because the radio version of *War of the Worlds* received so much attention, students can do a research project on what effects it had on listeners on that evening in 1938.

Hollister (1993) suggests the following activity in the *Mass Media Workbook* (pp. 122–124). In an exercise that helps underscore the advantages and limitations of different media, the teacher provides students with various scenes and asks them to analyze how radio and televison would handle them. In the first scene students are asked to describe an invasion of their community by ants, killer bees, roaches or rats. A second scene presents students with a little green Martian, a reptilian Venusian, or an extraterrestrial creature that looks like a normal earth person.

The teacher can show students a radio dial and explain the AM and FM bands. Students are then asked to listen to the radio and identify four stations on each band. They should take notes and be able to explain what kinds of programming are found on each station, such as music, public affairs, or news. A companion activity is to have students conduct a radio survey among their fellow students and adults of all ages. They can find out what stations different groups listen to, as well as when they listen and why. After the students have become familiar with the different types of radio stations and audiences, the teacher can lead a discussion on how stations try to deliver different market segments to advertisers.

In the absence of visual imagery, sound effects play an important role in radio programming. Have students work in groups and experiment with creating a variety of different sound effects and record them. Students can share their recordings and see if other groups can identify the sounds. Then they can talk about how the different effects they have created might be used in radio programming.

Schrank recommends that students identify and interview older persons who remember the early days of radio. The students can ask the interviewees about their favorite programs, how radio changed their daily activities, and how the introduction of television replaced radio. Another activity Shrank suggests is to have students listen to an hour of several different stations and list the products advertised during the hour. Students then examine their lists and find the relationship between the products advertised, the station format, and the intended audience [from Shrank (1991) pp. 262, 265].

POPULAR MUSIC

Middle and high school students can readily identify with popular music because it is so much a part of their environment. Teenagers will enjoy studying the early history of rock 'n roll in the 1950s. Today, the music recording industry is heavily dependent upon the adolescent market. Moreover, as noted previously, the electronic media (of which the recording industry is a part) try to create an environment to which youth turn to fulfill various needs. It is here, perhaps more than with any other media, that middle and high school students need to become aware of how the economics of the recording industry work, since they are one of the segments of the population most affected. The authors of *Media Literacy* note that the recording industry is the largest entertainment industry in the world, with sales of $5.5 billion in North America alone. Successful marketing is contingent upon promoting big stars. Promotional budgets typically exceed production costs, with adolescents making up the largest market.

As with other media some understanding of the technology for the production of music is necessary. This can easily be tied into a history of the recording industry, beginning with the early phonograph of Edison and extending to today's compact disc (CD). Students will learn that, just as recording technology has changed, so, too, have musical tastes over the decades, and as advances are made in recording technology, the potential for greater profitability increases! For example, following the development of the CD and it growing popularity, recording companies have made millions of dollars re-releasing older recordings on CD.

As noted at the beginning of this chapter, a key concept of media literacy is that the media construct reality. Because of the tremendous popularity of music among adolescents, this concept of reality construction has particular relevance. The addition of the music video provides a visual field that not only reinforces the power of music to construct reality, but also creates an additional reality in and of itself. Recall the research cited earlier on music television videos and commercials and gender roles.

> The lyrics of popular music have always played a major role in the construction of reality, particularly in the area of romance and love, and have influenced such associated constructs as masculinity, femininity, and the relationship between the sexes. These constructs are enhanced and intensified by the elements of rock video. The music contains melodic catch phrases called "hooks," the images are slickly designed, and the length, only three minutes on average, limits the images to intense flashes and impression. The result is a product that tends towards a construct that often reinforces sex roles, legitimizes violence, and stereotypes race as well. (Ministry of Education, 1989, p. 123)

Aiding students in their understanding of how popular music constructs reality can employ a number of approaches. Clearly, helping students explore how they resonate with music emotionally (and socially) is a good beginning. Helping students understand how music affects them provides a good point of departure for understanding the impact of music on society as a whole.

Classroom Applications

Because popular music is so important to adolescents, students will most certainly want to talk about this medium. The following are recommended in *Media Literacy* (Ministry of Education, 1989, p. 121) as good questions for generating discussion among students:

- What are some of the different types of popular music, and how do they differ in their lyrics, melody, and beat?
- Why are young people so intensely loyal to their favorite music (and antagonistic to other types)?
- What role does popular music play in your life? How does it influence your friendships? Does it give you a sense of identity?
- Why do young people think that popular music and rock videos "belong" to them? To what extent is this belief true?
- What feelings, needs, and wants of young people are communicated by the music, by the lyrics, and by the images of a specific rock video?

In his essay *Popular Music and Communication* Lull (1992) writes:

Audiences participate in popular music in ways that are physical (singing along, tapping, clapping, dancing, sexual arousal, and so on); emotional ("feeling" the music, reminiscing, romanticizing, achieving a spiritual "high," and the like); and cognitive (processing information, learning, stimulating thought, contributing to memory, framing perceptions, and so forth). (p. 19)

Share these three categories with students and discuss what they mean and how students experience music in these three ways in their own lives.

The teacher can explain to students that musical technology, like the sequencer and digital sampling music computer, can create music that is so flawless that the music must be "humanized," by programming irregularities into it so that it does not sound so sterile. For example, the Roland R8 drum machine includes a "feel" function that allows the user to add varying degrees of random error to make it sound like a "real" drumming sequence that includes human errors. The teacher can then share with the students Glenn Gould's observation as well. A concert pianist, Gould remarked, "Concerts as they are now known will not outlive the 20th century." Based upon these observations the teacher can have students discuss the implications of technology upon the recording industry. Does it have any impact upon them?

Once students have identified the impact of music on their own lives, they can examine its impact within the context of broader social issues. The power of a message set to music can be explored through the protest folk songs and rock music of the 1960s. Again, music was a critical component in the development of a youth culture in post–World War II America. The portrayal of drugs in music can be explored. Many adolescents number rock stars among their heroes. What does this say about our society?

MUSIC VIDEO

Few media innovations have impacted adolescent media consumption as much as music videos. Originally, European dance clubs played music videos to give music groups more exposure. Eventually, some of the videos made their way to the United States where cable television stations used them as filler between movies. When Warner Communications launched MTV in 1981, it quickly became one of the most popular cable stations with adolescents and young adults. To say that MTV has exercised a profound impact upon the entertainment industry would be an understatement. Not only the recording industry, but the television and film industry as well, have adopted an MTV format to broaden the appeal of their programs and products. Even educational television has taken its cue from MTV to make its programming more attractive. Political advertisements have been influenced as well. Finally, there is in advertising what Graham and Hamdan (1987), two youth marketing specialists, call an "MTV approach" in which brand information is presented in a "visually hip" way.

Because MTV acutally combines three media—popular music, television, and film—it shares some of the formal structures of each. The teacher can have students analyze music videos in this light and identify those features, for example, camera angles and rapid cuts. Criticisms of MTV range from being a "time waster" to promoting sexual violence to being a nonstop advertisement leading youth culture down the path of materialism. Because it represents a significant media experience for many adolescents, it is important to get them to learn how to become critical viewers/listeners. In *Media Literacy* (Ministry of Education, 1989) teachers are encouraged to get students to decode music videos from three perspectives: content, values, and aesthetics. This resource guide provides a number of excellent activities to help students accomplish these tasks.

Classroom Applications

Middle and High School

In his book *Music for Pleasure,* Simon Frith (1988), a sociologist of pop music, notes that there are three basic types of music videos: performance, narrative, and conceptual. Students can discuss what these categories mean, and the teacher can have students identify examples of each. Questions for discussion can include how they are similar or different. Do some videos combine elements of each?

An activity suggested in *Media Literacy* is to have students identify a rock video with which they are quite familiar. The teacher then asks the students to quote the lyrics from memory and then to reconstruct the visuals from memory. Students are then asked which of the two they remember most vividly? Why? Does this vary for different students [from Ministry of Education (1989), p. 127]?

The teacher can suggest that students perform a "gender check" on several videos. Things the students might look for are the differences in the way men and women are depicted. When and where do women appear in videos? Is there a difference in the way males and females are clothed? How are the relationships between the two genders portrayed? Is there a difference in the way the two genders act? How many men appear in rock videos in comparison to the number of women? Similar questions might be asked of commercials on music video stations as well. With a little training students might even want to conduct their own gender content analysis of rock videos and tabulate the results. The teacher can assist the students in brainstorming various categories that they might want to use to measure the differences between the genders. Groups of students are then assigned to watch music television at different times and count the number of times these measures appear. The teacher should inform parents of the nature of this kind of activity because some parents find watching music television objectionable. For more advanced students the teacher might want to share some of the findings from research on this topic, which can be found in the bibliography.

Again, in another exercise from *Media Literacy,* the teacher has students count the number of "jolts" in a variety of rock videos and then compare their findings for rock videos with those for sitcoms, cop shows, commercials, or scenes from feature films. The teacher then encourages students to offer explanations for the results [from Ministry of Education (1989), p. 127].

The teacher asks students to consider whether the media, including rock videos, are a source of values for young people and adults. Students then identify some of the values that are most important to them and write them on the board. A list of those values that seem to be most important to the class is compiled. Students than analyze a series of rock videos and identify those values which the videos seem to portray. What values are presented with which they agree or disagree?

ADVERTISING

Without advertising, most of the media would cease to exist. Schrank (1991) provides an excellent brief history of advertising in which he weaves the various approaches to selling products throughout its history. He notes, for example, that, before the nineteenth century, most advertising was informational in nature. The plethora of manufactured goods coming out of the second Industrial Revolution led producers to begin using an attention approach, for example, various styles of type and borders. Soon, this approach gave way to the repetition approach, which came into being when large newspapers insisted on a standardized type to insure that every advertiser was treated fairly. Beginning with a history of advertising allows students to see that the heart of the advertising industry is about economics, particularly selling products, and provides a good starting place for helping students to understand some of the basic economic realities underlying this particular industry. Part of acquainting students with the economics of advertising consists of having them develop an understanding of what a market is and, more specifically, how children and adolescents are viewed as an important part of the multi-billion dollar youth market. An additional feature of becoming literate in this area is for students to develop an appreciation for the variety of different kinds of advertising in the various media.

There are two essential components in developing media literacy regarding advertising. The first is to enable students to analyze and be critical of advertising claims. The second is to teach students the formal techniques and elements that go into a commercial to make products appealing. Because there are a plethora of products, often with few differences, companies rely on the power of advertising to get consumers to purchase their product over another. There are over 1200 shampoos on the market, for example.

Schrank identifies eleven different kinds of claims that one can find in advertising. Among these claims is "the weasel word" claim, which employs words that sound convincing, but really don't tell the consumer very much, such as "helps," "virtually," "refreshed," "enriched," "better." The "we're different and unique" claim invests the advertised product with an aura of superiority. Other claims Schrank includes are the endorsement or testimonial (often by a celebrity), the scientific or statistical claim, and the "water is wet" claim, which says something about a product that is true for any brand of the given product. For a complete listing and explanation of these claims, see "A Short Course in Advertising," *Understanding Mass Media,* Schrank (1991), pp. 86–92.

Just as there are different topologies for the variety of different kinds of claims that advertisers make, so, too, there are similar lists of the various kinds of appeals that advertisers use. Generally, advertising appeals are of one of two kinds: intellectual or emotional, with the latter being the most often employed. Considine and Haley (1992) note that most advertising is consumer-centered, rather than product-centered, with advertisers creating associations with attitudes and lifestyles that appeal to the intended audience/market.

The teacher may want to read Jib Fowles's (1986) "Advertising's Fifteen Basic Appeals" (based upon psychologist Henry A. Murray's list of needs) and Considine and Haley's (1992) list of associations and appeals to get a full range of the different kinds of appeals that advertisers use. While there is some overlap, each includes appeals not mentioned by the other. Fowles's essay originally appeared in *Et cetera* [39(3), Fall 1982] and sometimes appears in anthologies on mass media. Considine and Haley's list appears in *Visual Messages* (pp. 101–102). Lloyd-Kolkin and Tyner (1991) include a list of persuasive appeals as well in *Media & You* (pp. 115–116). Some of the appeals Fowles describes are the need for affiliation, achievement, attention, to feel safe, to satisfy curiosity, and guidance. The list from *Media & You* includes testimonials, using "plain folks," the big question ("Does she or doesn't she?"), and humor.

Classroom Applications

Because advertising is so ubiquitous and comes in so many varieties, there are countless activities that teachers can have students do in virtually any subject in the curriculum.

Elementary, Middle and High School
Before beginning a unit on advertising, the teacher might want to have students go to a store and record how many different brands of products there are. Student should look for products that are of particular interest to them. For example, elementary students could go to a toy store or a grocery store and look at breakfast cereals. Older students might look at clothing or personal care products. Students can share their results and discuss whether there are any major differences in brands.

Elementary
Lloyd-Kolkin and Tyner (1991) offer the following activity for introducing advertising to elementary students. The teacher prepares by collecting advertisements from several different media, including a newspaper, a magazine, a school lunchbox, radio, and television. The ads should be ones that the students will recognize and enjoy. Products from two of the ads should be brought to class as well. The teacher begins by telling the students that they are going to discuss advertising, and they are asked if they know what the word means. Definitions are recorded on the board. After several definitions have been shared, the teacher and students come up with a class definition. Lloyd-Kolkin and Tyner point out that the teacher needs to make sure that the ad has the following elements: a product/idea is presented, an advertiser pays for the presentation, it happens in the media, and the purpose is to persuade.

Students are then asked to think about ads that they remember. After several ads have been mentioned, the teacher shares some of the ads that he or she has brought to class. Unexpected ads such as for a T-shirt or an ad on a lunchbox are pointed out to the students and the teacher asks if they are surprised by them. The teacher then puts a chart on the chalkboard with the following headings:

Ad Product Medium Technique Message Purchase Evaluation

Using these headings as a guideline, students discuss a product. In the evaluation portion of the discussion, the teacher asks the students if anyone has purchased the advertised product. If so, did it work as the ad said? Because of the popularity of this medium with elementary students, most ads will come from television. As a follow-up assignment for homework, the teacher can request that students find an ad from a print medium for the next class [from Lloyd-Kolkin & Tyner (1991), pp. 119–121].

Elementary, Middle and High School

Another activity designed by Lloyd-Kolkin and Tyner, which helps students develop a better awareness of product appeal, as well as the concept of the targeted audience, requires several copies of magazines and/or newspapers. The teacher explains that the purpose of the activity is to help students learn about targeted audiences. Each student is given a newspaper or magazine and asked to find ads that appeal to three different audiences: mothers, children, and older people. The students cut out the ads, mount them on construction paper, and label them according to the audience for which the ad is intended. While designed for elementary students, this activity can be modified to be used with older students as well. For example, they might be asked to find ads that appeal to teenagers as well [from Lloyd-Kolkin & Tyner (1991), p. 127].

Product placement in commercial films represents a fairly recent venue of which advertisers do not make use. Companies pay hundreds of thousands of dollars to have their products featured in films. In this activity the teacher assigns students to watch several films appropriate to their age level and watch for products that are conspicuously featured in films. In preparation the teacher might tell them that, when Coca-Cola® purchased 49% of Columbia Pictures, Coke found its way into films made by Columbia until it sold out to Sony several years later. Students should also be alerted to the fact that product placement varies in degrees of subtlety. The teacher's resource guide for *The*

Glitter: Sex, Drugs and the Media contains a reproducible chart for students to record the products they find in the movies, as well as an extensive list of prepared questions for students to answer after they have recorded their data [from Human Relations Media (1994), pp. 31–33].

An activity that works well with all ages is what Golay (1994) calls "Rip Up Ads." The lesson has two parts. The first part helps students understand the generic, interchangeable basics of advertising images. Students are instructed to go through printed materials and look for examples of advertising where they can identify the brand name or image of a product, as well as an image of a person(s). The image of the person(s) might be a positive one, for example, happy, or negative, for example, sad or disappointed. The students then rip the ads into two parts, separating the product or brand name from the image. The torn ads are separated into two stacks. The teacher then has the students experiment, juxtaposing images from one ad with brand names or products from another. Golay suggests that students try it with different products and with several ads for the same product as well. As the students play with the images, they begin to see that they are interchangeable and that there is no intrinsic correlation between the image and the product advertised. Rather, the creator of the ad is using images to play on our needs and fears.

In the second part of this exercise, the teacher has students collect ads and sort them according to similar images, for example, idyllic couples or successful businessmen. The students produce the effect of saturation by then covering a wall or bulletin board with these ads. Golay maintains that "this saturation like a magnifying glass or an enlarger, allows the targeted audiences to discover in them a fantasy or a particular receptivity to these kinds of seductive images" [from Golay (1994), pp. 10–11].

Middle and High School

With practice, students can become very adept at analyzing advertising appeals and claims. The teacher can obtain copies of Lloyd-Kolkin and Tyner (1991), Schrank (1991), Considine and Haley (1992), and/or Fowles's (1986) lists and share them with the students. It helps to give them a copy of each list for this activity. Students are divided into groups, and each group is made responsible for collecting and recording advertisements and commercials from one of the mass media: television, radio, popular magazines, and music television. The teacher should try to have students cover as many different television stations and magazines as possible. Once the advertisements have been collected, the teacher has the students analyze each one and determine what kind of appeal or claim is being made.

Schrank points out that the teacher can spark some interesting discussion among students by finding some old advertisements – either in magazines at least ten years old or in books that reprint old ads. The ads can be photocopied and brought into the classroom. Students then examine how advertising has changed over the years and discuss whether the changes in ads mirror changes in society [from Schrank (1991), p. 99].

Students need to understand that advertisers begin to try to establish brand loyalty among children as young as three years of age. The teacher can encourage students to recall some of their own memories of advertisements, particularly from Saturday mornings. As a follow-up assignment, students can go to a toy store or grocery store (particularly the cereal aisle!) and watch children shop with their parents. Students should note children's reactions to the products and what kind of items they request. After students have shared the results of their store observations, they can discuss what they have learned regarding advertisements designed for children.

Advertisers are very adept at using language. The following activity can be useful in helping students appreciate the power of language in advertising:

> David Ogilvy, a very successful advertising executive, said that the first thing an advertisement has to do is to get the audience's attention. Vivid or unusual ways of saying something will often be an "attention grabber." Look at these examples:

Straightforward facts	Vivid language
Cancer can sometimes be cured.	Cancer is a word, not a sentence.
Sussan's has a wide range of clothing.	This goes with that at *Sussan's*.
Phone your family overseas.	Go home on the telephone.

> Collect some examples of advertisements that use "attention grabbing" language. Think up some catchy lines to advertise the following:
>
> (a) the post office

(b) save water

(c) road safety. [from Livesley et al. (1990), p. 38]

An element often overlooked is how products are packaged. Ewry (1988) classifies packaging as "permanent media" because it often remains unchanged for long periods of time. In his essay "The Power of Packaging," Ewry demonstrates the considerable research and marketing that goes into this endeavor. He provides case studies that the teacher can share with students. For example, Ewry shares how his company prepared a European chocolate product popular at Eastertime for the American market. By changing the name and the packaging, sales in the United States soared after it was introduced into this country. This case study is also interesting because this product, a chocolate egg, was marketed to children. The teacher can share Ewry's essay with students and then have them go to various types of stores and examine how different products are packaged. After the students compare notes, they can discuss packaging as a form of advertisement.

Elementary, Middle and High School

Students can participate in an "ad up." The teacher divides the class into groups and has them tally the number of ads they see over the course of a day (or week). Billboards should be included. The teacher may want to have students tabulate how many ads they would be exposed to in a week, a year, or a lifetime! Discuss with the students what effect encountering so many advertisements might have. To make this activity more effective, students can categorize the advertisements by kinds of products being advertised, for example, alcohol, tobacco products, beauty ads, or clothing.

An activity suggested in many resources is to have students create their own advertisement or commercial. It can be an ad for a real product or for some new kind of product. For example, the teacher resource book that accompanies the media literacy video *The Glitter* includes an activity based upon marketing an edible necktie. The same resource guide also includes a media activity entitled "Are you a Human Billboard?" Students are asked to guess how many "branded" products they own. Students then take inventory of how many things they own in which they are acting as a billboard for the company's name, which appears on their bodies [from Human Relations Media (1994), pp. 37, 51].

NEWSPAPERS

Because the freedom of press played such a significant role in the founding of the United States, students should be exposed to an overview of the history of newspapers in this country. The role of yellow journalism in the Spanish-American War can make an excellent case study. Students need to have an understanding of the major positions of those involved in producing a newspaper, from the publisher down to the reporter. They also need to learn the basic steps in a newspaper's production.

The teacher will want to acquaint the student with what a layout is and what factors go into making decisions about what is placed where. Schrank (1991) observes that there are only two kinds of space in a newspaper: advertising and the news hole. How each is filled is an important part of the layout process. Students also need to understand the formal features of a newspaper. Why are different kinds and sizes of type used? When and why are photographs employed? Newspapers have a number of different sections and "pages" with which students should familiarize themselves, such as the local section and editorial page. They should learn how newspapers rely on wire services.

Although advertising is explored as a separate unit of study, students need to realize that, over time, newspapers have printed less and less news and more advertising. Themes that work especially well for newspapers as a medium are the issue of objectivity and the difference between fact and opinion.

Classroom Applications

Elementary School

Lloyd-Kolkin and Tyner (1991) suggest the following activity to introduce the newspaper as a topic for study. While developed for elementary students, it will work well for middle school students as well. In preparation the teacher brings several issues of the daily paper to class. The teacher goes through the newspaper, pointing out each section and writing it on the chalkboard. Students learn that the newspaper not only contains stories about what is going on in the world, but also all sorts of other useful information such as television listings and the weather. The teacher points out that the newspaper makes its money from ads to pay reporters and the costs of production. Particular attention is paid to the front page. The teacher identifies the basic parts of the front page (see Figure 10.3) for the students and explains each one,

Your Name: _____

The Newspaper

Write the name of the newspaper part on the correct line.
Use the list of terms at the bottom of the page.

Figure 10.3 From Media & You: An Elementary Media Literacy Curriculum *by Donna Lloyd-Kolkin and Kathleen Tyner (1991). Used with permission.*

noting that the most important stories are on the front page, with the most important one receiving a headline.

After this orientation to the newspaper, the teacher divides the students into groups of four and gives them a copy of the newspaper. Students are then given a list of specific information to find and are instructed to write it down. Students then share their information with each other [from Lloyd-Kolkin & Tyner (1991), pp. 139–141].

Middle and High School

The teacher has students take a survey among their classmates to determine how many read the newspaper. Students who use the newspaper are then surveyed to find out how often they read, how long they read, and what sections of the paper they read.

To stimulate interest in reading the newspaper, the teacher can clip a newspaper story that is of interest to students. After the students discuss the story, they write a letter to the editor.

Schrank (1991, p. 229) suggests the following issue for students to discuss:

> A fairly large percentage of news that makes up the main section of a newspaper is crime: murders, robberies, arson, riots. What do you think is the effect on readers of the news decision that crime is front page news. Do you think crime should be so important? What kinds of crimes are rarely reported?

If possible, the teacher can obtain copies of press releases from a local government office, school, or business. After the releases are read, the teacher has the students analyze the releases and discuss what kinds of information they provide. How is the information presented? The students then write press releases about an event(s) at their school.

Elementary, Middle, and High School

Producing a newspaper on a daily basis is a highly complex process. Most major newspapers will provide students with a tour. If the teacher can schedule a tour of the local newspaper, students are asked to record all of the steps that go into its production as they take the tour. An optional pre-activity is to have students do a little research on newspaper production in the past. Today, the use of computer technology is revolutionizing the way newspapers are produced. Students might even speculate about what form a newspaper might take in the year 2014!

The next two activities from *Media Literacy* (Ministry of Education, 1989) were designed for middle and high school students but can be used with elementary students with some modifications.

> Discuss with students the way newspaper copy gives the reader the story in the inverted pyramid structure (in order of descending importance). Why does a newspaper usually structure its facts in this way? What does it tell us about the factor of speed in newspaper work? About the factors of space and layout? (Reporters may not always know how long their stories will be or how, exactly, their stories will appear on the page. Sometimes, the editors have to cut the story at the last minute, and most editors will begin cutting from the bottom.) (p. 158)

This activity provides students with an opportunity to use what they have learned about newspapers (Ministry of Education, 1989):

> Have students prepare a newspaper front page. Such an activity requires students to enact the various specialized jobs of newspaper publica-tion—reporter, editor, sub-editor, photographer, illustrator, advertiser, publisher—as well as reader. In addition, in writing and rewriting assignments, students will fulfill many of the traditional aims of the language-arts program. Final drafts of news items can be prepared by hand or by using computer software programs, which enable students to set columns, design graphics, and, generally, create a professional look. (p. 163)

Middle and High School

The teacher can have students research some of the statistical data on the newspaper publishing industry. Their research is guided by a number of questions. How many newspapers are there in the country? How many were there twenty years ago? How many are now owned by chains? Have there been any trends in ownership? What is the reader-ship of those newspapers that are owned by major newspaper publish-ing companies versus those that are not? The teacher may even wish to share sections of Bagdikian's *Media Monopoly* (1992) with students.

Middle School

In *Living History in the Classroom* (1993, pp. 81–87) Selwyn devel-ops media projects that combine media literacy and social studies. One activity he suggests is to have students create a Revolutionary War Era newspaper. After students have been sufficiently oriented to the newspaper, they can write stories on events from the war as if they were eyewitnesses.

NEWS MEDIA

Research suggests that adults, as well as children and adolescents, tend to assign to the news media a level of credibility and objectivity that is not always warranted. Teaching students to approach sources of news critically has long-term implications, particularly in the area of citizenship. Some media literacy resources do not treat the news media as a separate medium because there is a news element to many of the mass media. Much like advertising, a good case can be made for examining this area independently, particularly for students growing up in the information age.

Schrank (1991) and Considine and Haley (1992) identify a number of elements that go into helping students become news literate. Schrank suggests beginning the study of news media by asking students how they would define news. Then he poses the question, "What is news?" He explains that several characteristics make something newsworthy: timeliness, significance of events, closeness to audience, importance of the people involved, dramas of human interest, and unusual events. Considine and Haley begin with the same question, noting that this question gives rise to four other questions: 1) Is news new? 2) To whom is it news? 3) Who determines what is newsworthy? and 4) Is it *all* the news? In attempting to answer these questions, students can learn to approach the news media critically. Within the context of answering these questions, students need to explore the concepts of hard and soft news.

The production process for reporting the news varies from medium to medium. Students need to explore what those differences are. A key concept here goes to Considine and Haley's question of who determines what is newsworthy. Exploring the concept of gatekeeping is essential with middle and high school students. Students should also appreciate that literally thousands of newsworthy things happen daily, but only a small number are actually reported in the news. Exploring who and how those decisions are made is of the utmost importance.

The question of objectivity in the gathering and presentation of the news needs to be examined at a basic level. Objectivity is one of the myths regarding news production. News is often staged and slanted. Sometimes what is not reported makes a more important statement than what is. Africa, for example, despite its size and population, receives scant attention in the news. And what coverage does occur is usually related to some crisis or disaster. This is the case because news is now a product that is sold much like any other commodity. In fact, students might want to examine how the major networks advertise their own news programs to get viewers to tune in. Students should also learn the role wire services play in providing a great deal of the news to the media.

Distinguishing fact from opinion is typically identified as a thinking skill. The study of newspapers provides an excellent forum for exploring this skill. After the teacher has explained the difference between the two, students can read the editorial section of the newspaper. Editorials usually represent a combination of facts and opinions. After the teacher makes copies of several editorials, they are distributed to the class. Working either individually or in groups, students read the editorials. Using two different colored markers, they highlight facts in one color and opinions in another. The students then discuss their findings. Some local news stations contain a daily editorial. As an optional activity students can be assigned to watch the news and listen to the editorial and note what the facts are that are presented or what the opinions are.

Classroom Activities

Exploring the news can occur at a number of different levels. The activities below, taken from various media literacy resources, point to some of the possibilities.

Elementary

To orient students to the concept of the news, Lloyd-Kolkin and Tyner (1991) suggest that the teacher tell the students that they are going to talk about how they know some of the things that they know. In preparation the teacher preselects two pieces of information. The first is a prominent news story that the students are likely to know something about. The second is an idea or piece of information that has been introduced in the class previously through media. Lloyd-Kolkin and Tyner note that it might be information about a distant country taken from an educational television program or a unique song learned from a record used in class. The students are asked what they know about the prominent news story or current event selected by the teacher. After they have shared what they know, the teacher asks them how they learned about the event. Students may mention a media source, a teacher, or a parent. If they learned the information from adults, the teacher asks them where the adults learned about it. As Lloyd-Kolkin and Tyner point out, the answer always comes back to the media as a source of information.

The next question posed to the students is about how the media learn about what is happening in the world. The teacher explains that it is the job of *reporters* to gather information. Reporters may work for local news media or for big television networks or news services. They are stationed in places all over the world. When something happens, they send their stories by telephone or another means of communication to their news organization, which either prints or broadcasts the story.

Finally, the teacher asks for a volunteer to tell the class something about the second idea or piece of information the teacher selected previously. Then the teacher asks the students how they found out the information. Again, the teacher directs the students to realize that the information was introduced to the class through a mass medium. The teacher concludes by pointing out to the students that much of what they learn beyond their immediate environment comes through the mass media [from Lloyd-Kolkin & Tyner (1991), pp. 137–140].

Middle and High School

Considine and Haley (1992) note the importance of visual analysis of the news. An activity they suggest is examining how the evening news opens. The following activity below is from their book *Visual Messages:*

> *The opening.* The beginning of the evening news is prepackaged to convey a sense of importance and authority. Some of this occurs visually and some of it occurs aurally. Compare the opening of the news on two or more networks.
> — What type of music is used? What does it suggest?
> — Is there a voice-over introduction to the news? What does it say? What is the tone? Is it a male or female voice?
> — Does the introduction begin with a logo or some form of graphics? If so, what is it?
> — Does the program start with the formal introduction of the top story, or does it use a "hook" and quickly preview the top two or three stories to grab your attention?

—When the first anchor appears, how do we first see him or her? Is the anchor in the studio or on location? Is the anchor sitting or standing? What is the anchor wearing? Is it a long shot, a close-up or a medium shot?
(p. 167)

After students have studied the concepts of hard and soft news, the teacher divides them into groups. Each group is assigned a different news medium. Each group analyzes the content of their medium for the amount of hard versus soft news. Both a national news and a local news broadcast should be included in this activity. The teacher then leads a discussion based on the following questions. Do some media report more soft news than others? If so, why? If the students served as news gatekeepers, would they change the mix between the two? Why or why not?

Elementary, Middle and High School

After students investigate how many television stations there are locally, the teacher can try to set up a tour of one of them. If possible, students should take the tour at a time when they can watch a live broadcast of the news. Students can also meet with one of the local news personalities and interview him/her about what he/she does.

The teacher creates a series of ten newsworthy events. They can be fictional or real. A copy of the list of events is given to each student, and they are instructed to rank them in order of importance from one to ten. Students share their rankings and explain why they ranked them as they did. With some modifications this activity can be used with elementary students as well. A more complex version of this activity can be found in *Critical Viewing* by O'Reilly and Splaine (1987, pp. 16–19). They offer twenty-five news stories. Students have to choose which stories and how long they would devote to each story. Moreover, the stories must fit within a nineteen-minute time frame because eleven minutes out of a thirty-minute newscast is devoted to commercials!

MAGAZINES

Developing media literacy regarding magazines has two critical components: the economics of the magazine industry and the messages of different types of magazines. Teachers should explain to students that the primary purpose of magazines is to develop a particular market segment to advertisers. This is not the reason students and adults buy magazines, but this is the reason publishers print them. The messages that magazines deliver depend on the particular magazine. Students should be familiar with the major magazine genres and be able to examine their content critically.

Classroom Applications

Elementary, Middle and High School

The following project is one developed by language arts teacher Diane Koch, who also teaches a media course to middle school students. It can be modified for all grade levels. After the students have studied magazines, Diane has the class create its own magazine. The only charge students are given is to create a news magazine that reflects their interests. Some of the stories and advertisements they may borrow from other magazines, and some are written by the students themselves. The class also conducts surveys on favorite television shows, movies, and athletes. This open-ended approach allows students to be creative and apply what they have learned in the class.

Schrank (1991) offers another idea that can be adapted for all grade levels:

> Using either *Writer's Market* or another reference source, find the name and address of a magazine that interests you. The magazine should be one you have not read before, perhaps one that is not readily available in your town. Write for a sample copy, explaining that it is for a school project; be sure to send the amount listed as the single copy price. Keep the magazines in a classroom collection for the duration of this course so others can see the variety that is available. (p. 245)

Younger children may want to talk to a librarian for ideas of magazines, rather than using *Writer's Market.*

Middle and High School

With 12,000 magazines in print, bookstores and newsstands carry a wide variety of magazines. To help students develop an appreciation for the number and variety of magazines, the teacher can have them go to a bookstore and survey the number of magazines they find. Moreover, students should try to identify the market for the magazines that they identify, as well as how many magazines are targeted at that market.

This activity combines the study of magazines and news. A question suggested for discussion in *Understanding the Media* (Schrank, 1991) is: "Do you think the need to show a profit and to sell advertising influences the kind of news the various media report?" After the students have discussed this question, they can conduct a content analysis of the advertisements in several women's magazines. What kinds of products are advertised? The teacher then explains to the students that cigarettes are the leading cause of cancer among women. Students are now prepared to discuss whether they think a magazine that accepts tobacco advertising would run an article on the health risks of smoking. The teacher might want to share some of the results of studies cited earlier on this issue in the section on media and health.

INTEGRATING MEDIA LITERACY INTO THE CONTENT AREAS: AN OVERVIEW

Language Arts

Studying media literacy in language arts is a natural. The National Council of Teachers of English has been at the forefront of promoting media studies for decades. Many of the books included on reading lists for students of all grade levels are also available on video. Language arts teachers can approach movies from any number of angles by combining the use of literature and film. With modest background reading, teachers can be ready to provide an overview of the formal features of film. The most direct approach is to compare these two media. Before viewing the films, some of the basic formal features of films can be explored. Students can then decide how these features affect the message and impact of the film. This kind of lesson can be a powerful tool for helping students to understand visual imagery, which is such an important part of today's culture.

One of the goals of language arts is to help students appreciate and use the power of the written word. As noted previously, advertisers are very adept at using language and, therefore, can provide still another avenue for exploring the power of language.

Math

While language arts and social studies have traditionally been viewed as the subject areas most accessible to media literacy efforts, math and science should not be overlooked. Because much of the media is a "numbers game," there are many different activities that students can do that tie in with this subject. The most obvious is collecting and processing data. Students can conduct media use surveys that include themselves, parents, and/or other adults. The data can be organized by any number of graphs. The advantage of these surveys is that it helps students to understand the pervasiveness of our media culture.

Social Studies

From current events to the Constitution, social studies provides many opportunities for teaching media literacy. For example, students can read the First Amendment to the Constitution of the United States and discuss the "free speech" clause and what it means. The teacher then brings to class a copy of a recording that contains the parental advisory label regarding explicit lyrics. The teacher explains to students that this is a warning that recording companies voluntarily place on recordings that contain lyrics that may be objectionable. Students then discuss the issue of censorship and free speech within the context of these advisory labels.

The media have dramatically altered the way politics are conducted in this country. One of the most obvious influences is on political campaigns. Teachers can obtain copies of one of the back issues of *Media & Values* on media and politics, which contain articles that make excellent discussion starters. Students can also explore the concept of the pseudo event, which takes any number of forms. Shrank (1991) defines this as "an event staged for the purpose of gaining time or space in mass media" (p. 359). Politics uses a number of these pseudo events, including the press conference. Students can analyze a press conference and look at the staged elements. In their work *Critical Viewing: Stimulant to Critical Thinking,* O'Reilly and Splaine (1987) offer a number of excellent activities for helping students explore politics and the mass media.

One of the greatest influences on political life in the last three decades has been the political advertisement. Because these advertisements are frequently used to make judgments on the worthiness of candidates, they need careful examination. They can be approached on a number of different levels. One question that is of great importance is the cost. In a national election candidates must raise hundreds of thousands of dollars, much of it used for advertisements. A question students might debate is how this affects the political process. How do politicians raise this kind of money? Does the best candidate necessarily win if he/she does not raise sufficient funds to mount a successful advertising campaign? These questions have profound implications for the country's future citizenry.

While advertising has been around for a long time, it became increasingly important with the advent of mass production, beginning with the second Industrial Revolution. Manufacturers, such as Henry Ford, had to find a way to sell the products that factories were producing at an unprecedented rate. This is an excellent opportunity for introducing students to the concept of advertising and the economics behind this business. As industry grew, advertising became an industry in and of itself.

Science

Many of the technological developments in the media lend themselves to the exploration of students. In fact, by using the media as a starting place for science concepts such as radio and sound waves, motion, light, lasers, and chemical reactions, these topics have increased relevance.

For those adults not in scientific occupations, the media serve as their primary, if not only source of scientific developments taking place in the world. Teachers can explain this to students and then have them do a content analysis of the popular media for science information. Not only should they look for how much attention the media give to science, but also what areas of science. Students can discuss their findings, as well as any implications they see in the coverage of science by the media.

Because technology is the application of scientific knowledge, students can explore any of the developments in the media industry that have taken place, particularly in the past two decades. For example, some students will find that there is a great deal of science behind recording technology. Students could do research on their favorite music groups and find out how much synthesized music is used in their recordings. Then they could do a research project on the "science of synthesized music."

Health/Physical Education

Historically, one of the appeals of many products, particularly cigarettes, is that they are somehow healthy. As this country has become increasingly more health conscious, advertisers have tapped into this concern among consumers. The teacher can have students collect advertisements for a variety of products that play on this concern about health and then analyze the ads carefully. How is the connection between products and health made? Sometimes they are overt and at other times more subtle. Cigarette advertisements, for example, almost never show smoke. People may be outfitted in exercise apparel. Health might be associated with being attractive. After students have analyzed the advertisements, the teacher should have them discuss how effective these ads are. What impact do they have on them?

The Center for Media Literacy (see Appendix) has produced *Selling Addiction: A Workshop Kit on Tobacco and Alcohol Advertising*. The kit includes a video that is used in conjunction with lessons, as well as a leader's guide with reproducible masters. Students examine how these two industries target populations and encourage them to start smoking and drinking and how they keep them engaged in these behaviors. The video includes commentary by health professionals, as well as young people.

O'Reilly and Splaine (1987) help students see how much and what kinds of advertising go into televised sports. Their lesson includes an account of a professional basketball game on television, in which students can see how many commercials are interspersed throughout a televised sporting event. Of equal importance are the kinds of products advertised, of which beer is one of the most prominent. O'Reilly and Splaine provide a series of probing questions for students to consider, for example, what message viewers might get when beer and car commercials are juxtaposed.

CONCLUSION

Making media literacy a viable part of the curriculum will occur only after teachers begin to view the mass media as both an opportunity and an appropriate subject worthy of serious academic inquiry. In a period of diminishing resources in education, the mass media provide a ready-made laboratory for study. Most of the activities contained in this chapter require minimal resources and can be accomplished

Integrating Media Literacy into the Curriculum

Medium	Subject		
	Language Arts	Social Studies	Math
Introducing media literacy	Defining mass media Defining communication Identifying media use/habits Functions of mass communication	The economics of the mass media: ownership/production	Analyzing media use
TV	Identifying different program genres Visual and aural codes	History of TV Social reality of TV, e.g., violence stereotypes	
Movies	Identifying various film genres Film analysis (writing movie reviews) Comparing print and film	History of the movies Comparing print and film Historical figures in film Stereotypes	
Radio		History of radio, e.g., depression and 1950s	Conducting and analyzing radio use surveys
Popular music	Analyzing lyrics	The economics of the recording industry Popular music and social issues Popular music's construction of social reality Values in popular music	

(continued)

Integrating Media Literacy into the Curriculum (continued)

| Medium | Subject | | |
	Language Arts	Social Studies	Math
Music videos	Analyzing lyrics	The economics of making music videos: music videos as advertisement The construction of social reality, e.g., genre Music videos as a source of values	
Advertising	Kinds of advertising Advertising claims/appeals	History of advertising Economics of advertising, e.g., markets, product placement How products are packaged Political advertisements Consumerism and commercialism	Conducting content analysis, e.g., "ad up"
Newspapers	Formal features of newspapers Elements of a news story: how stories are written	History of newspapers Censorship and freedom of the press Elements of a newspaper Advertising and the economics of the newspaper industry Newspapers as a source of information	Conducting and analyzing a readership survey

(continued)

Integrating Media Literacy into the Curriculum (continued)

Medium	Subject		
	Language Arts	Social Studies	Math
News media	Defining news What is newsworthy?	Defining news What is newsworthy? Gatekeeping Economics of news: news as a product News as a source of information about the world Hard and soft news What is objectivity? Distinguishing fact from opinion	
Magazines		Economics of magazine industry delivering a market	

Medium	Science	Health	Other	Not Subject Specific
Introducing media literacy	The role of technology in mass media	Media habits Functions of mass communications		
TV		Social reality of TV		Features of a TV camera Pace of TV TV audiences

(continued)

255

Integrating Media Literacy into the Curriculum (continued)

Medium	Subject			
	Science	Health	Other	Not Subject Specific
Movies	History of movies (persistence of vision)		Study foreign language through films	Camera shots Editing techniques
Radio	How radio works, e.g., sound waves		In music radio can be explored as an important medium for music	
Popular music	Recording technology, e.g., CD, synthesizers	Health related messages, e.g., drug usage	Identifying music genres	The targeted audience
Music videos				Pace of music vidoes
Advertising	Analyzing health related advertisements	Analyzing health related advertisements	Advertising design can be integrated into art	
Newspapers			Newspaper photographs can be explored in art Computer classes can examine the critical role this technology plays in the newspaper production process	
News media	How is scientific information reported in the news			How news is gathered Visual components of the news

with surplus media materials, such as magazines, from around the home or school. Ideally, a time will arrive when all school districts will provide the resources and teacher training, and media literacy will take its place as a mandated part of the curriculum. In the meantime, working on their own or in small groups, teachers can search through the existing curriculum for opportunities to help their students to critically analyze and reflect on one of the most important cultural forces at work in our society today.

RESOURCES

Considine, David M. & Haley, Gail E. (1992). *Visual messages: Intergrating imagery into instruction.* Englewood, CO: Teacher Ideas Press.

Costanzo, William (1992). *Reading the movies: Twelve great films on video and how to teach them.* Urbana, IL: National Council of Teachers of English.

Creating critical TV viewers. (1992). Denver, CO: Pacific Mountain Network.

DeGaetano, Gloria (1993). *Television and the lives of our children: A manual for teachers and parents.* Redmond, WA: Train of Thought Publishing.

Dorman, William A. (1994). Mass media and logic: An oxymoron. *Educational Vision,* 2(2):35.

Ewry, Edwin E. (1988). The power of packaging. In A. A. Berger (Ed.), *Media USA: Process and Effect* (pp. 445–455). New York: Longman.

Fowles, Jib (1986). Advertising fifteen basic appeals. In R. Atwan, B. Orton, & W. Vesterman (Eds.), *American mass media: Industries and issues* (pp. 43–54). New York: Random House.

Frith, Simon (1988). *Music for Pleasure.* New York: Routledge.

Golay, Jean-Pierre (1994). Rip up ads. *Telemedium: The Journal of Media Literacy,* 40(3–4):10–11, Madison, WI: National Telemedia Council.

Hollister, Bernard C. (1993). *Mass media workbook.* Lincolnwood, IL: National Textbook Co.

Human Relations Media (1994). *The glitter: sex, drugs and the media.* Pleasantville, NY: Human Resources Media.

Inge, Thomas M. (Ed.). (1982). *Concise histories of American popular culture.* Westport, CT: Greenwood Press.

Limpus, Bruce (1994). *Lights, camera, action: A guide to using video production and instruction in the classroom.* Waco, TX: Prufrock Press.

Livesley, Jack, McMahan, Barrie, Pungente, John J., & Robyn Quin, S. J. (1990). *Meet the media.* Canada: Globe/Modern Curriculum Press.

Lloyd-Kolkin, Donna & Tyner, Kathleen R. (1991). *Media & you: An elementary media literacy curriculum.* Englewood Cliffs, NJ: Educational Technology Publications.

Lull, James (Ed.). (1992). *Popular music and communication.* Newbury Park, CA: Sage Publications.

Lusted, David (1991). *The media studies book: A guide for teachers.* London: Routledge.

Mallery, David (1994). The power of film. *NAIS: Academic Forum* (Spring):11–13.

Masterman, Len (1985). *Teaching the Media.* London: Routledge.

Ministry of Education. (1989). *Media literacy: Resource guide.* Ontario, Canada: Ministry of Education.

O'Reilly, Kevin & Splaine, John (1987). *Critical viewing: Stimulant to critical thinking.* Pacific Grove, CA: Midwest Publications.

Selling addiction: A media literacy workshop kit. (1992). Los Angeles, CA: Center for Media Literacy.

Selwyn, Douglas (1993). *Living history in the classroom: Integrative activities for making social studies meaningful.* Waco, TX: Prufrock Press.

Schrank, Jeffrey (1991). *Understanding mass media.* Lincolnwood, IL: National Textbook Co.

Note: The resources listed here are by no means exhaustive. Two other important resources have been developed since this writing. *Images in Language, Media, and Mind,* edited by Roy Fox and published by the National Council of Teachers of English, contains several excellent essays on media images. The Center for Media Literacy has recently completed the development of *Beyond Blame: Challenging Violence in the Media.* These materials are available for both children and adult levels. The children's resource package has both an elementary and middle school curriculum, while the adult program is geared for both teenagers and adults. The Center for Media Literacy has recently expanded its catalog to include a large number of materials in addition to the many resources produced by the Center itself (see Appendix for address).

Add Busters/Media Foundation
1243 W. 7th Ave.
Vancouver, British Columbia
V6H 1B7 Canada
604-736-9401

Assembly of Media Arts
National Council of Teachers of English
Robert Happ
Hemstead High School
3715 Pennsylvania Ave.
Dubuque, IA 52001
319-588-5172

Center for Media Literacy
1962 Shenandoah
Los Angeles, CA 90034
1-800-226-9494
http://www.medialit.org

Center for the Study of Commercialism
1875 Connecticut Ave., NW
Suite 300
Washington, DC 20009
202-797-7080

Citizens for Media Literacy
381/2 Battery Park Ave.

Suite G
Asheville, NC 28001
704-255-0182
Fax: 704-254-2286

Consumers Union Education Services
101 Truman Ave.
Yonkers, NY 10703
914-378-2436

Educational Video Center
60 East 13th St.
New York, NY 10003
212-254-2848
Fax: 212-777-7940

National Telemedia Council, Inc.
120 E. Wilson St.
Madison, WI 53703
608-257-7712
Fax: 608-257-7714

Strategies for Media Literacy
1095 Market St.
Suite 410
San Francisco, CA 94103
415-621-2911
Fax: 415-255-9392

The Foundation for Media Education
26 Center St.
Northampton, MA 01060
413-586-4170
Fax: 413-586-8398

The Video Support Group
Park Tower #908
1617 27th St.
Lubbock, TX 79405
806-763-1458

Abelman, R. (1992). *Some children under some conditions: TV and the high potential kid.* Storrs, CT: National Research Center on the Gifted and Talented.

Adams-Price, C. & Greene, A. L. (1990). Secondary attachments and self concept during adolescence. *Sex Roles,* 22:187–198.

Adoni, H. (1979). The function of mass media in the political socialization of adolescents. *Communication Research,* 6(1):84–106.

Aiken, P. P., Leathar, D. S., & O'Hagan, F. (1985). Children's perceptions of advertisements for cigarettes. *Social Science & Medicine,* 21:785–797.

Aitken, P. P. (1989). Television alcohol commercials and under-age drinking. *International Journal of Advertising,* 8(4):133–150.

Alexander, A. (1985). Adolescents' soap opera viewing and relational perspectives. *Journal of Broadcasting and Electronic Media,* 29(3):295–308.

Allen, R. L. (1993). Conceptual models of an African-American belief system: A program of research. In G. L. Berry & J. K. Asamen (Eds.), *Children & television: Images in a changing sociocultural world* (pp. 155–176). Newbury Park, CA: Sage.

Alper, W. S. & Leidy, T. R. (1969/70). The impact of information transmission through television. *Public Opinion Quarterly,* 33(4):556–562.

Altheide, D. L. (1974). *Creating reality: How TV news distorts reality.* Beverly Hills, CA: Sage Publications.

Altman, D. G., Slater, M. D., Albright, C. L., & Maccoby, N. (1987). How an unhealthy product is sold: Cigarette advertising in magazines, 1960–1985. *Journal of Communication,* 37(4):95–106.

American Academy of Pediatrics News. November 1988.

American Psychological Association. (1993) *Violence & youth: Psychology's response. Vol. 1. Summary report of the American Psychological Association Commission on Violence and Youth.* Washington, DC: American Psychological Association.

261

American Psychological Association. (1985). *Violence on television*. Washington, DC: American Psychological Association Board of Social and Ethical Responsibility for Psychology.

Anderson, D. R. & Collins, P. A. (1988). *The impact on children's education: Television's influence on cognitive development*. Washington, DC: U.S. Department of Education.

Anderson, D. R. & Levin, S. R. (1976). Young children's attention to *Sesame Street*. *Child Development*, 47(3):806–811.

Anderson, D. R. & Lorch, E. P. (1983). Looking at television: Action or reaction? In J. Bryant & D. R. Anderson (Eds.), *Children's understanding of television* (pp. 1–33). New York: Academic Press.

Anderson, J. A. & Ploghoft, M. E. (1993). Children and media in media education. In G. L. Berry & J. K. Asamen (Eds.), *Children & television: Images in a changing sociocultural world* (pp. 89–102). Newbury Park, CA: Sage.

Andreyenkov, V., Robinson, J. P., & Popov, N. (1989). News media use and adolescents' information about nuclear issues: A Soviet-American comparison. *Journal of Communication*, 39(2):95–104.

Arias, M. B. (1982). Educational television: Impact on the socialization of the Hispanic child. In G. L. Berry & C. Mitchell-Kernan (Eds.), *Television and the socialization of the minority child* (pp. 203–211). New York: Academic Press.

Arnold, J. (1993). *A curriculum to empower young adolescents*. Midpoints (Fall). Columbus, OH: National Middle School Association.

Arnstine, A. (1977). Learning, aesthetics, and schooling: The popular arts as textbook on America. *Educational Theory*, 27(4):261–273.

Asante, M. K. (1976). Television and black consciousness. *Journal of Communication*, 26(4):137–141.

Association for Supervision and Curriculum Development Panel on Moral Education. (1988). *Moral education in the life of the school: A report from the ASCD Panel on Moral Education*. Alexandria, VA: Association for Supervision and Curriculum Development.

Atkin, C. K. (1983). Effects of realistic TV violence on aggression. *Journalism Quarterly*, 60(4):614–621.

Atkin, C. K. (1982). Television advertising and socialization to consumer roles. In D. Pearl, L. Bouthilet, & J. Lazar (Eds.), *Television and behavior: Ten years of scientific progress and implications for the eighties* (Vol. 2) (pp. 191–200). Rockville, MD: National Institute for Mental Health.

Atkin, C. K. (1981). Mass media effects on voting: recent advances and future priorities. *Political Communication Review*, 13–19.

Atkin, C. K. (1977). Effects of campaign advertising on children. *Journalism Quarterly*, 54(3):503–508.

Atkin, C. K. & Block, M. (1983). Effectiveness of celebrity endorsers. *Journal of Advertising Research,* 23:57–62.

Atkin, C. K. & Gantz, W. (1978). Television news and political socialization. *Public Opinion Quarterly,* 42(2):183–198.

Atkin, C. K., Greenberg, B. S., & McDermott, S. (1983). Television and race role socialization. *Journalism Quarterly,* 60(3):407–415.

Atkin, C. K., Hocking, J., & Block, M. (1984). Teenage drinking: Does advertising make a difference? *Journal of Communication,* 44:(2)157–167.

Atkin, C. K., Neuendorf, K., & McDermott, S. (1983). The role of alcohol advertising in excessive and hazardous drinking. *Journal of Drug Education,* 13(4):313–325.

Atwan, R., Orton, B., & Vesterman, W. (1986). *American mass media: Industries and issues.* New York: Random House.

Aufderheide, P. (1992). *Media literacy: A report of the National Leadership Conference on Media Literacy.* Queenstown, MD: The Aspen Institute.

Aufderheide, P. (1990). Good soldiers. In M. Crispin (Ed.), *Seeing through movies* (pp. 81–111). New York: Pantheon Books.

Aufderheide, P. (1986). Music videos. The look of sound. *Journal of Communication,* 36(1):57–78.

Austin, E. W. & Nelson, C. L. (1993). Influences of ethnicity, family communication, and media on adolescents' socialization to U.S. politics. *Journal of Broadcasting & Electronic Media,* 37(4):419–435.

Avery, R. K. (1979). Adolescents' use of the mass media. *American Behavioral Scientist,* 23:53–70.

Bagdikian, B. H. (1992). *The media monopoly.* Boston: Beacon Press.

Ball, S. & Bogatz, G. A. (1972). Summative research on *Sesame Street:* Implications for the study of preschool children. In A. D. Pick (Ed.), *Minnesota symposium on child psychology* (Vol. 6), (pp. 3–17). Minneapolis: University of Minnesota Press.

Ball, S. & Bogatz, G. A. (1970). *The first year of* Sesame Street: *An evaluation.* Princeton, NJ: Educational Testing Service.

Ball, S., Palmer, P., & Millward, E. (1986). Television and its educational impact: A reconsideration. In J. Bryant & D. Zillmann (Eds.), *Perspectives on media effects* (pp. 129–142). Hillsdale, NJ: Lawrence Erlbaum.

Bandura, A. & Walters, R. H. (1963). *Social learning theory and personality development.* New York: Holt, Rinehart & Winston.

Baranowski, M. D. (1971). Television and the adolescent. *Adolescence,* 23(6):369–396.

Barcus, F. E. (1983). *Images of life on children's television: Sex roles, minorities, and families.* New York: Pragers.

Baron, J. N. & Reiss, P. C. (1985). Same time next year: Aggregate analysis of the mass media and violent behavior. *American Sociological Review,* 50:347–363.

Barthel, D. (1988). *Putting on appearances: Gender and advertising.* Philadelphia: Temple University Press.

Baxter, R. L., De Reimer, C., Landini, A., Leslie, L., & Singletary, N. W. (1985). A content analysis of music videos. *Journal of Broadcasting and Electronic Media,* 29(3):333–340.

Benninga, J. S. (Ed.). (1991). *Moral, character, and civic education in the elementary school.* New York: Teachers College Press.

Beniger, J. R. (1987). Personalization of mass media and the growth of pseudo-community. *Communication Research,* 14(3):352–371.

Berger, J. (1972). *Ways of seeing.* London: Penguin Books.

Berman, D. R. & Stookey, J. R. (1980). Adolescents, television, and support for government. *Public Opinion Quarterly,* 44(3):330–340.

Berry, G. L. (1980). Television and Afro-Americans: Past legacy and present portrayals. In S. B. Withey & R. P. Abeles (Eds.), *Television and social behavior: Beyond children and violence* (pp. 231–248). Hillsdale, NJ: Lawrence Erlbaum.

Berry, G. L. & Asamen, J. K. (Eds.). (1993). *Children and television: Images in a changing sociocultural world.* Newbury Park, CA: Sage.

Berry, V. (1992). From *Good Times* to *The Cosby Show:* Perceptions of changing televised images among black fathers and sons. In S. Craig (Ed.), *Men, masculinity, and the media* (pp. 93–110). Newbury Park, CA: Sage.

Betterton, R. (Ed.). (1987). *Looking on: Images of femininity in the visual arts and media.* New York: Pandora.

Beuf, A. (1974). Doctor, lawyer, household drudge. *Journal of Communication,* 24(2):142–145.

Beyer, B. K. (1988). *Developing a thinking skills program.* Boston: Allyn & Bacon, Inc.

Birchall, G. & Faichney, G. (1985). Images of Australia in elementary social studies texts. *Social Studies,* 76(3):120–124.

Bird, S. E. & Dardenne, R. W. (1988). Myth, chronicle, and story: Exploring the narrative qualities of news. In J. W. Carey (Ed.), *Media, myths and narratives: Television and the press* (pp. 67–86). Newbury Park, CA: Sage.

Black, J. & Whitney, F. C. (1988). *Introduction to mass communication.* Dubuque, IA: William C. C. Brown.

Bogatz, G. A. & Ball, S. (1972). *The second year of* Sesame Street: *A continuing evaluation* (2 vols.). Princeton, NJ: Educational Testing Service.

Bollen, K. A. & Phillips, D. P. (1982). Imitative suicides: A national study of the effects of television news stories. *American Sociological Review,* 47:802–809.

Boorstin, D. (1981). The road to diplopia. In B. Cole (Ed.), *Television today:*

A close-up view. Readings from TV Guide. Oxford: Oxford University Press.

Booth, W. C. (1982). The company we keep: Self-making in imaginative art, old and new. *Daedelus,* 111(4):33–59.

Bowen, W. (1992). Not a bang, but a whimper. Citizens want to participate, but the media's roar drown out their voices. *Media & Values,* 58:15–17.

Brabant, S. (1976). Sex role stereotyping in Sunday comics. *Sex Roles,* 2(4):331–337.

Brabant, S. & Mooney, L. (1986). Sex role stereotyping in the Sunday comics: Ten years later. *Sex Roles,* 14(3/4):141–148.

Bracey, G. W. (1994). The media's myth of school failure. *Educational Leadership,* 52(1):80–83.

Brecher, E. J. (1993). Malled in your living room. *Miami Herald* (14 June).

Breed, W. J. & DeFoe, J. R. (1984). Drinking and smoking on television. 1950–1982. *Journal of Public Health,* 5(2):257–270.

Breed, W. J. & DeFoe, J. R. (1981). The portrayal of the drinking process on prime time television. *Journal of Communication,* 31(1):58–67.

Brody, R. A. (1989). Why study politics? In *Charting a course: Social Studies for the 21st century. A report of the curriculum task force of the National Commission on Social Studies in the Schools.* Washington, DC: National Commission on Social Studies in the Schools.

Bronfenbrenner, U. (1970). *Two worlds of childhood: U.S. and U.S.S.R.* New York: Russel Sage.

Brown, J. D. & Campbell, K. (1986). Race and gender in music videos: The same beat but a different drummer. *Journal of Communication,* 36(1):94–106.

Brown, J. D., Campbell, K., & Fischer, L. (1986). American adolescents and music videos: Why they watch? *Gazette,* 37(1):19–32.

Brown, J. D., Childers, K., Bauman, K., & Koch, G. (1990). The influence of news media and family structure on young adolescents' TV and radio use. *Communication Research,* 17(1):65–81.

Brown, J. D. & Schulze, L. (1990). The effects of race, gender, and fandom on audience interpretations of Madonna's music videos. *Journal of Communication,* 40(2):88–102.

Brown, J. F. (1993). Helping black women build high self-esteem. *American Counselor,* 2(1):9–11.

Brown, J. R., Cramond, J. K., & Wilde, R. J. (1974). Displacement effects of television and the child's functional orientation to media. In J. G. Blumler & E. Katz (Eds.), *The uses of mass communications: Current perspectives on gratifications research* (pp. 93–112). Beverly Hills, CA: Sage Publications.

Bryant, J. & Rockwell, S. C. (1994). Effects of massive exposure to sexually oriented prime-time television programming on adolescent moral judgement. In D. Zillman, J. Bryant, & A. C. Huston (Eds.), *Media, children, and the family: Social scientific, psychodynamic, and clinical perspectives* (pp. 183–195). Hillsdale, NJ: Lawrence Erlbaum.

Bryant, J., Alexander, A. F., & Brown, D. (1983). Learning from educational programs. In M. J. A. Howe (Ed.), *Learning from television: Psychological and educational research* (pp. 1–30). London: Academic Press.

Bryant, J. & Zillman, D. (1983). Sports violence and the media. In J. H. Goldstein (Ed.), *Sports violence* (pp. 195–211). New York: Springer-Verlag.

Buckingham, D. (1991). Teaching about the media. In D. Lusted (Ed.), *The media studies book: A guide for teachers* (pp. 12–35). New York: Routledge.

Buerkel-Rothfuss, N. L., Strouse, J. S., Pettey, G., & Shatzer, M. (1993). Adolescents' and young adults' exposure to sexually oriented and sexually explicit media. In B. S. Greenberg, J. D. Brown, & N. L. Buerkel-Rothfuss (Eds.), *Media, sex and the adolescent* (pp. 61–98). Cresskill, NJ: Hampton Press.

Burton, S. G., Calonico, J. M., & McSeveney, D. R. (1979). Effects of pre-school television watching on first grade children. *Journal of Communication, 29(3):164–170.*

Busby, L. J. (1985). The mass media and sex-role socialization. In J. R. Dominick and J. E. Fletcher (Eds.), *Broadcasting research methods* (pp. 267–295). Boston: Allyn & Bacon, Inc.

Busch, J. S. (1978). Television's effects on reading: A case study. *Phi Delta Kappan, 59(10):668–672.*

Campaine, B. M. (1980). The magazine industry: Developing the special interest audience. *Journal of Communication, 3(2):98–103.*

Cantor, J. (1994). Confronting children's fright responses to mass media. In D. Zillman, J. Bryant, & A. C. Huston (Eds.), *Media, children, and the family: Social scientific, psychodynamic, and clinical perspectives* (pp. 139–150). Hillsdale, NJ: Lawrence Erlbaum Associates.

Cantor, J. & Hoffner, C. (1990). Children's fear reactions to a televised film as a function of perceived immediacy of depicted threat. *Journal of Broadcasting & Electric Media. 34(4):421–442.*

Cantor, J., Mares, M., & Oliver, M. B. (1993). Parents' and children's emotional reactions to TV coverage of the Gulf War. In B. S. Greenberg & W. Gantz (Eds.), *Desert Storm and the mass media* (pp. 325–340). Cresskill, NJ: Hampton Press.

Cantor, J., Wilson, B. J., & Hoffner, C. (1986). Emotional responses to a televised nuclear holocaust film. *Communication Research, 13:257–277.*

Carnegie Council on Adolescent Development. (1993). *A matter of time: Opportunities in the nonschool hours.* Washington, DC: Carnegie Council on Adolescent Development.

Carnegie Council on Adolescent Development. (1989). *Turning points: Preparing youth for the 21st century.* Washington, DC: Carnegie Council on Adolescent Development.

Carroll, R. L., Silbergleid, M. I., Beachum, C. M., Perry, S. D., Pluscht, P. J., & Pescatore, M. J. (1993). Meanings of radio to teenagers in a niche-programming era. *Journal of Broadcasting and Electronic Media,* 37(2):159–176.

Chaffee, S. H., Jackson-Beeck, M., Durall, J., & Wilson, D. (1977). Mass communication in political socialization. In S. Renshon (Ed.), *Handbook of political socialization* (pp. 223–258). New York: Free Press.

Chaffee, S. H., Ward, L. S., & Tipton, L. P. (1970). Mass communication and political socialization. *Journalism Quarterly,* 47(4):647–659, 666.

Charles, J., Shore, L., & Todd, R. (1979). The *New York Times* coverage of Equatorial and Lower Africa. *Journal of Communication,* 29(2):148–155.

Childers, P. R. & Ross, J. (1973). The relationship between viewing television and student achievement. *Journal of Educational Research,* 66(7):317–319.

Chlubna, D. (1991). Childhood's end: A profile of the 11-year-old. *Advocate* (15 September).

Christenson, P., Begert, B., & Gunther, A. (1989). I sort of want my MTV: Children's use of music television. Paper presented to Western Speech Communication Association, Spokane, Washington.

Christenson, P. G. & Roberts, D. F. (1990). *Popular music in early adolescence.* Working Paper Series. Washington, DC: Carnegie Council on Adolescent Development.

Christenson, P. G. & Roberts, D. F. (1983). The role of television in the formation of children's social attitudes. In M. J. A. Howe (Ed.), *Learning from television: Psychological and educational research* (pp. 79–99). London: Academic Press.

Christian-Smith, L. K. (1991). Readers, texts, and contexts: Adolescent romance fiction in schools. In M. W. Apple & L. K. Christian-Smith (Eds.), *The politics of the textbook* (pp. 191–212). New York: Routledge.

Cobb, C. J. (1986). Patterns of newspaper readership among teenagers. *Communication Research,* 13(2):299–326.

Collins, W. A. (1983). Interpretation and inference in children's television viewing. In J. Bryant & D. R. Anderson (Eds.), *Children's understanding of television* (pp. 125–150). New York: Academic Press.

Collins, W. A. (1982). Cognitive processing and television viewing. In D. Pearl, L. Bouthilet, and J. Lazar (Eds.), *Television and behavior: Ten years of scientific progress and implications for the eighties* (Vol. 2) (pp. 9–23). Rockville, MD: National Institute of Mental Health.

Collins, W. A. (1973). The effect of temporal separation between motivation, aggression, and consequences: A developmental study. *Developmental Psychology,* 8(2):215–221.

Collins, W. A., Berndt, T. J., & Hess, V. L. (1974). Observational learning of motives and consequences of television aggression: A developmental study. *Child Development,* 45:799–802.

Compaine, B. M. (1980). The magazine industry: Developing the special interest audience. *Journal of Communication,* 3(2):98–103.

Comstock, G. (1989). *The evolution of American television.* Newbury Park, CA: Sage.

Comstock, G. (1980). *Television and America.* Beverly Hills, CA: Sage Publications.

Comstock, G., Chaffee, S., Katzman, N., McCombs, M., & Roberts, D. (1978). *Television and human behavior.* New York: Columbia University Press; originally published by RAND.

Comstock, G. & Cobbey, R. E. (1982). Television and the children of ethnic minorities: Perspectives from research. In G. L. Berry & C. Mitchell-Kernan (Eds.), *Television and the socialization of the minority child* (pp. 245–259). New York: Academic Press.

Considine, D. (1994). Media literacy and multicultural education. *Telemedium: The Journal of Media Literacy,* 40(1):8–14.

Considine, D. M. (1992). Media literacy: An instructional imperative. *Telemedium,* 38(1/2):1–2, 9–11.

Considine, D. M., & Haley, G. E. (1992). *Visual messages: Integrating imagery into instruction.* Englewood, CO: Teacher Ideas Press.

Conway, M. M., Stevens, A. J., & Smith, R. G. (1975). The relation between media use and children's civic awareness. *Journalism Quarterly,* 52(3):531–538.

Cook, T. D., Appleton, H., Conner, R. F., Shaffer, A., Tamkin, G., & Weber, S. J. (1975). Sesame Street *revisited.* New York: Russel Sage.

Cook, T. D., Kendzierski, D. A., & Thomas, S. V. (1983). The implicit assumptions of television. An analysis of the 1982 NIMH report on television and behavior. *Public Opinion Quarterly,* 47(2):161–201.

Corteen, R. S. & Williams, T. (1986). Television and reading skills. In T. Williams (Ed.), *The impact of television: A natural experiment in three communities* (pp. 39–84). Orlando, FL: Academic Press.

Costanzo, W. (1992). *Reading the movies: Twelve great films on video and how to teach them.* Urbana, IL: National Council of Teachers of English.

Covell, K. (1992). The appeal of image advertisements: Age, gender, and product differences. *Journal of Early Adolescence,* 12(1):46–60.

Cowan, G. & O'Brien, M. (1990). Gender and survival vs. death in slasher films: A content analysis. *Sex Roles,* 23(3/4):187–196.

Crabb, P. B. & Goldstein, J. H. (1991). The social psychology of watching sports: From illium to living room. In J. Bryant & D. Zillman (Eds.),

Responding to the screen: Reception and reaction processes (pp. 355–372). Hillsdale, NJ: Lawrence Erlbaum.

Crane, D. (1992). *The production of culture: Media and the urban arts.* Newbury Park, CA: Sage Publications.

Dale, E. (1935). *Children's attendance at motion pictures.* New York: Macmillan Company. Reprint edition, Arno Press. 1970.

Dates, J. (1980). Race, racial attitudes and adolescent perceptions of black television characters. *Journal of Broadcasting,* 24(4):548–560.

Davidson, E. S., Yasuna, A., & Tower, A. (1979). The effects of television cartoons on sex-role stereotyping in young girls. *Child Development,* 50(2):597–600.

Davidson, J. W. & Lytle, M. H. (1986). From Rosie to Lucy: The mass media's image of women in the 1950s. In J. W. Davidson & M. H. Lytle (Eds.), *After the fact: The art of historical detection* (pp. 364–392). New York: Alfred A. Knopf.

Davies, J. P. (1993a). Growing up in a media world: The case for media literacy in the middle school. Paper presented to the National Middle School Association, Portland, Oregon.

Davies, J. P. (1993b). The impact of the mass media upon the health of early adolescents. *Journal of Health Education,* 24(6):S28–S35.

Davies, J. P. (1991a). Transescents and the mass media: The need for a new literacy. Paper presented to National Middle School Association, San Antonio, Texas.

Davies, J. P. (1991b). TV and transescent social and emotional development. *Transescence,* 8(2):29–26.

Davies, J. P. (1990). The impact of television on transescent physical and intellectual development. *Transescence,* 9(1):44–52.

Davis, D. M. (1990). Portrayals of women in prime-time network television. Some demographic characteristics. *Sex Roles,* 23(5/6):325–332.

Deacon, J. (1994). Biceps in a bottle. *Macleans,* 2:52.

DeGaetano, G. (1993). *Television and the lives of our children: A manual for teachers and parents.* Redmond, WA: Train of Thought Publishing.

Denski, S. & Sholle, D. (1992). Metal men and glamour boys: Gender performance in heavy metal. In S. Craig (Ed.), *Men, masculinity, and the media* (pp. 41–60). Newbury Park, CA: Sage.

DeVaney, A. (1994). *Watching Channel One: The convergence of students, technology, and private business.* New York: State University of New York Press.

Dietz, W. H. & Gortmaker, S. L. (1985). Do we fatten our children at the TV set? Television viewing and obesity in children and adolescents. *Pediatrics,* 75:807–812.

DiFranza, J. R., Richards, J. W., Paulman, P. M., Wolf-Gillespie, N., Fletcher, C., Jaffe, R. D., & Murray, M. (1991). RJR Nabisco cartoon camel promotes Camel cigarettes to children. *Journal of the American Medical Association,* 266(22):3152–3158.

Dohrmann, R. (1975). A gender profile of children's educational TV. *Journal of Communication,* 25:56–65.

Dominick, J. R. (1984). Videogames, television violence, and aggression in teenagers. *Journal of Communication,* 34(2):136–147.

Dominick, J. R. (1974). Children's viewing of crime shows and attitudes on law enforcement, *Journalism Quarterly,* 51(1):5–12.

Dominick, J. R. (1972). Television and political socialization. *Educational Broadcasting Review,* 6(1):48–56.

Dominick, J. R. & Greenberg, B. S. (1972). Attitudes toward violence: The interaction of television exposure, family attitudes, and social class. In G. A. Comstock and E. A. Rubenstein (Eds.), *Television and social behavior (Vol. 3), Television and adolescent aggressiveness* (pp. 314–335). Washington, DC: Government Printing Office.

Dorman, W. A. (1994). Mass media and logic: An oxymoron. *Educational Vision* 2(2):35.

Dorr, A. (1982). Television and the socialization of the minority child. In G. L. Berry & C. Mitchell-Kernan (Eds.), *Television and the socialization of the minority child* (pp. 15–35). New York: Academic Press.

Dorr, A. (1980). When I was a child I thought as a child. In S. B. Withey & R. P. Abeles (Eds.), *Television and social behavior: Beyond violence and children* (pp. 191–230). Hillsdale, NJ: Lawrence Erlbaum.

Dorr, A., Graves, S. B., & Phelps, E. (1980). Television literacy for young children. *Journal of Communication,* 30(3):71–83.

Downs, A. C. & Harrison, S. K. (1985). Embarrassing age spots or just plain ugly? Physical attractiveness stereotyping as an instrument of sexism on American television commercials. *Sex Roles,* 13(1/2):9–19.

Drew, D. G. & Reeves, B. B. (1980). Children and television news. *Journalism Quarterly,* 57(1):45–54, 114.

Durkin, K. (1985). Television and sex-role acquisition. 2: Effects. *British Journal of Social Psychology,* 24:191–210.

Dwyer, J. (1982). Shaping up: The teenage diet. In M. Schwartz, (Ed.), *TV and teens: Experts look at the issues* (pp. 15–21), Reading, MA: Addison-Wesley.

Dysinger, W. S. & Ruckmick, C. A. (1933). *The emotional response of children to the motion picture situation.* New York: Macmillan Co., Reprint edition, Arno Press, 1970.

Edwards, O. (1990/91). Doing the right thing. *Special Reports* (November 1990/January 1991):8–9.

Elkind, D. (1986). Stress and the middle-grader. *Education Digest,* 51:30–34.

Elkind, D. (1981). *The hurried child: Growing up too fast too soon.* Reading, MA: Addison-Wesley.

Ellis, D. (1984). Video arcades, youth and trouble. *Youth and Society,* 16(1):47–65.

Ellis, G. J. (1983). Youth and the electronic environment: An introduction. *Youth and Society* 15(1):3–12.

Ellis, G. J., Streeter, S. K., & Englebrecht, J. D. (1983). Television characters as significant others and the process of vicarious role taking. *Journal of Family Issues,* 4(2):367–384.

England, D. A. (1983). *A survey of teachers' attitudes about television and television education.* Washington, DC: National Association of Broadcasters.

Erdman, B. (1994). Form, style, and lesson: An analysis of commercially produced school news programs. In A. De Vaney (Ed.), *Watching Channel One: The convergence of students, technology, and private business* (pp. 153–166). Albany: State University of New York Press.

Ewry, E. E. (1988). The power of packaging. In A. A. Berger (Ed.), *Media USA: Process and effect* (pp. 445–453). New York: Longman.

Faber, R., Brown, J. D., & McLeod, J. M. (1979). Coming of age in the global village: Television and adolescence. In E. Wartella (Ed.), *Children Communicating* (pp. 215–249). Beverly Hills, CA: Sage Publications.

Fedler, F., Hall, J., & Tanzi, L. (1982). Popular songs emphasize sex, deemphasize romance. *Mass Communications Review,* 9:10–15.

Fejes, F. J. (1992). Masculinity as a fact: A review of empirical mass communication research on masculinity. In S. Craig (Ed.), *Men, masculinity, and the media* (pp. 9–22). Newbury Park, CA: Sage.

Feshbach, N. D. (1988). Television and the development of empathy. In S. Oskamp (Ed.), *Television as a social issue* (pp. 261–269). Newbury Park, CA: Sage.

Feshbach, N. D., Dillman, A. S., & Jordan, T. S. (1979). Portrait of a female on television. Some possible effects on children. In C. B. Kopp (Ed.), *Becoming female: Perspectives on development* (pp. 363–385). New York: Plenum Press.

Feshbach, S. (1961). The stimulating vs. cathartic effects of a vicarious aggressive activity. *Journal of Abnormal and Social Psychology,* 63:381–385.

Fetler, M. (1984). Television viewing and school achievement. *Journal of Communication,* 34(2):104–118.

Fitch, M., Huston, A. C., & Wright, J. C. (1993). From television forms to genre schemata: Children's perceptions of television reality. In G. L. Berry & J. K. Asamen (Eds.), *Children and television: Images in a changing sociocultural world* (pp. 38–52). Newbury Park, CA: Sage Publications.

Fontana, L. A. (1988). Television and the social studies. *Social Education,* 52(5):348–350.

Fore, W. F. (1990). *Mythmakers: Gospel, culture and the media.* New York: Friendship Press.

Fowles, J. (1986). Advertising fifteen basic appeals. In R. Atwan, B. Orton, W. Vesterman (Eds.), *American mass media: Industries and issues* (pp. 43–54). New York: Random House.

Freedman, J. L. (1988). Television violence and aggression: What the evidence shows. In S. Oskamp (Ed.), *Television as a social issue* (pp. 144–162). Newbury Park, CA: Sage.

Freedman, J. L. (1984). Effects of television violence on aggressiveness. *Psychological Bulletin,* 96(2):227–246.

Frith, M. & Frith, K. (1993). Creating meaning from media messages: Participatory research and adolescent health. In R. M. Lerner (Ed.), *Early adolescence: Perspectives on research, policy, and intervention* (pp. 419–430). Hillsdale, NJ: Lawrence Erlbaum.

Frith, S. (1988). *Music for pleasure.* New York: Routledge.

Frueh, T. & McGhee, P. E. (1975). Traditional sex role development and amount of time spent watching television. *Developmental Psychology,* 11(1):109.

Gadberry, S. (1980). Effects of restricting first graders TV-viewing on leisure time use, IQ change and cognitive style. *Journal of Applied Developmental Psychology,* 1:45–57.

Gantz, W. (1993). Introduction. In B. S. Greenberg & W. Gantz (Eds.), *Desert Storm and the mass media.* Cresskill, NJ: Hampton Press.

Geiogamah, H. & Pavel, D. M. (1993). Developing television for American Indian and Alaska native children in the late 20th century. In G. L. Berry & J. K. Asamen (Eds.), *Children & television: Images in a changing sociocultural world* (pp. 191–204). Newbury Park, CA: Sage.

Gelman, E., Starr, M., Anderson, M., & Carrol, G. (1985). MTV's message. *Newsweek* (30 December):54–56.

Gerbner, G. (1973). Teacher image in mass culture. Symbolic functions of the Hidden Curriculum. In G. Gerbner, L. P. Gross, W. H. Melody (Eds.), *Communications technology and social policy* (pp. 265–286). New York: John Wiley & Sons.

Gerbner, G. & Gross, L. (1976). Living with television: The violence profile. *Journal of Communication,* 26(2):173–199.

Gerbner, G., Gross, L., Eleey, M. F., Jackson-Beeck, M., & Jeffries-Fox, S. (1977). TV Violence Profile No. 8: The highlights. *Journal of Communications.* 27(2):171–180.

Gerbner, G., Morgan, M., & Signorielli, N. (1982). Programming health portrayals: What viewers see, say and do. In D. Pearl, L. Bouthlet, & J. Lazar (Eds.), *Television and behavior: Ten years of scientific progress and implications for the eighties* (Vol. 2) (pp. 291–307). Rockville, MD: National Institute of Mental Health.

Gerson, W. M. (1966). Mass media and socialization behavior: Negro-white differences. *Social Forces,* 45:40–50.

Gitlin, T. (1982). Prime time ideology: The hegemonic process in television entertainment. In H. Newcomb (Ed.), *Television: The critical view* (pp. 426–454). New York: Oxford University Press.

Glasser, P. (1990–91). TV guidance. *Special Reports* (November 1990–January 1991):38–39.

Goffman, E. (1979). *Gender advertisements.* Cambridge, MA: Harvard University Press.

Golay, J. (1994). Rip up ads. *Telemedium: The Journal of Media Literacy,* 40(3–4):10–11.

Goldberg, M. E. & Gorn, G. J. (1983). In M. J. A. Howe (Ed.), *Learning from television: Psychological and educational research* (pp. 125–151). London: Academic Press.

Goldstein, J. H. & Bredemeir, B. J. (1977). Socialization: Some basic issues. *Journal of Communication,* 27(3):154–159.

Gore, T. (1987). *Raising PG kids in an X-rated society.* New York: Bantam Books.

Gorn, G., Goldberg, M., & Kanugo, R. (1976). The role of educational television in changing the intergroup attitudes of children. *Child Development,* 47(1):277–280.

Gould, M. S. & Shaffer, D. (1986). The impact of suicide in television movies: Evidence of imitation. *New England Journal of Medicine,* 315(11):690–694.

Gow, J. (1993). Music video as persuasive form: The case of the pseudo-reflexive strategy. *Communication Quarterly,* 41(3):318–327.

Graham, L. & Hamdan, L. (1987). *Capturing the $200 billion youth market.* New York: St. Martin's Press.

Graves, S. B. (1982). The impact of television on the cognitive and affective development of minority children. In G. L. Berry & C. Mitchell-Kernan (Eds.), *Television and the socialization of the minority child* (pp. 37–67). New York: Academic Press.

Graves, S. B. (1980). Psychological effects of black portrayals on television. In S. B. Withey and R. P. Abeles (Eds.), *Television and social behavior: Beyond violence and television* (pp. 259–289). Hillsdale, NJ: Lawrence Erlbaum.

Graves, S. B. (1975). Racial diversity in children's television: Its impact on racial attitudes and stated program preferences. *Dissertation Abstracts,* 36:4464.

Greenberg, B. S. (1988). Some uncommon television images and the drench hypothesis. In S. Oskamp (Ed.), *Television as a social issue* (pp. 88–102). Newbury Park, CA: Sage.

Greenberg, B. S. (1972). Children's reactions to television blacks. *Journalism Quarterly,* 49(1):5–14.

Greenberg, B. S. & Brand, J. E. (1993). Cultural diversity on Saturday morning television. In G. L. Berry & J. K. Asamen (Eds.), *Children and television: Images in a changing sociocultural world* (pp. 132–142). Newbury Park, CA: Sage.

Greenberg, B. S. & Brand, J. E. (1993/94). Channel One: But what about advertising? *Educational Leadership,* 51(4):56–58.

Greenberg, B. S. & Gantz, W. (Eds.) (1993). *Desert Storm and the mass media.* Cresskill, NJ: Hampton Press.

Greenberg, B. S. & Gordon, T. F. (1972). Social class and racial differences in children's perceptions of television violence. In G. A. Comstock, E. A. Rubenstein, & J. P. Murray (Eds.), *Television and social behavior. Vol. V. Television's effects: Further explorations* (pp. 185–210). Washington, DC: Government Printing Office.

Greenberg, B. S. & Heeter, C. J. (1987). VCRs and young people: The picture at 39% penetration. *The American Behavioral Scientist,* 30:509–521.

Greenberg, B. S., Ku, L., & Li, H. (1989). *Young people and their orientation to the mass media: An international study. Study #2: United States.* East Lansing: Michigan State University, Department of Communications.

Greenberg, B. S., Linsangan, R., Soderman, A., Heeter, C., Lin, C., Stanley, C., Siemicki, M. (1993). Adolescents' exposure to television and movie sex. In B. S. Greenberg, J. D. Brown, & N. L. Buerkel-Rothfuss (Eds.), *Media, sex and the adolescent* (pp. 61–98). Cresskill, NJ: Hampton Press.

Greenberg, B. S., Siemicki, M., Dorfman, S., Heeter, C., Stanley, C., Soderman, A., & Linsangan, R. (1993). Sex content in R-rated films viewed by adolescents. In B. S. Greenberg, J. D. Brown, & N. L. Buerkel-Rothfuss (Eds.), *Media, sex, and the adolescent* (pp. 45–58). Cresskill, NJ: Hampton Press.

Greene, A. L. & Adams-Price, C. (1990). Adolescents' secondary attachments to celebrity figures. *Sex Roles,* 23(7/8):335–347.

Greenfield, P. M. (1984). *Mind and media: The effects of television, video games, and computers.* Cambridge, MA: Harvard University Press.

Greenfield, P. M., Bruzzone, L., Koyamatsu, K., Satuloff, W., Nixon, K., Brodie, M., & Kingsdale, D. (1987). What is rock music doing to the minds of our youth? A first experimental look at the effects of rock music lyrics and music videos. *Journal of Early Adolescence,* 7(3):315–329.

Greenfield, P. M., Yut, E., Chung, M., Land, D., Kreider, H., Pantoja, M., & Horsley, K. (1993). The program-length commercial: A study of the effects of television/toy tie-ins on imaginative play. In G. L. Berry & J. K. Asamen (Eds.), *Children & television: Images in a changing sociocultural world* (pp. 53–72). Newbury Park, CA: Sage

Greenstein, J. (1054). Effects of television upon elementary school grades. *Journal of Educational Research,* 48(3):161–176.

Greenwald, J. (1990). Shooting the works. *Time* (21 May).

Griswold, W. J. (1975). *The image of the Middle East in secondary school textbooks.* New York: Middle East Studies Association of North America, Inc.

Gross, L. & Jeffries-Fox, S. (1978). What do you want to be when you grow up, little girl? In G. Tuchman, A. K. Daniels, & J. Benet (Eds.), *Hearth and home: Images of women in the mass media* (pp. 240–265). New York: Oxford University Press.

Gross, L. & Morgan, M. (1985). Television and enculturation. In J. R. Dominick & J. E. Fletcher (Eds.), *Broadcasting research methods* (pp. 221–234). Boston: Allyn & Bacon, Inc.

Grossman, H. & Grossman, S. H. (1994). *Gender issues in education.* Boston: Allyn & Bacon, Inc.

Guerrero, E. (1993). *Framing blackness: The African-American image in film.* Philadelphia: Temple University Press.

Hall, S. J. (1977). *Africa in U.S. educational materials: Thirty problems and responses.* New York: Afro-American Institute.

Hamamoto, D. (1993). They're so cute when they're young: The Asian-American child on television. In G. L. Berry & J. K. Asamen (Eds.), *Children & television: Images in a changing sociocultural world* (pp. 205–215). Newbury Park, CA: Sage.

Hamburg, B. A. (1974). Early adolescence: A specific and stressful stage in the life cycle. In G. Coelho, D. Hamburg, & J. Adams (Eds.), *Coping and adaptation* (pp. 101–124). New York: Basic Books.

Hamelink, C. J. (1986). Is there life after the information revolution? In M. Traber (Ed.), *The myth of the information revolution: Social and ethical implications of communication technology* (pp. 7–20). Newbury Park, CA: Sage Publications.

Harris, R. J. (1989). *A cognitive psychology of mass communication.* Hillsdale, NJ: Lawrence Erlbaum.

Harrison, L. F. & Williams, T. M. (1986). Television and cognitive development. In T. M. Williams (Ed.), *The impact of television: A natural experiment in three communities* (pp. 87–142). Orlando, FL: Academic Press.

Haskell, M. (1973). *From reverence to rape: The treatment of women in the movies.* New York: Holt, Rinehart, & Winston.

Havighurst, R. J. (1972). *Developmental tasks and education.* New York: David Mckay Co.

Hawkins, R. P. & Pingree, S. (1982). TV influence on social reality and conceptions of the world. In D. Pearl, L. Bouthilet, and J. Lazar (Eds.). *Television and behavior: Ten years of scientific progress and implications for the eighties* (Vol. 2) (pp. 224–247). Rockville, MD: National Institute of Mental Health.

Hawkins, R. P., Pingree, S., & Roberts, D. (1975). Watergate and political socialization. *American Politics Quarterly,* 3(4):406–422.

Hawkins, R. P., Pingree, S., Smith, K. A., & Bechtolt, W. E. (1979). Adolescents' responses to issues and images. In S. Krauss (Ed.), *The great debates: Carter vs. Ford* (pp. 368–383). Bloomington: Indiana University Press.

Healy, J. M. (1990). *Endangered minds: Why our children don't think.* New York: Simon and Schuster.

Hechinger, F. M. (1992). *Fateful choices: Healthy choices for the 21st century.* Washington, DC: Carnegie Council on Adolescent Development.

Heeter, C. (1988). Gender differences in viewing styles. In C. Heeter & B. S. Greenberg (Eds.), *Cableviewing* (pp. 151–166). Norwood, NJ: Ablex.

Henderson, A. (1992). Media and the rise of the celebrity culture. *Magazine of History,* 6(4):49–54.

Herbst, J. (1994). *How school materials teach and misteach world affairs: Africa.* Washington, DC: American Federation and Teachers and Freedom House.

Hirsch, H. (1971). *Poverty and politicization.* New York: Free Press.

Hoffner, C. & Cantor, J. (1991). Perceiving and responding to mass media characters. In J. Bryant & D. Zillman (Eds.), *Responding to the screen: Reception and reaction processes* (pp. 135–168). Hillsdale, NJ: Lawrence Erlbaum.

Hoffner, C. & Cantor, J. (1990). Forewarning of threat and prior knowledge of outcome: Effects on children's emotional responses to a film sequence. *Human Communication Research,* 16:323–354.

Hoffner, C. & Haefner, M. J. (1993). Children's affective responses to news coverage of the war. In B. S. Greenberg & W. Gantz (Eds.), *Desert Storm and the mass media* (pp. 364–380). Cresskill, NJ: Hampton Press.

Hollander, N. (1971). Adolescents and the war: The sources of socialization. *Journalism Quarterly,* 58(3):472–79.

Hollenbeck, A. R. & Slaby, R. G. (1979). Infant visual and vocal responses to television. *Child Development,* 50(1):41–45.

Hollister, B. C. (1993). *Mass Media Workbook.* Lincolnwood, IL: National Textbook Company.

Hornick, R. C. (1981). Out-of-school television and schooling: Hypotheses and methods. *Review of Education Research,* 51(2):193–214.

Hornick, R. (1978). Television access and the slowing cognitive growth. *American Educational Research Journal,* 15(1):1–15.

Howard, M. (1985). Postponing sexual involvement among adolescents: An alternative approach to prevention of sexually transmitted diseases. *Journal of Adolescent Health Care,* 6:271–277.

Huesmann, L. R. & Eron, L. D. (Eds.). (1986). *Television and aggressive child: A cross-national comparison.* Hillsdale, NJ: Lawrence Erlbaum.

Hughes, C. E. & Dobrow, J. R. (1988). The VCR and the adolescent: Patterns of use. Paper presented to the International Communication Association: New Orleans.

Human Relations Media. (1994). *The glitter: Sex, drugs, and the media.* Pleasantville, NY: Human Relations Media.

Huston, A. C., Donnerstein, E., Fairchild, H., Feshbach, N. D., Katz, P. A., Murray, J., Rubinstein, E. A., Wilcox, B., & Zuckerman, D. (1992). *Big world, small screen: The role of television in American society.* Lincoln: University of Nebraska Press.

Huston, A. C. & Wright, J. C. (1983). Children's processing of television: The informative functions of formal features. In J. Bryant & D. R. Anderson (Eds.), *Children's understanding of television: Research on attention and comprehension* (pp. 35–68). New York: Academic Press.

Iiyama, P. & Kitano, H. H. L. (1982). Asian Americans and the media. In G. L. Berry & C. Mitchell-Kernan (Eds.), *Television and the socialization of the minority child* (pp. 151–186). New York: Academic Press.

Inge, M. T. (Ed.). (1982). *Concise histories of American popular culture.* Westport, CT: Greenwood Press.

Jackson-Beeck, M. (1979). Interpersonal and mass communication in children's political socialization. *Journalism Quarterly,* 56(1):48–53.

Jacobson, M. F., Atkins, R., & Hacker, G. (1983). Booze merchants cheer on teenage drinking. *Business and Society Review,* 46:46 51.

Janis, I. (1980). The influence of television on personal decision-making. In S. Withey & R. Abels (Eds.), *Television and social behavior* (pp. 161–189). Hillsdale, NJ: Lawrence Erlbaum.

Jeffres, L. W. (1986). *Mass media processes and effects.* Prospect Heights, IL: Waveland Press.

Jhally, S. (1991). *Dreamworlds: Sex/desire/power in rock video.* Northampton, MA: Foundation for Media Education.

Johnston, J., Anderman, E. M., Milne, L., & Klenk, L. (1994). *Improving civic discourse in the classroom.* Ann Arbor, MI: Institute for Social Research, University of Michigan.

Johnston, J. & Brzezinski, E. J. (1992). *Taking the measure of Channel One: The first year. Executive summary.* Ann Arbor, MI: Institute for Social Research, University of Michigan.

Johnston, J., Brezezinski, E. J., & Anderman, E. M. (1994). *Taking the measure of Channel One: A three year perspective.* Ann Arbor, MI: Institute for Social Research, University of Michigan.

Johnston, J. & Ettema, J. S. (1982). *Positive images: Breaking stereotypes with children's television.* Beverly Hills, CA: Sage Publications.

Johnstone, J. W. C. (1974). Social integration and mass media use among adolescents: A case study. In J. G. Blumler & E. Katz (Eds.), *The uses of mass communications: Current perspectives on gratifications research* (pp. 35–47). Beverly Hills, CA: Sage Publications.

Jönsson, A. (1986). TV–a threat or a complement to school. *Gazette,* 37(1):51–61.

Jowett, G. (1982). They taught it at the movies: Film models for learned sexual behavior. In S. Thomas (Ed.), *Film/culture: Explorations of cinema in its social context* (pp. 209–221). Metuchen, NJ: Scarecrow Press.

Joy, L. A., Kimball, M. M., & Zabrack, M. L. (1986). Television and children's aggressive behavior. In T. M. Williams (Ed.), *The impact of television: A natural experiment in three communities* (pp. 303–360). Orlando, FL: Academic Press.

Kane, M. & Greendorfer, S. L. (1994). The media's role in accommodating and resisting stereotyped images of women in sport. In P. Creedon (Ed.), *Women, media, and sport: Challenging gender values* (pp. 28–44). Thousand Oaks, CA: Sage.

Kaplan, G. R. (1992). *Images of education: The mass media's version of American schools.* Washington, DC: Institute for Educational Leadership.

Kaplan, G. (1990). TV's version of education (and what to do about it). *Phi Delta Kappan,* 71(5):K1–K12.

Katz, E. (1988). On conceptualizing media effects: Another look. In S. Oscamp (Ed.), *Television as a social issue* (pp. 361–374). Newbury Park, CA: Sage.

Katz, E., Blumler, J. G., & Gurevitch, M. (1974). Utilization of mass communication by the individual. In J. G. Blumler & E. Katz (Eds.), *The use of mass communication. Current perspectives on gratifications research* (pp. 93–112). Beverly Hills, CA: Sage Publications.

Kessler, L. (1989). Women's magazines' coverage of smoking related health hazards. *Journalism Quarterly,* 66(2):316–322, 444.

Kilbourne, J. (1991). Deadly persuasion: 7 myths alcohol advertisers want you to believe. *Media & Values,* 54–55:10–12.

Kilbourne, J. (1989). Beauty and the beast of advertising. *Media & Values,* 49:8–10.

Kilpatrick, W. (1992). *Why Johnny can't tell right from wrong: Moral illiteracy and the case for character education.* New York: Simon & Schuster.

Kimball, M. M. (1986). Television and sex-role attitudes. In T. M. Williams (Ed.), *The impact of television: A natural experiment in three communities* (pp. 265–302). Orlando, FL: Academic Press.

Kindem, G. & Teddlie, C. (1982). Film effects and ethnicity. In S. Thomas (Ed.), *Film/culture: Explorations of cinema in its social context* (pp. 195–208). Metuchen, NJ: Scarecrow Press.

Knupfer, N. N. & Hayes, P. (1994). The effects of the Channel One broadcast on students' knowledge of current events. In A. De Vaney (Ed.), *Watching Channel One: The convergence of students, technology, and private business* (pp. 42–60). New York: State University of New York Press.

Kozol, W. (1989). Representations of race in network news coverage of South

Africa. In G. Burns & R. J. Thompson (Eds.), *Television studies: Textual analysis* (pp. 165–182). New York: Praeger.

Krendl, K. A., Clark, G., Dawson, R., & Troiano, C. (1993). Preschoolers and VCRs in the home: A multiple methods approach. *Journal of Broadcasting and Electronic Media,* 37(3):293–312.

Krull, R. & Husson, W. (1979). Children's attention. The case of TV viewing. In E. Wartella (Ed.), *Children communicating: Media and development of thought, speech, understanding* (pp. 83–114). Beverly Hills, CA: Sage Publications.

Kubey, R. (1990/91). Growing up in a media world. *Media & Values,* 52/53:8–10.

Kubey, R. & Csikszentmihalyi, M. (1990). *Television and the quality of life: How viewing shapes everyday experience.* Hillsdale, NJ: Lawrence Erlbaum Associates, Publishers.

Kubey, R. & Larson, R. (1990). The use and experience of the new video media among children and young adolescents. *Communication Research,* 17(1):107–130.

Kubey, R. W. & Peluso, T. (1990). Emotional response as a cause of interpersonal news diffusion: The case of the space shuttle tragedy. *Journal of Broadcasting and Electronic Media,* 34(1):69–76.

Kunkel, D. (1988). From a raised eyebrow to a turned back: The FCC and children's product-related programming. *Journal of Communication,* 38(4):90–108.

Lambert, W. E. & Klineberg, O. (1967). *Children's views of foreign peoples: A cross-national study.* New York: Appleton-Century-Crofts.

Lampton, D. M., Linden, C. A., Ricks, T. M., Child, J., Nyang, S. S. (1990). Studying world affairs: Five regions and their importance. *NASSP Bulletin,* 74(522):48–63.

Langston, K. P. (1969). *Political socialization.* New York: Oxford University Press.

Larson, J. F. (1986). Television and U.S. foreign policy: The case of the Iran hostage crisis. *Journal of Communication,* 36(4):108–130.

Larson, J. F. (1984). *Television's window on the world: International affairs coverage on the U.S. networks.* Norwood, NJ: Ablex.

Larson, J. F. (1979). International affairs coverage on U.S. network television. *Journal of Communication,* 29(2):136–147.

Larson, R. & Kubey, R. (1983). Television and music: Contrasting media in adolescent life. *Youth and Society,* 15(1):13–31.

Lasch, C. (1979). *The culture of narcissism: American life in an age of diminishing expectations.* New York: Warner Books.

Lawrence, J. (1989). Nonsense as knowledge. *Media & Values,* 47:7–8.

Laybourne, G. (1993). The Nickelodeon experience. In G. L. Berry & J. K.

Asamen, *Children & television: Images in a changing sociocultural world* (pp. 303–307). Newbury Park, CA: Sage.

Lee, B. (1988). Prosocial content on prime-time television. In S. Oskamp (Ed.), *Television as a social issue* (pp. 238–246). Newbury Park, CA: Sage.

Leifer, A. D. & Roberts, D. F. (1972). Children's response to television violence. In J. P. Murray, E. A. Rubenstein, & G. Comstock (Eds.), *Television and social behavior: Vol. II. Television and social learning.* Washington, DC: U.S. Government Printing Office.

Leming, J. S. (1987). Rock music and the socialization of moral values in early adolescence. *Youth & Society,* 18(4):363–383.

Lesser, G. S. (1974). *Children and television: Lessons from* Sesame Street. New York: Random House.

Levine, G. F. (1977). Learned helplessness and the evening news. *Journal of Communication,* 27(4):100–105.

Lichter, S. R. & Lichter, L. S. (1988). Does TV shape ethnic images? *Media & Values,* 43:5–7.

Lickona, T. (1991). *Educating for character: How our schools can teach respect and responsibility.* New York: Bantam Books.

Liebert, R. M. & Poulos, R. W. (1979). Television as a moral teacher. In B. Logan (Ed.), *Television awareness training: The viewer's guide for family and community* (pp. 243–250). Nashville, TN: Abingdon Press.

Liebert, R. M. & Sprafkin, J. (1988). *The early window: Effects of television on children and youth.* New York: Pergamon Press.

Limpus, B. (1994). *Lights, camera, action! A guide to using video production and instruction in the classroom.* Waco, TX: Prufrock Press.

Linn, M. C., de Benedictis, T., & Delucchi, K. (1982). Adolescent reasoning about advertisements: Preliminary investigations. *Child Development,* 53:1599–1613.

Linz, D., Donnerstein, E., & Penrod, S. (1984). "The effects of multiple exposures to filmed violence against women." *Journal of Communication,* 34(2):130–147.

Livesley, J., McMahon, B., Pungente, J. J., & Quin, R., (1990). *Meet the media.* Canada: Globe/Modern Curriculum Press.

Lloyd-Kolkin, D. & Tyner, K. R. (1991). *Media & you: An elementary media literacy curriculum.* Englewood Cliffs, NJ: Educational Technology Publications.

Locke, M. (1993). In the news. *Science and Children,* 30(5):6.

Lorch, E. P., Anderson, D. R., & Levin, S. R. (1979). The relationship of visual attention to children's comprehension of television. *Child Development,* 50(3):722–727.

Louis Harris and Associates, Inc. (1988). *Sexual material on American network television during the 1987–88 season.* New York: Planned Parenthood Federation of America.

Louis Harris and Associates. (1986). *American teens speak: Sex, myths, TV, and birth control.* New York: Planned Parenthood Federation of America.

Loundsbury, J. (1987). What values are we teaching, should we teach at the middle school level? *Schools in the middle: A report on trends and practices* (May). Reston, VA: National Association of Secondary School Principals.

Lovdale, L. T. (1989). Sex role messages in television commercials: An update. *Sex Roles,* 21(11/12): 715–724.

Lull, J. (Ed.). (1992). *Popular music and communication.* Newbury Park, CA: Sage.

Lull, J. (1985). The naturalistic study of media use and youth culture. In K. E. Rosengren, L. A. Wenner, & P. Palmgreen (Eds.), *Media gratification research: Current perspectives* (pp. 209–224). Beverly Hills, CA: Sage Productions.

Luker, R. & Johnston, J. (1988). TV and teens: Television in adolescent social development. *Social Education,* 52(5):350–353.

Lumpkin, A. & Williams, L. D. (1991). An analysis of *Sports Illustrated* feature articles, 1954–1987. *Sociology of Sport Journal,* 8:1–15.

Lusted, D. (1991). *The media studies book: A guide for teachers.* London: Routledge.

Lyle, J. & Hoffman, H. R. (1972). Children's use of television and other media. In E. S. Rubinstein, G. A. Comstock, & J. P. Murray (Eds.), *Television in day-to-day life: Patterns of use* (pp. 129–256). Washington, DC: Government Printing Office.

MacNeil, R. (1983). Is television shortening our attention span? *New York University Educational Quarterly,* 14(2):2–5.

Mallery, D. (1994). The power of film. *NAIS: Academic Forum* (Spring):11–13.

Mander, G. (1978). *Four arguments for the elimination of television.* New York: Quill.

Masterman, L. (1985). *Teaching the media.* London: Routledge.

Matelski, M. J. (1985). Image and influence: Women in public television. *Journalism Quarterly,* 6(1):147–150.

Mattes, J. & Cantor, J. (1982). Enhancing responses to television advertisements via the transfer of residual arousal from prior programming. *Journal of Broadcasting,* 26:55–556.

Mayes, S. L. & Valentine, K. B. (1979). Sex role stereotyping in Saturday morning cartoon shows. *Journal of Broadcasting,* 23(1):41–45.

McArthur, L. Z. & Eisen, S. V. (1976). Television and sex-role stereotyping. *Journal of Applied Social Psychology,* 6(4):329–351.

McGhee, P. E. & Frueh, T. (1980). Television viewing and the learning of sex-role stereotypes. *Sex Roles,* 6(2):179–188.

McIntyre, J. J. & Teevan, J. J., Jr. (1972). Television violence and deviant behavior. In G. A. Comstock & E. A. Rubinstein (Eds.), *Television and social behavior. Vol. III. Television and adolescent aggressiveness.* Washington, DC: U.S. Government Printing Office.

McLeod, J. M., Atkin, C. K., & Chaffee, S. H. (1972a). Adolescents, parents, and television use: Adolescent self-report measures from Maryland and Wisconsin samples. In G. A. Comstock & E. A. Rubenstein (Eds.), *Television and social behavior. Vol. III. Television and adolescent aggressiveness.* Washington, DC: U.S. Government Printing Office.

McLeod, J. M., Atkin, C. K., & Chaffee, S. H. (1972b). Adolescents, parents, and television use: Self-report and other-report measures from the Wisconsin sample. In G. A. Comstock & E. A. Rubenstein (Eds.), *Television and social behavior. Vol. III. Television and adolescent aggressiveness.* Washington, DC: U.S. Government Printing Office.

McLeod, J. M. & Reeves, B. (1980). On the nature of mass media effects. In S. B. Withey & R. P. Abeles (Eds.), *Television and social behavior: Beyond violence and children* (pp. 17–54). Hillsdale, NJ: Lawrence Erlbaum.

McLuhan, M. (1978). The brain and the media: The Western hemisphere. *Journal of Communication,* 28(4):54–60.

McNeal, J. U. (1992). The littlest shoppers. *American Demographics,* 14(2):48–52.

McPhail, T. L. (1987). *Electronic colonialism: The future of international broadcasting and communication.* Newbury Park, CA: Sage.

Medhurst, M. J. (1989). Propaganda techniques in documentary film and television: AIM vs. PBS. In G. Burns & R. J. Thompson (Eds.), *Television studies: Textual analysis* (pp. 183–204). New York: Praeger.

Medrich, E. A., Roizen, J. A., Rubin, V., & Buckley, S. (1982). *The serious business of growing up: A study of children's lives outside school.* Berkeley: University of California Press.

Mee, C. S. (1994). Too much of a good thing? Overexercising. *Current Health,* 21(1):18–20.

Meline, C. W. (1976). Does the medium matter? *Journal of Communication,* 26(3):81–89.

Merelman, R. M. (1972). The adolescence of political socialization. *Sociology of Education,* 45(2):132–166.

Meringoff, L. K., Vibbert, M. M., Char, C. A., Fernie, D. E., Banker, G. S., & Gardner, H. (1983). How is children's learning from television distinctive? Exploiting the medium methodologically. In J. Bryant & D. R. Anderson (Eds.), *Children's understanding of television* (pp. 151–179). New York: Academic Press.

Metabane, P. W. (1988). Television and the black audience: Cultivating moderate perspectives on racial integration. *Journal of Communication,* 38(3):21–31.

Meyer, K., Seidler, J., Curry, T., & Aveni, A. (1980). Women in July Fourth cartoons: A 100-year look. *Journal of Communications,* 30(1):21–30.

Meyrowitz, J. (1985). *No sense of place: The impact of electronic media on social behavior.* New York: Oxford University Press.

Miedzian, M. (1991). *Boys will be boys: Breaking the link between masculinity and violence.* New York: Doubleday.

Milavsky, J. R. (1988). Television and aggression once again. In S. Oscamp (Ed.), *Television as a social issue* (pp. 163–170). Newbury Park, CA: Sage.

Milavsky, J. R., Kessler, R., Stipp, H. H., & Rubens, W. S. (1982). *Television and aggression: A panel study.* New York: Academic Press.

Milgram, S. & Shotland, R. L. (1973). *Television and antisocial behavior: A field experiment.* New York: Academic Press.

Miller, M. C. (1990). Advertising: End of story. In M. C. Miller (Ed.), *Seeing through movies* (pp. 186–246). New York: Pantheon Books.

Ministry of Education. (1989). *Media literacy: Resource guide.* Ontario, Canada: Ministry of Education.

Molitor, F. & Sapolsky, B. S. (1993). Sex, violence, and victimization in slasher films. *Journal of Broadcasting and Electronic Media,* 37(3):233–242.

Moody, K. (1980). *Growing up on television: A report to parents.* New York: McGraw-Hill.

Morgan, M. (1987). Television, sex-role attitudes, and sex-role behavior. *Journal of Early Adolescence,* 7(3):269–282.

Morgan, M. (1982). Television and adolescents' sex-role stereotypes: A longitudinal study. *Journal of Personality and Social Psychology,* 43(5):947–955.

Morgan, M. (1980). Television viewing and reading: Does more equal better? *Journal of Communication,* 30(1):159–165.

Morgan, M. & Gross, L. (1982). Television and educational achievement and aspiration. In D. Pearl, L. Bouthilet, & J. Lazar (Eds.), *Television and behavior: Ten years of ascientific projects and implications for the eighties* (Vol. 2) (pp. 78–90). Rockville, MD: National Institute of Mental Health.

Morgan, M. & Gross, L. (1980). Television viewing, IQ, and academic achievement. *Journal of Broadcasting,* 24:117–133.

Morgan, M. & Rothschild, N. (1983). Impact of the new technology: Cable TV, peers, and sex-role cultivation in the electronic environment. *Youth and Society,* 15(1):33–50.

Morris, J. S. (1982). Television portrayal and the socialization of the American Indian child. In G. L. Berry & C. Mitchell-Kernan (Eds.), *Television and the socialization of the minority child* (pp. 187–202). New York: Academic Press.

Morrison, D. & MacGregor, B. (1993). Anxiety, war and children: The role of television. In B. S. Greenberg & W. Gantz (Eds.), *Desert Storm and the mass media* (pp. 353–363). Cresskill, NJ: Hampton Press.

Muffoletto, R. (1994). Drawing the line: Questions of ethics, power, and symbols in state policy and the Whittle concept. In A. De Vaney (Ed.), *Watching Channel One: The convergence of students, technology, and private business* (pp. 189–207). New York: State University of New York Press.

Murray, J. P. (1993). The developing child in a multimedia society. In G. L. Berry & J. K. Asamen (Eds.), *Children and television: Images in a changing sociocultural world* (pp. 9–22). Newbury Park, CA: Sage.

Murray, J. P. (1980). *Television and youth: 25 years of research and controversy.* Boys Town, NE: Boys Town Center for the Study of Youth Development.

National Leadership Conference on Media Literacy. (1992). *Media literacy: A report of the National Leadership Conference on Media Literacy.* Washington, DC: Aspen Institute.

National Science Foundation. (1977). *Research on the effects of television advertising on children: A review of the literature and recommendations for future research.* Washington, DC: National Science Foundation.

Neuman, S. B. (1982). Television viewing and leisure reading: A qualitative analysis. *Journal of Educational Research,* 75(5):299–304.

Newspaper Readership Project. (1980). *Mass media in the family setting: Social patterns in media availability and use by parents.* New York: Newspaper Advertising Bureau.

Nias, D. K. B. (1983). The effects of televised sex and pornography. In M. J. A. Howe (Ed.), *Learning from television: Psychological and educational research* (pp. 179–192). London: Academic Press.

Noble, G. (1983). Social learning from everyday television. In M. J. A. Howe (Ed.), *Learning from television: Psychological and educational research* (pp. 101–124). London: Academic Press.

Noble, G. (1975). *Children in front of the small screen.* Beverly Hills, CA: Sage Publications.

Noden, M. (1994). Dying to win. *Sports Illustrated* (8 August):52–60.

O'Brien, T. (1990). *The screening of America: Movies and values from* Rocky *to* Rainman. New York: Frederick Ungar.

Office of the Superintendent of Schools. (1989). *The wired bedroom: A report of the results of a media consumption survey conducted in Santa Barbara County.* Santa Barbara, CA: Office of the Superintendent of Schools.

O'Heffernan, P. (1993). Sobering thoughts on sound bites seen 'round the world. In B. S. Greenberg & W. Gantz (Eds.), *Desert Storm and the mass media* (pp. 19–28). Cresskill, NJ: Hampton Press.

Olson, D. R. (1988). Mind and media: The epistemic functions of literacy. *Journal of Communication,* 38(3):27–36.

O'Reilly, K. & Splaine, J. (1987). *Critical viewing: Stimulant to critical thinking.* Pacific Grove, CA: Midwest Publications.

Osborn, B. (1990/91). Altered states: How television changes childhood and challenges parents: An interview with Joshua Meyrowitz. *Media & Values,* 52/53:2–3.

Palmgreen, P., Wenner, L. A., & Rosengren, K. E. (1985). Uses and gratifications research: The past ten years. In K. E. Rosengren, L. A. Wenner, & P. Palmgren (Eds.), *Media gratifications research: Current perspectives.* Beverly Hills, CA: Sage Publications.

Papert, S. (1993). *The children's machine: Rethinking school in the age of the computer.* New York: Basic Books.

Parenti, M. (1992). *Inventing reality: The politics of the mass media.* New York: St. Martin's Press.

Paugh, R. (1988). Music video viewers. In C. Heeter & B. S. Greenberg (Eds.), *Cableviewing* (pp. 237–245). Norwood, NJ: Ablex.

Pearl, D., Bouthelet, L., & Lazar, J. (1982). *Television and behavior: Ten years of scientific progress and implications for the eighties (Vol. I).* Washington, DC: U.S. Government Printing Office.

Peck, R. (1982). Teenage stereotypes. In M. Schwartz (Ed.), *TV and teens: Experts look at the issues* (pp. 62–65). Reading, MA: Addison-Wesley.

Pecora, N. (1992) Superman/superboys/supermen: The comic book hero as socializing agent. In S. Craig (Ed.), *Men, masculinity, and the media* (pp. 61–77). Newbury, CA: Sage.

Peirce, K. (1990). A feminist theoretical perspective on the socialization of teenage girls through *Seventeen* magazine. *Sex Roles,* 23(9/10):491–500.

Phelan, J. M. (1977). *Mediaworld.* New York: Seabury Press.

Phillips, D. P. & Bollen, K. A. (1985). Same time, last year: Selective data dredging for negative findings. *American Sociological Review,* 50:364–371.

Phillips, D. P. & Carstensen, L. L. (1986). Clustering of teenage suicides after television news stories about suicide. *New England Journal of Medicine,* 315(11):685–689.

Phillips, D. P. & Paight, D. J. (1987). The impact of televised movies about suicide: A replicative study. *New England Journal of Medicine,* 317(13):809–811.

Phillips, G. (1989). Teacher as learner. Paper presented to the Florida Association of Supervision and Curriculum Development, Miami, Florida.

Pierce, C. M. (1980). Social trace contaminants: Subtle indicators of racism in TV. In S. B. Withey & R. P. Abeles (Eds.), *Television and social behavior: Beyond violence and television* (pp. 249–257). Hillsdale, NJ: Lawrence Erlbaum.

Pierce, J. P., Gilpin, E., Burns, D. M., Whalen, E., Rosbrook, B., Shopland, D., & Johnson, M. (1991). Does tobacco advertising target young people to start smoking? *Journal of the American Medical Association,* 266:3154–3158.

Pingree, S. (1978). The effects of nonsexist television commercials and perceptions of reality on children's attitudes about women. *Psychology of Women Quarterly,* 2(3):263–279.

Pingree, S. & Hawkins, R. P. (1980). Children and media. In M. Butler & W. Paisley (Eds.), *Women and the mass media: Source book for research and action.* New York: Human Sciences Press.

Ploghoft, M. E. & Anderson, J. A. (1982). *Teaching critical television viewing skills: An integrated approach.* Springfield, IL: Charles C. Thomas.

Ploghoft, M. E. & Anderson, J. A. (1981). *Education for the television age.* Springfield, IL: Charles C. Thomas.

Poindexter, P. M. & Stroman, C. (1981). Blacks and television: A review of the research literature. *Journal of Broadcasting,* 25(2):103–122.

Pollay, R. W. (1991). Cigarettes under fire: Blowing away the PR smoke-screen. *Media & Values,* 54–55:13–16.

Postman, N. (1985). *Amusing ourselves to death: Public discourse in the age of show business.* New York: Penguin Books.

Postman, N. (1982). *The disappearance of childhood.* New York: Delacourte Press.

Postman, N., Nystrom, C., Strate, L., & Weingartner, C. (1987). *Myths, men, & beer: An analysis of beer commercials on broadcast television, 1987.* Falls Church, VA: American Automobile Association.

Potts, R. & Sanchez, D. (1994). Television viewing and depression: No news is good news. *Journal of Broadcasting and Electronic Media,* 38(1):79–90.

Poulos, R. W., Rubinstein, E. A., & Liebert, R. M. (1975). Positive social learning. *Journal of Communication,* 25(4):90–97.

Powell, G. J. (1982). The impact of television on the self-concept development of minority children. In G. L. Berry & C. Mitchell-Kernan (Eds.), *Television and the socialization of the minority child* (pp. 105–131). New York: Academic Press.

Prothrow-Stith, D. (1990). The epidemic of violence and its imapct on the health care system. *Henry Ford Hospital Medical Journal,* 38(2/3):175–177.

Provenzo, E. F. (1991). *Video kids: Making sense of Nintendo.* Cambridge, MA: Harvard University Press.

Rabinovitch, M. S., McLean, Jr., M. S., Markham, J. W., & Talbott, A. D. (1972). Children's violence perception as a function of television violence. In *Television and social behavior. Vol. V. Television's effects: Further explorations.* Washington, DC: U.S. Government Printing Office.

Rank, H. (1993/94). Channel One: Asking the wrong questions. *Educational Leadership,* 51(4):52–55.

Rather, D. (1990). Journalism and the public trust. *The Humanist,* 50(6):5–8, 42.

Real, M. R. (1989). *Super media: A cultural studies approach.* Newbury Park, CA: Sage.

Real, M. R. (1977). *Mass-mediated culture.* Englewood Cliffs, NJ: Prentice-Hall.

Renshon, S. A. (1977). Assumptive frameworks in political socialization theory. In S. A. Renshon (Ed.), *Handbook of political socialization* (pp. 3–44). New York: Free Press.

Ritchie, D., Price, V., & Roberts, D. F. (1987). Television, reading, and reading achievement: A reappraisal. *Communication Research,* 14(3):292–315.

Roberts, E. J. (1982). Television and sexual learning in childhood. In D. Pearl, L. Bouthilet, & J. Lazar (Eds.), *Television and behavior: Ten years of scientific progress and implications for the eighties.* (Vol. 2) (p. 209–223). Rockville, MD: National Institute of Mental Health.

Robinson, J. P., Chivian, E., & Tudge, J. (1989). News media use and adolescents' attitudes about nuclear issues: An American-Soviet comparison. *Journal of Communication,* 39(2):105–113.

Robinson, R. S. (1994). Investigating Channel One: A case study report. In A. De Vaney (Ed.), *Watching Channel One: The convergence of students, technology, and private business* (pp. 21–41). Albany: State University of New York.

Roe, K. (1989). School achievement, self-esteem and adolescents' video use. In M. L. Levy (Ed.), *The VCR age: Home video and mass communication* (pp. 168–189). Newbury Park CA: Sage.

Rosenbaum, J. & Prinsky, L. (1987). Sex, violence, and rock 'n roll: Youth's perceptions of popular music. *Popular Music and Society,* 11(2):79–89.

Rosengren, K. E., Wenner, L. A., & Palmgreen, P. (Eds.). (1985). *Media gratification research: Current perspectives.* Beverly Hills, CA: Sage Publications.

Rubin, A. M. (1978). Child and adolescent television use and political socialization. *Journalism Quarterly,* 55(1):125–129.

Rubin, B. (1994). *How school materials teach and misteach world affairs: The Middle East.* Washington, DC: American Federation of Teachers and Freedom House.

Rushton, J. P. (1982). Television and prosocial behavior. In D. Pearl, L. Bouthilet, & J. Lazar (Eds.), *Television and behavior: Ten years of scientific progress and implications for the eighties* (Vol. 2) (pp. 248–258). Rockville, MD: National Institute of Mental Health.

Sadker, M. & Sadker, D. (1994). *Failing at fairness: How America's schools cheat girls.* New York: Charles Scribner's.

Salomon, G. (1983). Television watching and mental effort: A social psychological view. In J. Bryant & D. R. Anderson (Eds.), *Children's understanding of television* (pp. 181–198). New York: Academic Press.

Salomon, G. (1979). Shape, not only content. How media symbols partake in the development of abilities. In E. Wartella (Ed.), *Children communicat-*

ing: media and development of thought, speech, understanding (pp. 53–82). Beverly Hills, CA: Sage Publications.

Salomon, G. & Leigh, T. (1984). Predispositions about learning from print and television. *Journal of Communication,* 34(2):119–132.

Sanbonmatsu, D. M. & Fazio, R. H. (1991). Construct accessibility: Determinants, consequences, and implications for the media. In J. Bryant & D. Zillman (Eds.), *Responding to the screen: Reception and reaction processes* (pp. 45–62). Hillsdale, NJ: Lawrence Erlbaum.

Sawyer, F. (1988). Realities of television news programming. In S. Oskamp (Ed.), *Television as a social issue* (pp. 30–43). Newbury Park, CA: Sage.

Scales, P. C. (1991). *A portrayal of young adolescents in the 1990s: Implications for promoting healthy growth and development.* Chapel Hill, NC: Center for Early Adolescence.

Scanlon, C. (1993). The new "national crisis": Diet-crazed kids. *Miami Herald* (3 June).

Schmidt, B. C. (1994). The Edison Project's plan to redefine public education. *Educational Leadership,* 52(1):61–64.

Schramm, W., Lyle, J., & Parker, E. B. (1961). *Television in the lives of our children.* Stanford, CA: Stanford University Press.

Schrank, J. (1991). *Understanding mass media.* Lincolnwood, IL: National Textbook Company.

Schultze, Q. J., Anker, R. M., Bratt, J. D., Romanowski, W. D., Worst, J. W., & Zuidervaart, L. (1991). *Dancing in the dark: Youth, popular culture and the electronic media.* Grand Rapids, MI: William B. Eerdmans.

Schwartz, L. A. & Markham, W. T. (1985). Sex stereotyping in children's toy advertisements. *Sex Roles,* 12(1/2):157–170.

Schwartz, R. & Perkins, D. (1990). *Teaching thinking: Issues and approaches.* Pacific Grove, CA: Midwest Publications.

Seefeldt, V., Ewing, M., & Walk, S. (n.d.). *Overview of youth sports programs in the United States.* Washington, DC: Carnegie Council on Adolescent Development.

Seidman, S. A. (1992). An investigation of sex-role stereotyping in music videos. *Journal of Broadcasting & Electronic Media,* 36(2):209–216.

Seiter, E. (1987). Semiotics and television. In R. C. Allen (Ed.), *Channels of discourse: Television and contemporary criticism* (pp. 17–41). Chapel Hill: University of North Carolina.

Selling addiction: A media literacy workshop kit. (1992). Los Angeles, CA: Center for Media Literacy.

Selnow, G. W. (1990). Values in prime-time television. *Journal of Communication,* 40(2):64–74.

Selnow, G. W. (1984). Playing video games: The electronic friend. *Journal of Communication,* 34(2):148–156.

Selwyn, D. (1993). *Living history in the classroom: Integrative arts activities for making social studies meaningful.* Tucson, AZ: Zephyr Press.

Shaheen, J. G. (1984). *The TV Arab.* Bowling Green, OH: Bowling Green State University Popular Press.

Sherman, B. L. & Dominick, J. R. (1986). Violence and sex in music videos: TV and rock and roll. *Journal of Communications, 36*:79-93.

Signorielli, N. (1990a). Children, television, and gender roles: Messages and impact. *Journal of Adolescent Health Care,* 11(1):50-58.

Signorielli, N. (1990b). Television and health: Images and impact. In C. Atkin & L. Wallack (Eds.), *Mass communication and public health: Complexities and conflicts* (pp. 96-113). Newbury Park, CA: Sage.

Signorielli, N. (1989). Television and conceptions about sex roles: Maintaining conventionality and status quo. *Sex Roles,* 21(5/6):341-360.

Signorielli, N. (1987). Drinking, sex, and violence on television: The cultural indicators perspective. *Journal of Drug Education,* 17:245-260.

Signorielli, N. (1985). The measurement of violence in television programming: Violence indices. In J. R. Dominick & J. E. Fletcher (Eds.), *Broadcasting research methods* (pp. 235-251). Boston: Allyn & Bacon, Inc.

Signorielli, N. (1985). *Role portrayal and stereotyping on television: An annotated bibliography of studies relating to women, minorities, aging, sexual behavior, health, and handicaps.* Westport, CT: Greenwood Press.

Signorielli, N., McLeod, D., & Healy, E. (1994). Gender stereotypes in MTV commercials: The beat goes on. *Journal of Broadcasting & Electronic Media,* 38(1):91-101.

Silverglade, B. A. (1990). Regulatory policies for communicating health information. In C. Atkin & L. Wallack (Eds.), *Mass communication and public health: Complexities and conflicts* (pp. 88-95). Newbury Park, CA: Sage.

Silverstein, B., Perdue, L., Peterson, B., & Kelly, E. (1986). The role of the mass media in promoting a thin standard of bodily attractiveness for women. *Sex Roles,* 14(9/10):519-532.

Singer, D. G. (1983). A time to reexamine the role of television in our lives. *American Psychologist,* 38(7):815-816.

Singer, D. G. (1982). Television and the developing imagination of the child. In D. Pearl, L. Bouthilet, & J. Lazar (Eds.), *Television and behavior: Ten years of scientific progress and implications for the eighties* (Vol. 2) (pp. 39-52). Rockville, MD: National Institute of Mental Health.

Singer, D. G. & Singer, J. L. (1983). Learning how to be intelligent consumers of television. In M. J. A. Howe (Eds.), *Learning from television: Psychological and educational research* (pp. 203-222). London: Academic Press.

Singer, D. G. & Singer, J. L. (1981a). Television and the developing imagination of the child. *Journal of Broadcasting,* 4:337-387.

Singer, D. G. Zuckerman, D. M., & Singer, J. L. (1980). Helping elementary school children learn about TV. *Journal of Communication,* 30(3):84–93.

Singer, E. & Endreny, P. (1986). The reporting of social science research in the mass media. In S. J. Ball-Rokeach & M. G. Cantor (Eds.), *Media, audience, and social structure* (pp. 293–312). Newbury Park, CA: Sage.

Singer, J. L. & Singer, D. G. (1983). Psychologists look at television: Cognitive, developmental, personality, and social policy implications. *American Psychologist,* 38(7):826–834.

Singer, J. L. & Singer, D. G. (1981b). Come back, Mr. Rogers, come back. In C. Lowe (Ed.), *Television and American culture* (pp. 124–128). New York: H. W. Wilson Co.

Singer, J. L. & Singer, D. G. (1981c). *Television, imagination, and aggression: A study of preschoolers.* Hillsdale, NJ: Lawrence Erlbaum.

Singer, J. L. & Singer, D. G. (1976). Can TV stimulate imaginative play? *Journal of Communication,* 26(3):74–80.

Singer, J. L., Singer, D. G., & Rapaczynski, W. S. (1984). Family patterns and television viewing as predictors of children's beliefs and aggression. *Journal of Communication,* 34(2):73–89.

Slater, B. R. (1965). An analysis and appraisal of the amount of televiewing, general school achievement and socio-economic status of third grade students in selected public school in Erie County, New York. *Dissertation Abstracts,* 25:5651–5652.

Sleeter, C. E. & Grant, C. A. (1991). Race, class, gender, and disability in current textbooks. In M. W. Apple & L. K. Christian-Smith (Eds.), *The politics of the textbook* (pp. 78–110). New York: Routledge.

Smillie, J. & Bowen, W. (1993). *Get a life! or the awakening of Billy Bored.* Asheville, NC: Citizens for Media Literacy.

Smith, R. (1986). Television addiction. In J. Bryant & D. Zillman (Eds.), *Perspectives on media effects* (pp. 109–128). Hillsdale, NJ: Lawrence Erlbaum.

Snow, R. P. (1987). Youth and rock 'n roll, and electronic media. *Youth & Society,* 18(4):326–343.

Snow, R. P. (1983). *Creating media culture.* Beverly Hills, CA: Sage Publications.

Spangler, L. C. (1992). Buddies and pals: A history of male friendships on prime-time television. In S. Craig (Ed.), *Men, masculinity, and the media* (pp. 93–110). Newbury Park, CA: Sage.

Sprafkin, J., Gadow, K. D., & Abelman, R. (1992). *Television and the exceptional child: A forgotten audience.* Hillsdale, NJ: Lawrence Erlbaum.

Spring, J. (1990). *The American school.* New York: Longman.

Steenland, S. (1986). *Women in focus: An analysis of TV's female characters and their jobs.* Washington, DC: National Commission on Working Women.

Steenland, S. (1985). *Trouble on the set: An analysis of female characters on 1985 television programs.* Washington, DC: National Commission on Working Women.

Steenland, S. (n.d.). *Primetime women: An analysis of older women on entertainment television.* Washington, DC: National Commission on Working Women.

Stevenson, H. C. (1980). The mass media and popular culture. In M. Johnson (Ed.), *Toward adolescence: The middle school years* (pp. 74–93). Chicago: NSSE Yearbook.

Strasburger, V. C. (1989). Adolescent sexuality and the media. *Pediatric Clinics of North America,* 36(3):747–773.

Strate, L. (1992). Beer commercials: A manual on masculinity. In S. Craig (Ed.), *Men, masculinity, and the media* (pp. 78–92). Newbury Park, CA: Sage.

Strickland, D. E. (1983). Advertising exposure, alcohol consumption and misuse of alcohol. In M. Grant, M. Plant, & A. Williams (Eds.), *Economics and alcohol: Consumption and controls* (pp. 201–222). New York: Gardner Press.

Sun, S. & Lull, J. (1986). The adolescent audience for music videos and why they watch. *Journal of Communication,* 36(1):115–125.

Takanishi, R. (1982). The influence of television on the ethnic identity of minority children: A conceptual framework. In G. L. Berry & C. Mitchell-Kernan (Eds.), *Socialization of the minority child* (pp. 81–104). New York: Academic Press.

Tan, A. S. (1979). TV beauty ads and the role expectations of adolescent female viewers. *Journalism Quarterly,* 56(2):283–288.

Tannenbaum, P. H. (1985). "Play It Again, Sam": Repeated exposure to television programs. In D. Zillman & J. Bryant (Eds.), *Selective exposure to communication* (pp. 225–241). Hillsdale, NJ: Lawrence Erlbaum.

Tannenbaum, P. H. (1980). Entertainment as vicarious emotional experience. In P. H. Tannenbaum (Ed.), *The entertainment function of television* (pp. 107–131). Hillsdale, NJ: Lawrence Erlbaum.

Tavris, C. (1988). Beyond cartoon killings: Comments on two overlooked effects of television. In S. Oskamp (Ed.), *Television as a social issue* (pp. 189–197). Newbury Park, CA: Sage.

Thoman, E. (1992). In the light of the fires. *Media & Values,* 58:2.

Tiene, D. (1993). Channel One, good or bad news for our schools? *Educational Leadership,* 50(8):46–51.

Tolley, H. (1977). Childhood learning about war and peace: Coming of age in the Nuclear Era. In S. A. Renshon (Ed.), *Handbook of political socialization* (pp. 389–410). New York: Free Press.

Tolley, H. (1973). *Children and war: Political socialization to international conflict.* New York: Teachers College Press.

Traber, M. (Ed.). (1986). *The myth of the information revolution: Social and ethical implications of communication technology.* Newbury Park, CA: Sage.

Travis, L. D. & Violato, C. (1981). Mass media use, credulity and beliefs about youth: A survey of Canadian education students. *The Alberta Journal of Educational Research,* 27(1):16–34.

Tuchman, G. (1981). The symbolic annihilation of women by the mass media. In S. Cohen & J. Young (Eds.), *The manufacture of news: Social problems, deviance, and the mass media* (pp. 169–185). Beverly Hills, CA: Sage Publications.

Tucker, L. A. (1986). The relationship of television viewing to physical fitness and obesity. *Adolescence,* 21:797–806.

Ukadike, N. F. (1990). Western images of Africa: Geneology of an ideological formulation. *Black Scholar,* 21(2):30–48.

UNESCO Declaration on Media Education. (1982). Reprinted in L. Masterman (1985). *Teaching the media* (pp. 340–341). London: Routledge.

United States Department of Health and Human Services. (1991). *Youth and Alcohol: A National Survey. Drinking Habits, Access, Attitudes, and Knowledge.* Washington, DC: Office of the Inspector General.

van der Voort, T. H. A. (1986). *Television violence: A child's-eye view.* Amsterdam, Netherlands: Elsevier Science Publishers.

van der Voort, T. H. A., van Lil, J. E., & Vooijs, M. W. (1993). Parent and child emotional involvement in the Netherlands. In B. S. Greenberg & W. Gantz (Eds.), *Desert Storm and the mass media* (pp. 341–352). Cresskill, NJ: Hampton Press.

Vande Berg, L. R. & Streckfuss, D. (1992). Prime-time television's portrayal of women and the world of work: A demographic profile. *Journal of Broadcasting & Electronic Media,* 36(2):195–208.

Wade, S. (1971). Adolescents, creativity, and media: An exploratory study. *American Behavorial Scientist,* 14(3):341–351.

Walker, J. R. (1987). The context of MTV: Adolescent entertainment media use and music television. *Popular Music and Society,* 11(3):1–9.

Wallack, L. (1983). Alcohol advertising reassessed: The public health perspective. In M. Grant, M. Plant, & A. Williams (Eds.), *Economics and alcohol: Consumption and controls* (pp. 243–248). New York: Gardner Press.

Wallack, L., Breed, W., & Cruz, J. (1987). Alcohol on prime time television. *Journal of Studies on Alcohol,* 48(1):33–38.

Wallack, L., Grube, T. W., Madden, P. A., & Breed, W. (1990). Portrayals of alcohol in prime-time television. *Journal of Studies on Alcohol,* 51(5):428–442.

Walsh-Childers, K. & Brown, J. D. (1993). Adolescents' acceptance of sex-role stereotypes and television viewing. In B. S. Greenberg, J. D. Brown,

& N. L. Buerkel-Rothfuss (Eds.), *Media, sex and the adolescent* (pp. 117–132). Cresskill, NJ: Hampton Press.

Walters, H. F. (1993). Another kind of superhero. *Newsweek* (16 August):58–59.

Ware, M. C. & Stuck, M. F. (1985). Sex-role messages vis-à-vis microcomputer use: A look at the pictures. *Sex Roles,* 13(3/4):205–214.

Wartella, E., Heintz, K. E., Aidman, A. J., & Mazzarella, S. R. (1990). Television and beyond: Children's video media in one community. *Communication Research,* 17(1):45–64.

Waters, H. F. (1993). Another kind of superhero. *Newsweek,* (16 August).

Weis, W. L. & Burke, C. (1986). Media content and tobacco advertising: An unhealthy addiction. *Journal of Communication,* 36(4):59–69.

Welch, R. L., Huston-Stein, A., Wright, J. C., & Plehal, R. (1979). Subtle sex-role cues in children's commercials. *Journal of Communication,* 29(3):202–209.

Wells, A. & Hakanen, E. A. (1991). The emotional use of popular music by adolescents. *Journalism Quarterly,* 68(3):445–454.

Wells, J. D. (1984). Music television video and the capacity to experience life. *Journal of Popular Music and Society,* 9(4):1–6.

Williams, J. D. (1993). Minority adolescents, alcohol consumption, and media effects: A review of issues and research. In R. M. Lerner (Ed.), *Early adolescence: Perspectives on research, policy, and intervention* (pp. 431–446). Hillsdale, NJ: Lawrence Erlbaum.

Williams, J. D. & Frith, K. (1993). Adolescents and the media. In R. M. Lerner (Ed.), *Early adolescence: Perspectives on research, policy, and intervention* (pp. 401–406). Hillsdale, NJ: Lawrence Erlbaum.

Williams, P. A., Haertel, E. H., Haertel, G. D., & Walberg, H. J. (1982). The impact of leisure-time television on school learning: A research synthesis. *American Educational Research Journal,* 18(1):19–50.

Winick, C. (1988). The functions of television: Life without the big box. In S. Oscamp (Ed.), *Television as a social issue* (pp. 217–237). Newbury Park, CA: Sage.

Winick, M. P. & Winick, C. (1979). *The television experience: What children see.* Beverly Hills, CA: Sage.

Winn, M. (1977). *The plug-in drug.* New York: Viking Press.

Winston, M. R. (1982). Racial consciousness and the evolution of mass communication in the United States. *Daedelus,* 111(4):171–182.

Woll, A. L. (1980). *The Latin image in American film.* Berkeley: University of California Press.

Wooley, O. W. & Wooley, S. (1982). The Beverly Hills eating disorder. The mass marketing of anorexia nervosa. *International Journal of Eating Disorders,* 1(3):57–69.

Wright, J. C. & Huston, A. C. (1983). A matter of form: Potentials of television for young viewers. *American Psychologist,* 38(7):835–843.

Wright, J. C., Kunkle, D., Pinon, M., & Huston, A. C. (1989). How children reacted to televised coverage of the space shuttle disaster. *Journal of Communication,* 39(2):27–45.

Wynne, E. A. & Ryan, K. (1992). *Reclaiming our schools: A handbook on teaching character, academics, and discipline.* New York: Merrill.

Wysocki, D. & Harrison, R. (1991). AIDS and the media: A look at how periodicals influence children and teenagers in the knowledge of AIDS. *Journal of Health Education,* 22:20–23.

Yankelovich, Skelly, and White, Inc. (1979). *The General Mills American family report 1978–79: Family health in an era of stress.* Minneapolis, MN: General Mills.

Zillman, D. (1991). Empathy: Affect from bearing witness to the emotions of others. In J. Bryant & D. Zillman (Eds.), *Responding to the screen: Reception and reaction processes* (pp. 135–168). Hillsdale, NJ: Lawrence Erlbaum.

Zillman, D. & Bryant, J. (1985). Affect, mood, and emotion as determinants of selective exposure. In D. Zillman & J. Bryant (Eds.), *Selective exposure to communication* (pp. 157–190). Hillsdale, NJ: Lawrence Erlbaum.

Zillman, D., Bryant, J., & Sapolsky, B. S. (1979). The enjoyment of watching sport contests. In J. H. Goldstein (Ed.), *Sports, games and play: Social and psychological viewpoints* (pp. 297–335). Hillsdale, NJ: Lawrence Erlbaum Associates.

Zillman, D., Hezel, R. T., & Medoff, N. J. (1980). The effect of affective states on selective exposure to televised entertainment fare. *Journal of Applied Social Psychology,* 10(4):323–339.

John Davies is the middle school director at Miami Country Day School in Miami, Florida where he also teaches courses on film. He received his BA in philosophy from Merrimack College and an MA in history from Texas A&M University. Currently he is a doctoral candidate in Educational Leadership at Florida International University.

The author of several articles on media literacy, he frequently speaks on the subject to educational and other community groups. His current research interests include popular culture, the image of educators in popular media, and how the media help us construct images of our selves.